ISBN 978-1-333-32402-5
PIBN 10490591

1 MONTH OF
FREE
READING

at
www.ForgottenBooks.com

By purchasing this book you are eligible for one month membership to ForgottenBooks.com, giving you unlimited access to our entire collection of over 1,000,000 titles via our web site and mobile apps.

To claim your free month visit:
www.forgottenbooks.com/free490591

English
Français
Deutsche
Italiano
Español
Português

www.forgottenbooks.com

Mythology Photography **Fiction**
Fishing Christianity **Art** Cooking
Essays Buddhism Freemasonry
Medicine **Biology** Music **Ancient**
Egypt Evolution Carpentry Physics
Dance Geology **Mathematics** Fitness
Shakespeare **Folklore** Yoga Marketing
Confidence Immortality Biographies
Poetry **Psychology** Witchcraft
Electronics Chemistry History **Law**
Accounting **Philosophy** Anthropology
Alchemy Drama Quantum Mechanics
Atheism Sexual Health **Ancient History**
Entrepreneurship Languages Sport
Paleontology Needlework Islam
Metaphysics Investment Archaeology
Parenting Statistics Criminology
Motivational

THE FIRST

VOYAGE ROUND THE WORLD,

BY

MAGELLAN.

TRANSLATED FROM THE ACCOUNTS OF

PIGAFETTA,

AND OTHER CONTEMPORARY WRITERS.

Accompanied by Original Documents, with Notes and an Introduction,

BY

LORD STANLEY OF ALDERLEY.

LONDON:

PRINTED FOR THE HAKLUYT SOCIETY.

M.DCCC.LXXIV.

T. RICHARDS, 37, GREAT QUEEN STREET.

COUNCIL

OF

THE HAKLUYT SOCIETY.

CONTENTS.

PLATES AND MAPS.

INTRODUCTION

AND

LIFE OF MAGELLAN.

—— Teucer Salamina patremque
Quum fugeret, tamen uda Lyæo
Tempora populeâ fertur vinxisse coronâ,
   Sic tristes affatus amicos :
Quo nos cunque feret melior Fortuna parente,
   Ibimus, o socii comitesque !
Nil desperandum Teucro duce et auspice Teucro ;
   Certus enim promisit Apollo
Ambiguam tellure novâ Salamina futuram.
   O fortes, pejoraque passi
Mecum sæpe viri, nunc vino pellite curas :
   Cras ingens iterabimus æquor.

THOUGH Magellan's enterprise was the greatest ever undertaken by any navigator, yet he has been deprived of his due fame by the jealousy which has always existed between the two nations inhabiting the Peninsula : the Spaniards would not brook being commanded by a Portuguese, and the Portuguese have not yet forgiven Magellan for having abandoned them to serve Castile. But Magellan really had no choice ; for if the western passage which he expected to discover was to be sought for, it could only be under the auspices of Spain, within whose demarcation those waters lay.

b

It would seem that D. Manuel had only himself to blame for the loss of Magellan's services ; and, as M. Amoretti well observes, D. Manuel ought to have been well aware of the value of those services, since Charles V knew it, and showed his appreciation of them. It is difficult to believe that the injury of which Magellan complained, and which led him to seek other service, was merely, as Osorio says, the refusal of promotion in palace rank, and which he had well deserved, especially since the motive ascribed by Osorio to the king's refusal, namely the necessity of avoiding a bad precedent, was not alone a sufficient affront to account for Magellan's sacrificing all his hopes and property in his own country, had he not also felt that the king was condemning him to inaction, obscurity, and uselessness. Barros, indeed, says that :

"The favours of princes given for services are a retributive justice, which must be observed equally with all, with regard to the quality of each man : and that if a man's portion be denied him, though he endures it ill, yet he will have patience ; but if he see the advancement of those who have profited more by artifice and friends than by their own merits, he loses all patience ; indignation, hatred, and despair arise, and he will commit faults injurious to himself and others. And what outraged Magellan more than the refusal of the half ducat a month, was that some men who were with him at Azamor, said that his lameness was feigned to support his petition."

The king, moreover, refused to receive Magellan, and showed his ill-will against him. It is therefore highly probable that before Magellan took the step of leaving Portugal, D. Manuel, prompted by his niggardly disposition, had refused to entertain Magellan's desire for employment at sea, or his projects of discovery, from which no immediate profit was to be expected. This is apparent from the statement of Barros, *Decad.* III, lib. v, cap. viii, that letters of Magellan to Francisco Serrano were found after the death of the latter in Maluco, in which Magellan said that he should soon see him ; and, if it were not by way of Portugal, it would be by way of Castile, and that Serrano should therefore wait for him there. Further on, Barros says that recourse to Castile appears from these letters to have been in Magellan's mind some time before the occurrence of the king's dismissal of his business : and that this was shown by his always associating with pilots, and occupying himself with sea-charts.

The Portuguese exaggerated very much the injury they expected to result, and, later, which they thought had resulted from Magellan's voyage, which could not change the position of the Moluccas, nor consequently the Portuguese title to them ; but the apprehensions which they felt, arose from their fear of others sharing in the spice trade, and from the limited geographical knowledge of the period, which left both parties very much in doubt as to the true position of those islands, or as to the extent of the circumference of the globe. The question of the exact position of the Moluccas was not definitely ascertained till much later, though a compromise was arrived at in 1529 by the treaty between Spain and Portugal, by which Charles V gave up whatever rights to the Moluccas he imagined he possessed, to Portugal, for a sum of three hundred and

fifty thousand ducats.[1] As late as 1535, Gaspar Correa
mentions, tom. iii, p. 661, a Dominican friar in Portuguese India, who was learned in cosmography, and
who asserted that the Moluccas fell within the demarcation of Castile.

The grounds of complaint of the Portuguese against
Magellan are, perhaps, best expressed, and in the
strongest terms, by Bishop Osorio, so it may be well to
quote from him the following passage. Lib. xi, § 23.

"About this time a slight offence on the part of the king
(D. Manuel) so grievously exasperated the mind of a certain
Portuguese, that, forgetful of all faith, piety, and religion, he
hastened to betray the king who had educated him, and the
country which had brought him forth; and he risked his
life amongst the greatest perils. Ferdinand Magellan, of
whom we have before spoken, was a man of noble birth, and
endued with a high spirit. He had given proofs in India, in
warlike affairs, of courage and perseverance in no small degree. Likewise in Africa he had performed his duties with
great ardour. Formerly it was the custom among the Portuguese that the king's servants should be fed in the palace
at the king's expense; but when the number of these servants had become so great (because the sons of the king's
officers retained the same station, and besides, many were
admitted for their services into the king's household), it was
seen to be very difficult to prepare the food of such a multitude. On this account it was determined by the Kings of
Portugal that the food which each man was to receive in the
palace should be provided by himself out of the king's
money. Thus it was settled that a certain sum of money
was assigned per month to each man. That money, indeed,

[1] See Appendix V, pp. 392-396, to De Morga's *Philippine
Islands*, Hakluyt Society, with respect to the negotiations about
the Moluccas.

when provisions were so cheap, provided abundantly for the men; but now that the number of men, and the prices of commodities had increased, it happened that the sum, which formerly was more than sufficient for their daily expenses, was now much too small. Moreover, as all the dignity of the Portuguese depends upon the king, this small sum of money is as eagerly sought after as though it were much more ample. And as the Portuguese think that the thing most to be desired is to be enrolled amongst the king's household, so also, they consider the greatest honour to consist in an increase of this stipend. For, as there are various ranks of king's servants, so the sum of money is assigned to each servant according to the dignity of his rank. The highest class is that of nobleman; but, as there are distinctions of nobility, so an equal salary is not given to all. Thus it happens that the nobility of each is estimated according to the importance of this stipend, and each one is held to be more noble in proportion to the more ample stipend which he receives. This judgment, indeed, as human affairs go, is often most false; for many obtain through ambition and pertinacity what ought to be assigned to deserts and innate nobleness. The Portuguese, however, since they are over anxious in seeking this nobility, and imagine that their nobility is increased by a small accession of salary, very often think that they must strive for this little sum of money, as though all their well-being and dignity depended upon it. Now, Magellan contended that for his services, his stipend should be increased monthly by half a ducat. The king refused it him, lest an entrance should be opened to ambitious persons. Magellan, excited by the injury of the refusal of this advantage to him at that time, abandoned the king, broke his faith, and brought the State into extreme danger. And whilst we ought to tolerate the injuries inflicted by the State, and to endure also the outrages of kings, who are the fathers of the republick, and whilst we ought to lay down our lives for the well-being of our country, which lives we owe to our country; this most

audacious man conceived such despite on account of half a
ducat, amounting to five denarii, which was refused to him,
that he opposed the State; he offended the king, who had
brought him up; and brought his country, for which he
should have died, into peril. For the affair reached such a
pitch that the danger of a perilous war impended over the
commonwealth. I do not know, indeed, whence so barbarous a custom has crept into the State: for, whilst the name
of a traitor is not only hateful and hated, but also burns in
the stain of everlasting dishonour upon a whole posterity;
yet men who determine upon breaking their faith, and op-
posing their kings or states, may reject the favours they
have received by formal letters, may abjure their fealty, and
despoil themselves of the rights and duties of the State; they
bid the king keep for himself that which belongs to him,
and they attest that thenceforward they will have nothing in
common with their country: then, at length, they contend
that it is allowable for them to commence war against their
country. Be it so: reject favours if it please you; contemn
the liberality of your country; grumble as much as you
please, that a reward equal to your dignity has not been
granted. But by what means can you betray the faith
which you have plighted? My country has inflicted on me
a severe outrage; it has inflicted, indeed, the worst. But
an outrage is not to be avenged, either upon parents or
upon one's country. I have abandoned, he says, all that I
had received from my country. Have you then rejected
life, disposition, and education? By no means. But all
these things; you received them, in the first place, from
God, and then from the laws, customs, and institutions of
your country. It will never be allowable to combat nature,
to injure your country, or to break faith, even should you
be laden with every injury. Nay, your life should be given
up, and the most extreme punishments should be under-
gone, sooner than break your faith, or betray your duty.
Abjure fealty as much as you please, attest your perfidy by
public letters, leave to posterity a notable memory of un-

speakable wickedness; yet you will not be able by any such document to avoid offending the Deity, nor the stain of an everlasting opprobrium."

Against this view of Osorio may be set the following passage from Vattel, which has all the more weight, in that it is simply an enunciation of law and right, and is not written to support or to denounce any particular person.

" Many distinctions will be necessary, in order to give a complete solution to the celebrated question, whether a man may *quit his country*, or *the society of which he is a member*. The children are bound by natural ties to the society in which they were born; they are under an obligation to shew themselves grateful for the protection it has afforded to their fathers, and are in a great measure indebted to it for their birth and education. They ought, therefore, to love it, as we have already shewn, to express a just gratitude to it, and requite its services as far as possible by serving it in turn. We have observed above, that they have a right to enter into the society of which their fathers were members. But every man is born free; and the son of a citizen, when come to the years of discretion, may examine whether it be convenient for him to join the society for which he was destined by his birth. If he does not find it advantageous to remain in it, he is at liberty to quit it, on making it a compensation for what it has done in his favour, and preserving, as far as his new engagements will allow him, the sentiments of love and gratitude he owes it."—*Chitty's translation of Vattel*, book I, cap. xix, § 220.

There are also some remarkable passages in a pamphlet by Condorcet, dated October 25th, 1791, named *Opinion sur les Emigrants*. This opinion deserves attention, both on account of its author and the time in which it was written, when popular passions and

prejudices were much excited against those who were
expatriating themselves from France.

Condorcet begins with the statement, that :

"It is a great error to imagine that the public utility is
not constantly to be found united with the rights of individuals, or that the public well-being may demand acts of
real injustice. This error has everywhere been the eternal
excuse for the inroads of tyranny, and the pretext for the
artful manœuvres employed to establish it.[1]

"On the contrary, in the case of every measure that is
proposed as useful, it must first be examined whether it is
just. Should it not be so, it must be concluded that it had
only an empty and fallacious appearance of utility.

.   .   .   .   .

"Nature concedes to every man the right of going out of
his country; the constitution guarantees it to every French
citizen, and we cannot strike a blow at it. The Frenchman
who wishes to leave his country, for his business, for his
health, even for the sake of his peace and well-being, ought
to have the fullest liberty to do so : he ought to be able to
use this liberty, without his absence depriving him of the
least of his rights. In a great empire, the variety of pro-
fessions, and inequality of fortunes, do not admit of residence
and personal service being regarded as a common obligation
which the law may impose upon all citizens. This rigorous obligation can only exist in the case of absolute necessity; to extend it to the habitual state of society, and even
to all periods when the public safety or tranquillity may
seem to be menaced, would be to disturb the order of useful labours, and to attack the sources of general prospe-
rity.

"Every man, moreover, has the right to change his country; he may renounce that in which he was born, to choose

[1] This opinion may be recommended to those who war on
"pious founders".

another. From that moment, as a citizen of his new country, he is only a foreigner in the first; but if some day he returns to it, if he has left any property in it, he ought to enjoy there to the full the rights of man; he has only deserved to lose those of a citizen.

"But here a first question presents itself. Is this citizen by his sole renunciation released from every obligation towards the body politic which he abandons? Does the society from which he separates himself lose immediately all its rights over him? Doubtless, not; and I do not speak only of those sentiments which a noble and grateful soul preserves for its country, even though it be unjust; I speak of rigorous obligations, of those which a man cannot fail to fulfil without becoming guilty of an offence: and I say that there exists a time during which a man placed between his ancient and his new country can only permit himself to express hopes as to the differences which arise between them: a time when that one of the two nations against which he might bear arms would have the right to punish him as an assassin; and when the man who might employ his riches or talents against his former countrymen, would really be a traitor.

"I will add that each nation has also the right to fix the time after which the citizen who abandons it is to be considered as free from all obligation, and to determine what are his duties until the expiration of that period, and what actions it still preserves the power to forbid him. To deny this principle, would be to break all the social bonds which can bind men together. This period, doubtless, is not an arbitrary one; it is that during which the citizen who abdicates can employ against his country the means which he has received from it, and during which he can do it more injury than could a foreigner."

Further on, Condorcet proposes two years as the period during which a citizen who renounces his nationality shall engage not to enter the service of any

X   INTRODUCTION AND

foreign power, unless he has been authorised so to do
by a decree of the national assembly. He also proposes
various measures for different classes of emigrants, and
the full enjoyment of their property on the same foot-
ing as foreigners, by those who sign an engagement
not to take foreign service for two years, nor during
that time to solicit the aid of any foreign power
against the nation or its constituted authorities.

Magellan fully satisfied the conditions specified by
Vattel, as may be seen by his conversations with
Sebastian Alvarez, the King of Portugal's agent: at
this date, also, it is sufficiently clear that Magellan not
only did no harm to his native country, but that he
increased its renown by his own services, and by those
of the other Portuguese officers whom he associated
with his labours. If his countrymen have preferred
Gama to him, it is because he only served the interests
of science, whilst Gama served the passions of his
countrymen, and aided them to enrich themselves.
After D. Manuel had refused employment and advancement to Magellan, and seemed inclined to leave him in
the obscurity of a small garrison in Africa, the Portuguese would seem to have no more right to complain
of Magellan's profiting by the opportunities offered by
Spain, than the Genoese would have had, if they had
reproached Columbus for availing himself in a similar
way of the resources of that country. D. Manuel, it
is true, made offers to Magellan if he would leave Spain
and return to Portugal, but it was then too late, for
the great navigator had already pledged his word to
Charles V.

There is another circumstance which justifies Magellan still more than if he had been an Englishman or
a Frenchman, a circumstance peculiar to Spain and
Portugal. In the Peninsula, the kingly power was of
recent origin, and had been divided amongst several
crowns : the wearers of these crowns had been at first
only the equals of other great lords, and, after they
had acquired these crowns, they were only the first
amongst their equals ; and such they recognised themselves to be by their coronation oaths, even long after
the time of Magellan. In these coronation oaths they
also bound themselves more than did other European
sovereigns to respect all the privileges of the great
nobles ; any infraction of which was held to justify
these in revolt from the sovereign. At the same time
there existed the custom and tradition of disnaturalisation, in accordance with which any noble who felt
aggrieved, formally renounced his fealty to the sovereign, and betook himself to some neighbouring state.
Osorio and Mariana, who wrote when the kingly power
had become consolidated, ridicule this custom ; but it
must have had the advantage of giving time and
opportunity for a peaceable settlement instead of an
immediate recourse to arms. But whether the custom
was good or bad, there is no doubt that it was generally and constantly acted upon ; and Magellan was
following precedents that were generally received in
the Peninsula. It is unfortunate that the document
mentioned by historians, by which Magellan formally
renounced fealty to D. Manuel, is not forthcoming in
the archives either of Spain or Portugal ; but it may

be supposed to be similar in substance to those renunci-
ations which Osorio mentions and reproves.

Among those who disnaturalised themselves may
be cited various Condes de Haro of Biscay, and Guzman, who gave his services to Marocco, and who bears
the title of El Bueno. With regard to Count Diego
de Haro, who in 1216 withdrew from Castile to
Navarre, Mariana makes the following observations.

" Several great lords of Castile, irritated against their
king, whose avarice they could not endure, had passed into
the kingdoms of Navarre and Aragon, after having renounced their right of naturalisation by a public deed, a
means formerly in use amongst those nations, in order not
to be regarded as traitors and rebels when they quitted the
states of their sovereign. . . Among the grandees who came
to take refuge in Navarre, the most illustrious beyond dispute was Don Diego de Haro. This lord had excellent
qualities : never were seen greater constancy, probity, or
zeal for the public service than his ; the slightest injustice
irritated him. It was in order not to see his country and
freedom oppressed, that he abandoned Castile."—*Mariana,
History of Spain,* book XIII.

" In the year 1276, Alfonso the Wise had defeated Yussuf,
the Emperor of Marocco, and made peace with him with
the assistance of Guzman : a tournament was held in Seville
in celebration of it, and King Alfonso having asked who
had most distinguished himself, was told D. Alonzo Perez.
He asked which of them, and D. Juan Ramirez de Guzman
replied : 'Alonzo Perez de Guzman, my brother of profit.'
This answer seemed ill to all, and especially to Guzman,
who saw that a slur was cast upon the illegitimacy of his
birth, for at that time they named children of profit (*ganan-
ciu*), those who were born of unmarried women, and his
mother had not been married. Guzman, irritated at-being
thus spoken of before the king and the court, then said :

'You speak truth, I am a brother of profit, but you are and will be one of loss; and were it not for the respect due to the presence in which we stand, I would teach you the manner in which you should treat me; but you are not to blame for it, but rather he who has brought you up and taught you so ill.' The king, against whom this complaint appeared to be directed, then said : ' Your brother does not speak ill, for so it is the custom in Castile to name those who are not children of women married to their husbands.' ' So also,' he replied, ' is it the custom of the nobles of Castile, when they are not well treated by their sovereigns, to go abroad to seek those who will treat them well; I will do likewise; and I swear not to return until with truth they may call me a man of profit. Grant me, therefore, the term which the privilege of the nobles of Castile gives, that I may go out of the kingdom, for from this day I disnaturalise myself, and take leave of being your vassal.' The king attempted to dissuade him, but his efforts being in vain, he had to grant him the term which he asked for; during which Guzman sold all that he had inherited from his father or acquired in the war, and went out from Castile, accompanied by thirty of his friends and servants."—Quintana, *Vidas de Españoles Celebres.*

There seems to be some inconsistency on the part of those who refuse to admit of disnaturalisation, yet at the same time maintain that rebellion can be justified. If there is a justification of rebellion, the right of expatriation, or of withdrawal from amongst those who provoke rebellion, must exist; and there can be no doubt that the peaceable withdrawal of those who are oppressed or injured is preferable in the interests of all to armed insurrection. Even Bishop Osorio and Mariana would probably admit that the disnaturalisation of Prim and Serrano would have been better than their treason, which has plunged Spain in anarchy and bloodshed for so many years.[1] Rebellions have almost always been conducted by minorities; and as their justification does not depend upon the numerical importance of those engaged in them, it would follow that in the case of disnaturalisation, where numbers are not requisite, as in the case of armed insurrection, the right would exist equally even if the minority consisted only of one.

There are some writers on the Law of Nations, with whom I am agreed in general, who disapprove of the Naturalisation and Disnaturalisation Act of the Session of 1869. I am compelled to differ from them with respect to that measure, for the foregoing reasons, and also because it seems to me that they have lost sight of another circumstance which affects the question. So long as kingly power was a reality, personal allegiance and duty to the sovereign was a reality also. But now that modern innovation and corruption have substituted the rule of majorities for the kingly power, the feeling of the personal duty of the subject is almost lost; and the subject, or citizen, has become only one of an aggregation of individuals, or of an association of persons with equal rights; and each member of such an association has clearly the right to choose whether he will form part of it or not : so that whatever rights of expatriation may have existed in

---

[1] Thus Hazelrigg, Hampden, Cromwell, and Pym, *are said* to have been prevented by the Government from emigrating to New England in 1638. See Palfrey's *Hist. of New England*, vol. i, pp. 502, 503.

the times of Magellan, Grotius, and Vattel, have become much stronger at the present time, when the conscience of the subject is no longer considered by some as held bound by duty to the sovereign, who has become almost impersonal : instead of loyalty and fealty, we have the duty of fair dealing as between partners and associates on equal terms, as is exemplified by the argumentation of Condorcet in the passage quoted above. That this view is in accordance with the common sense and consent of mankind is shown by the general repudiation of the pretension of the northern portion of the United States to term the secession of the southern states a rebellion ; and this pretension was seen to be especially illogical on the part of those who had repudiated the name of rebels when they departed from the duty of obedience to their lawful sovereign.

Magellan has not had the good fortune of Vasco da Gama, whose exploits have been narrated by Camoens and Gaspar Correa ; he did not survive to give his own account of his great voyage, and the only accounts preserved were written by two Italians of very small literary capacity. There are, however, more documents concerning Magellan in existence than are to be found with respect to Gama.

The birth-place of Magellan is doubtful ; according to his will executed in Lisbon, December 29th, 1504, in favour of his sister, Theresa de Magalhães, wife of Joan da Sylva Telles, he was born at Villa de Sabroza, in the district of Villa Real, Traz os Montes ; in his will of August 24th, 1519, he calls himself " Vezino de

Porto," or domiciled at Porto; documents quoted by M. Ferdinand Denis make him to be born at Villa de Figueiro in Portuguese Estremadura. His family was "hidalgo," with a known coat of arms, of which a plate is given in this volume.

The book of noble genealogies of Portugal, by Bernardo Pimenta do Avelar Portocarrero, states, in the vol. M, done and copied in the year 1721, fo. 641, that Ruy de Magalhaēs, whose parents are unknown, was Alcaide-mōr of Aveiro. He married Alda de Mesquita, daughter of Martin Gonzalves Pimentel and Ignez de Mesquita. Antonio de Lima (another genealogist) represents her as the wife of Gil de Magalhaēs, fifth son of Gil de Magalhaēs; and he gives her the same children as others give to Ruy de Magalhaēs: who had

Genebra de Magalhaēs, wife of Pero Cāo.

Fernāo de Magalhaēs, who married Da. Brites Barbosa, daughter of his relation Diogo Barbosa, alcaide-mōr of Seville, in the absence of D. Alvaro of Portugal; he had

Da. Anna de Magalhaēs, his heiress, the wife of D. Hernando de Henao e Avila, from whom his lineage continues. She was his only child.

This does not agree with the archives of Seville, from which it appears that Beatriz Barbosa was daughter of Diego Barbosa and Maria Caldera, and that Fernan Magalhaēs and Beatriz Barbosa had a son named Rodrigo; and that after the death of these three, Diego Barbosa became their heir; and he having died in 1525, his son Jayme inherited.

Fernan Magellan executed a will in Seville on the

24th day of August, 1519. He instituted by it a mayorazgo for his son, grandson, or relation, who should bear the name of Magallanes, and who should be bound to live in the kingdoms of Castille. He also bequeathed a sum of 12,500 maravedis to the Convent of N. S. de la Victoria in Triana.

Two facsimiles of the signature of Magellan are given, one taken from his signature to the protocol of the Council of War, held at Cochim in 1510 ; there is also a facsimile of the signature of another Magellan, taken from the book of Moradias or Palace stipends, attached to a receipt printed by Navarrete, who appears to have supposed it to have been that of the navigator: and a facsimile of the signature of Magellan's brother-in-law Duarte Barbosa.

Gaspar Correa states, in his *Lendas da India*, tom. II, p. 28, that, in January of 1510, Alfonso d'Alboquerque despatched the ships from Cochim to the kingdom.

"Two ships of Bastian de Sousa and Francisco de Sá convoyed this fleet, and at night they both struck on the shoals of Padua, which are opposite the Maldive Islands, and remained aground, upright, and without breaking up. Upon this they prepared the boats as well as they could, and raised their sides, and put inside water and biscuit, and victuals which did not require cooking. The captains and pilots, and as many men as could, got into these boats and returned to Cochym. The people who remained in the ships set shores[1] on each side of the ships, with the yards, which they cut. All this was arranged and commanded by an honourable gentleman, who remained as overseer, named Fernan de Magalhaēs, who had been much wounded in

[1] "Escoras."

c

Calecut. He took much care that the chests should not be
broken, and that there should be no robbery, because the
captains were going to request ships of the governor, with
which to return to the ships to save what goods had not
been wetted. These captains reached Cananor in eight
days, from whence they sent a message to the governor,
who at once sent Gonzalo de Crasto in a caravel, with two
pilots; and they went to the ships and put the best things
on board the caravel, until they could not load it any more,
and having recovered all the men, they set fire to the ships,
as they were already full of water. So they returned to
Cochim. In this Fernan de Magalhães worked hard, and
did much service, and attended well to everything.

"This Fernan de Magalhães was of the king's household,
and came to India with the Viceroy Dom Francisco [d'Al-
meida], and he was in the action with the Turks; and he
was always much wounded in the fleets and in Calecut; and
in these ships he lost his small portion of property,[1] and he
went away poor to Portugal, and went about with claims
for his services, and begged of the king a hundred reis increase of his palace stipend,[2] which the king did not choose
to grant, at which he was aggrieved, and went to Castile to
live at Seville, where he married. As he had much knowledge of the art of navigation, and enterprise, and devoted
himself to that, he came to an understanding with the
directors of the House of Trade of Seville, so that the emperor gave him a fleet of five ships, with which he navigated, discovering a new way to Maluco, which was in the
year 1519, as I will relate further on in its place; with
which he caused great difficulties to Portugal."

Correa again refers to the incident of Magellan
remaining with the wreck, in his tome II, p. 625,
where he says:

"Fernan de Magalhães, an honourable gentleman, who
served in these parts in the time of the Viceroy Afonso

---

[1] "Perdeo sua pobreza"   [2] "Moradia."

d'Alboquerque, of whom I made mention in the first book, with respect to two ships which were going to the kingdom, which were lost on the shoals of Padua, and their captains went back to Cochym in their boats, and this Fernan de Magalhães remained in the ships with the men taking care of the ships until caravels came from Cochim in which much property, belonging to the king and to private individuals, was saved. This Fernan de Magalhães, on going to the kingdom and bringing before the king his services, asked in satisfaction for them that he should have an increase in his palace stipend of a hundred reis a month, which the king refused him, because he did not find favour with him, or because it was so permitted to be. Fernan de Magalhães, offended at this, because he much entreated the king to do it, and he would not, asked his leave to go and live with whoever would show him favour, where he might obtain more good fortune than with him. The king told him to do as he pleased; for which he wished to kiss his hand, which the king did not choose to give him."

Castanheda, in relating the wreck on the Padua banks, says (lib. iii, cap. v) :

" There were disputes as to who should go away with the captains from the grounded vessels, and Magellan said that it was clear that all could not go away, and that to avoid strife, which was commencing, let the gentlemen and chief men go away with the captains, and he would remain with the sailors and other common people, provided they would promise to return for him, or get the governor to send for him. This they swore to, and Fernan de Magalhães stayed behind, the common people consented to remain, for otherwise there must have been strife. As Magalhães was in the boat, when it was nearly ready to go away, a sailor, thinking that he repented himself of remaining, said to him: 'Sir, did you not promise to remain with us?' He replied : 'Yes; and see, I am coming;' and went to them and remained with them. In this he shewed great courage, and confidence in the men."

Barros relates the incident of the two vessels wrecked on the banks of Padua, and says that Antonio Pacheco was sent with a caravel to their assistance ; and that:

"As much honour as Antonio Pacheco gained in the method with which he recovered these crews, with the differences which he had with them on account of some goods which the men took with them, so much honour also did Magellan gain by the good management of these men, which he shewed whilst waiting with them till they came to fetch them. And if he had had as much loyalty to his king and country, as he observed with a friend of his, on whose account he would not go away in company with Bastian de Sousa [the captain]; for they did not take away the other man, as he was not a man of much importance, perchance he would not have lost himself with a name of infamy, as will be seen further on."—*Decad.* II, lib. IV; chap. i.

Thus Castanheda and Barros, who are both of them very hostile to Magellan, have preserved one of the finest traits of his life: Whether the motive of Magellan in remaining by the wreck was fidelity to the interests of his friend, or devotion to the common seamen, or the repugnance of an officer and a gentleman to abandon a ship which had not broken up, this trait is alone sufficient to show that he was incapable of disloyalty, or of being influenced by pique, as the Portuguese historians have represented.

The next mention we find of Magellan is in the following document, preserved in the archives of Lisbon, which contains an account of a Council of War held by Albuquerque respecting his attack on Goa. This document confirms what Correa says of Albuquerque's departure from Cochym for Goa.

*Council held by Alfonso d'Albuquerque with the Captains
with respect to going to Goa.*

Torre do Tombo. Corpo Chron. Part 2a, Maç 23, Doc. 190.

Thursday, which was the tenth day of the month of October, of five hundred and ten, the captain-major ordered all the captains of the king our sovereign to be summoned in Cochim, in order to hold a council with them, to which council there came those named below, and no others. This council was as to whether, whilst the ships of burden remained in Cochim taking in their cargo, it seemed good to them to carry all their crews with them to the action of Goa, or not.

Fernan de Magalhães said that it seemed to him that the captain-major ought not to take the ships of burden to Goa, inasmuch as if they went thither they could not pass this year to Portugal, since we are at the twelfth of October; and that, making their shortest course without touching at Cananor, nor at any other port, it was not possible to lay the fleet before the port of Goa before the eighth of November,[1] as the winds were now contrary for that place : and with respect to the crews, let his worship say whether it was well that they should go, that it seemed to him that he ought not to take them, since there did not remain time for them to lay out their money, nor to do anything of what was necessary for the voyage ; and this said Fernan de Magalhães.

The following gave an opinion :

    Nuno Vaz, captain of the Rumesa.
    Antonio da Costa...Rei Pequeno.
    Duarte da Silva...Galé Grande.
    *Simão Martins.
    *D. João de Lima...Sta. Maria d'Ajuda.

[1] Albuquerque did not arrive before Goa till the 24th November. Correa, tom. II, p. 145.

*Sebastian de Miranda...Galé Pequeno.
Fernan de Magalhães.[1]
Jeronimo Teixeira...Sta. Maria do Campo.
*Jorge da Silveira.
Francisco de Sousa...Boa Ventura.
*Manuel da Cunha.
*Garcia de Sousa...Sta. Clara.
Francisco Corvinel...Sant-Iago.
Lourenço de Paiva.
Antonio Real, alcaìde-mór and captain of Cochim.
Gonzalo de Sequeira, captain-major of the fleet which had just come from Portugal.
Affonso d'Albuquerque said at the end what he determined to do.

(N.B. Albuquerque said at the end of these opinions that he was determined to sail on the following day, the eleventh of October, with the captains who wished to accompany him. Therefore, *we are at the twelfth of October,* means that that day was close at hand, and not that the council was held on that day.)

Gaspar Correa says, tome II, p. 138:

" When this was thus ended, the governor told all the captains that he was going immediately, and that he would sail from Cananor with all the ships and men that he could take, and go and take Goa, as he trusted in the Lord's Passion that He would assist him; and he gave them notice that so he would act, and not occupy himself with anything else : and he gave them all this notice, because he trusted in the Lord, that he should be able to send news to the king in these ships, that he was taking his rest inside the city of Goa : and, as it was already October, whoever had the will to serve the king, and win such great honour, as it would be to find oneself in such a noble action, would still have time enough to witness the action and return to embark in

---

[1] A facsimile of this signature is given in the plate.

his ship, carrying away so much honour from having been present in the action: and each one was to act according to his own will, for he would give an account of all to the king in his letters. But the captains, occupied with their profits of selling and taking in cargo, set little store by this, and the governor departed, saying that he was not going to take anyone away with him against his will."

Albuquerque then went to Cananor, which G. Correa says he again left on the 3rd October for Goa (tom. II, p. 140); *tres* is probably an error for *treze*, the 13th, which would be in accordance with the statement of the document that Albuquerque sailed from Cochim on the 11th of October. Gaspar Correa gives the following names of captains who accompanied Albuquerque against Goa.

*Joan de Lima.	Joan Serrano.
Jeronymo de Lima, his brother.	Diogo Mendes de Vascogon-
Manuel de Lacerda.	cellos.
Fernan Peres d'Andrade.	Pero Coresma.
Simão d'Andrade, his brother.	Baltesar da Silva.
Diogo Fernandes de Beja.	Mice Vinete Cerniche.
*Manuel da Cunha.	Antonio Raposo.
Duarte de Mello.	*Simão Martins.
Francisco de Tavora.	Gaspar de Paiva.
Vasco Fernandes Coutinho.	Francisco Pantoja.
*Gracia de Sousa.	*Bastian de Miranda, d'Azevedo.
Gaspar Cão.	Afonso Pessoa.
Lopo Vaz de Sampayo.	Jorge Martins de Lião.
Ayres da Silva.	Francisco Pereira.
Diniz Fernandes de Mello.	

Twenty-eight ships, and 1,700 Portuguese.

He also mentions, p. 145, the following gentlemen as being with Albuquerque in the attack on Goa:

* The names marked with an asterisk are among those who gave an opinion at the Council of War above mentioned.

Fernan Gomez de Lemos.

Nuno Vaz de Castello Branco.

*Jorge da Silveira.

Ruy de Brito.

Luis Coutinho, brother of Vasco Fernandes.

Simão d'Andrade, brother of Fernan Peres.

Gonzalo d'Almeida.

Simão Martins Henriques.

Payo Rodrigues de Sousa.

Diogo Pires de Miranda.

Duarte de Mello.

Alvaro Paçanha.

Luis Preto.

Pero d'Afonsequa.

Antonio de Matos.

Antonio Diniz.

And other gentlemen.

The supposition may be hazarded that it was this opinion which Magellan gave at the Council of War in opposition to Alfonso d'Albuquerque, which set D. Manuel against him. Such opposition was enough to have made Albuquerque write unfavourably of Magellan to D. Manuel; and the ill-will of D. Manuel to Magellan, and his refusal to grant him a due recognition of his services is not otherwise sufficiently accounted for. On the other hand, Gaspar Correa, who was Albuquerque's secretary at one time, does not indicate this; but Correa is the most friendly to Magellan of all the Portuguese historians, and does not appear, like the others, to have taxed Magellan with treason.

After this, Magellan appears to have left India, and to have been stationed at Azamor in Morocco, where, in a skirmish with the Arabs, he was wounded in the leg by a javelin, which left him somewhat lame. After that, some disputes arose as to the distribution amongst the townsmen of some cattle that had been captured from the Arabs. When João Soarez, Captain of Azamor, left that place, and was succeeded by D. Pedro de Sousa, Magellan left Azamor without leave from D. Pedro de Sousa, and came to Portugal;

his petition with regard to the increase of his palace
stipend had already been sent to D. Manuel; but
D. Pedro de Sousa having written to the king of Magellan having left Azamor without leave of absence,
and of the complaints made about the cattle, the king
refused to receive Magellan, and commanded him to
return at once to Azamor, and there give himself up
as he was accused. When he arrived there, as Barros
says, either because he was free from blame, or, as was
mostly asserted, because the frontier officers of Azamor,
in order not to vex him, would not accuse him, he
received a sentence of acquittal, and returned with it
to Portugal; but the king always bore ill-will to him,
and, Magellan's requests not being granted, he set about
that business of which he had written to his friend
Francisco Serrano, who was in Maluco.

After Magellan had disnaturalised himself, he took
refuge in Spain, accompanied by the astrologer Ruy
Faleiro, and having arrived at Seville on the 20th of
October, 1517, he entered upon negotiations with the
ministers of Charles V; and the King of Portugal did
his utmost, through his agents, to thwart him; Osorio
says that the king would have succeeded in dissuading
Charles V from employing Magellan, had not the
Spanish nobles persuaded him not to lose such an
opportunity of increasing the Spanish empire. Charles
V then ordered ships to be provided for Magellan,
by which he might discover a new way to the east.

Here follows an abstract of documents, copies of
which are contained in the Torre do Tombo, relating
to the appointment of Magellan, and the privileges and

powers conferred upon him : these documents are dated
in the spring of 1518, more than a year before Magellan sailed ; and it appears that delay was caused
partly through the procrastination of the Spanish
authorities in Seville, who were charged with equipping
the fleet, and partly by the intrigues of the agents of
the King of Portugal.   These intrigues appear to have
been partially successful, and to have caused delay. A
final order for the departure of Magellan was given in
Barcelona, April 19th, 1519. The original of this
document is preserved in the Lisbon archives, and it
was probably carried out with the fleet, and fell into
the possession of the Portuguese in the Moluccas after
Magellan's death ; a translation of this order is given
below, and the text is in the Appendix.

After this document, translations are given of two
letters (the text of which is given in the Appendix)
from Alvaro da Costa, the Portuguese ambassador in
Spain, and from Sebastian Alvarez, the Portuguese
factor, about the efforts made by them to prevent Magellan's expedition.   M. Ferdinand Denis, in the *Bio-
graphie Universelle*, mentions that Alvaro da Costa is
said to have pushed his zeal to the extremity of wishing to assassinate Magellan, and even his poor asso-
ciate, Ruy Faleiro ; this, with regard to the latter,
seems hardly probable, judging from Costa's own
letter.   Navarrete states that the Portuguese agents
succeeding in exciting the mob of Seville against
Magellan on the 22nd of October, 1518, under the
empty pretext that he was substituting the arms of
Portugal for those of Castile in his ships.   Faria y

Sousa, in his *Europa Portuguesa*, tom. II, pt. IV, cap. I, p. 543, says .

"D. Fernando de Vasconcellos, Bishop of Lamego, alone expressed the desire that the King of Portugal should either grant favours to him (Magellan) or else have him killed, because his intentions were most dangerous to the kingdom. The result of this (counsel) was that the kingdom received a great disappointment, and Magellan glorious and everlasting fame; since, whilst the world endures it will endure in the monument of his name, which has remained applied to all the South Sea and to his Straits."

> Que nunca se vera tão forte peito,
> Do Gangetico mar ao Gaditano;
> Nem das Boreaes ondas ao Estreito,
> Que mostrou o aggravado Lusitano.
>
> *Camoens*, Canto II, 55.

> And never will their prowess find its mate,
> No, not from Ganges to the Gadite shore,
> Not from Arcturus to the Southern Strait
> Which first an injured Lusian will explore.
>
> *Quillinan.*

> Eis aqui as nóvas portas do Oriente,
> Que vosoutros agora ao mundo dais,
> Abrindo a porta ao vasto mar patente,
> Que com tam forte peito navegais:
> Mas he tambem razaō, que no ponente
> De hum Lusitano hum feito inda vejais,
> Que de seu Rey monstrandose agravado,
> Caminho ha de fazer nunqua cuidado.
>
> *Camoens*, Canto x, 138.

> Thus hast thou all the regions of the East,
> Which by thee giv'n unto the world is now::
> Opening a way with an undaunted breast,
> Through that vast sea which none before did plough.
> But it is likewise reason, in the West
> That of a Lusian too one action thou
>   Shouldst understand, who (angry with his king)
>   Achieves a great and memorable thing.
>
> *Fanshaw.*

Contract and Agreement made by the King of Castile with Fernan Magellan for the discovery which he was to make, a copy of which he carried with him, signed by the Officers of the King of Castile, and made by his Secretary Fernan de los Cobos, and copied word for word.[1]

Gav. 18, Maço 10, No. 4.

Certificate given in Seville that the commendador Fernan de Magallanes, and the bachelor Ruy Faleiro, Portuguese, presented themselves at the Audiencia on the fourth of May, of 1518, before Dr. Sancho de Matienzo, the contador Juan Lopez de Ricalde, and the factor Juan de Aranda, judges and fiscals of their Highnesses, of the India House, residing in this city, in the presence of Juan Gutierrez Calderon, clerk of their H.H., and his Notary public, on behalf of Diego de Porras, chief clerk in civil and criminal causes of the said India House; and they presented to the judges two capitulations written on paper and signed by his Highness, and one sealed with a seal of coloured wax at the back and other necessary signatures, and two royal orders (*cedulas*) of H.H. signed with his royal name, all written by the secretary Fernan de los Cobos, the tenour of all which, one after another, is as follows.

The King:

"Since you, Fernando de Magallanes, a knight, native of the Kingdom of Portugal, and the bachelor Ruy Faleiro, also a native of that kingdom, wish to render us a great service in the limits which belong to us in the ocean within the bounds of our demarcation, we order the following capitulation to be established with you for that purpose."

---

[1] This document has been abridged here; it is taken from a copy in the Torre do Tombo, made from another copy, which is very illegible. The Spanish is rather antiquated, and much debased, apparently by Portuguese copyists, who have mixed up their own orthography. The Secretary's name was Francisco, not Fernan.

" Firstly : That you are to go with good luck to discover the part of the ocean within our limits and demarcation, and because it would not be in reason that, while you go to do the above mentioned, that other persons should cross you to do the same, and taking into consideration that you undertake the labour of this enterprise, it is my favour and will, and I promise that for the first ten following years we will not give leave to any person to go and discover by the same road and course by which you shall go ; and if anyone desire to undertake it and should ask our leave for it, before giving it, we will let you know of it in order that if you should be ready to make it in that time in which they offer, you should do so, providing an equal sufficiency and equipment, and as many ships as the other persons who may wish to make the said discovery : but, be it understood that, if we please to send to discover, or to give leave for it to such other persons as we please by way of the south-west in the parts of the islands and mainland, and all other parts which are discovered towards the part where they are to seek the strait of those seas (para buscar el estrecho de aquellas mares),[1] we may order it to be done, or give leave to other persons to do it, both of the mainland by the South Sea, which is discovered, or from the island of S. Miguel, if they wish to go and discover, they may do so. Also, if the governor and people who are now, by our orders, or may in future be in the said mainland, or other of our subjects may wish to discover in the South Sea, they may do so, notwithstanding the above, or any section or clause of this capitulation. Also, you may discover in any of those parts what has not yet been discovered, so that you do not discover nor do anything in the demarcation and limits of the most serene King of Portugal, my very dear and well-beloved uncle and brother, nor to his prejudice, but only within the limits of our demarcation."

---

[1] From this it appears that Magellan anticipated that America would end like Africa.

In consideration of their good-will and services, the next paragraph grants the right to levy upon any isles or countries settled by them after the expenses have been paid, a twentieth part, with the title of our Adelantados and Governors of the said countries and isles, "you, and your sons and rightful heirs for ever, so that they remain for us and the kings that may come after us, and your sons and heirs being natives of our realms and married in them; and of this we will send you your formal letter of privileges."

The next paragraph grants the right to invest in goods each year the value of a thousand ducats, cost price, to sell in the islands and countries, and bring back the returns, paying only a twentieth in duty to the king without other payment. This only after the return from the voyage, not during it.

Also to grant them greater favour, if more than six islands should be discovered; after six have been set apart for the king, they might mark out two from which they might take the fifteenth part of all the net profits and duties of the king after the expenses had been deducted.

Also of all the net profit that there may be for the king on the return of the fleet, after this first voyage, deducting its expense, they may take a fifth part.

"In order that you may better carry this out, I will order the equipment of five ships, two of one hundred and thirty tons each, and two others of ninety, and another of sixty tons, provided with men, victuals, and artillery; that is to say, that the said ships shall be supplied for two years, and there shall go in them two hundred and thirty-four persons for their management: amongst masters, mariners, ship-boys, and all other people that are of necessity, according to the memorial, and this we will order to be carried out by our officers in Seville."

Also if either of them died, this agreement was to be kept with, and by the other, as it would have been kept with both if they were alive.

The next paragraph says that a factor, a treasurer, an

accountant, and clerks of the said ships, shall keep the accounts of all the expenses of the fleet.

"All which I promise and plight my faith and royal word that I will order it to be observed to you, in all and for all, according as is contained above, and upon it I have ordered this present to be given, signed with my name. Dated in Valladolid, the twenty-second day of March, of five hundred and eighteen years.

"Yo el Rey.

"By order of the King,

"FRANCISCO DE LOS COBOS."

Another copy of the same document has the heading :—

Doña Juana and Don Carlos, her son, by the grace of God, Queen and King of Castile, Leon, Aragon, the two Sicilies, and Jerusalem, of Navarra, Granada, Toledo, Valencia, Galicia, the Mallorcas, Seville, Sardinia, Cordova, Corsica, Murcia, Jaen, the Algarves, of Aljazira, Gibraltar, of the Canary Isles, of the Indies, isles and mainland of the Ocean-sea, Counts of Barcelona, Lords of Biscay and Molina, Dukes of Athens and Neopatria, Counts of Roussillon and Cerdaña, Marquises of Euristan and Gociano, Archdukes of Austria, Dukes of Bergoña and Brabant, Counts of Flanders and Tirol, etc.

Another letter, also dated Valladolid, March 22nd, 1518, and signed by the king, and the secretary Francisco de los Cobos, and signed at the back by Joanes Beijamanse, Fonseca Archiepiscopus, Episcopus, registered, Johan de Samana, Guillermo Chancellor, confers upon Magellan the power of deciding and executing short and summary justice by sea or land in case of suits or disputes arising in the fleet.

Another royal letter of the same date as the above

orders the officers of the India House to provide Magellan with five ships, crews, provisions, etc., according to the memorial which is signed by our chancellor of Bargonha and by the Archbishop of Rosano and Bishop of Burgos ; and bids them use all dispatch.

Another royal letter, dated Aranda, 17th of April, 1518, to Magellan and Ruy Faleiro, says that if, after they shall have sailed, either or both of them should die, and that they should have given to the people in the fleet instructions and orders which should be necessary for the discovery ; and if they, profiting by them, should discover the isles and parts which they were going to discover, then their heirs and successors should enjoy the favours and privileges contained in the said capitulations.

The document then states that Magellan and Ruy Faleiro having presented the capitulations and letters and royal orders of his highness to the said judges, they summoned and required them to fulfil them according to their contents, and they requested this in the presence of the witnesses, Francisco de Santa Cruz, alguazil Lorenzo Pinelo, and Francisco de Collantes, porter of the Audiencia of the said House. Then the judges took the letters in their hands, and kissed them, and put them on their heads, as the orders of their king, and natural sovereign, whom may God suffer to live and reign many years ; and they would answer more at length in complying with the orders. Witnesses the above-named.

After that, on Monday, at the Audiencia de la Nona, on the thirty-first day of May of 1518, the said judges,

Dr. Sancho de Matienzo and the contador Juan Lopez de Ricalde, appeared before me, the said Juan Gutierrez Calderon, the above-mentioned clerk and notary, and presented an answer signed with their names to the presentation made by the Portuguese captains of the royal orders and letters. And this reply is as follows.

The said judges state, in reply, that the king's letters order them to provide five ships, and men and provisions as may be necessary, in conformity with a memorial which the captains bring, signed by the great Chancellor of Burgundy and by the very Reverend Archbishop of Rosano and Bishop of Burgos, which said memorial up to this time has not been shown to us, and without it we cannot undertake anything; so let his Highness send us orders according to that the said despatch signed, as has been said, by the chancellor and bishop; and we are ready to fulfil the orders which his Highness sends, having at the time moneys of his Highness in our power. This they said, and gave as their answers, and signed it with their names, Doctor Matienzo, Juan Lopez de Ricalde.

Magellan and Ruy Faleiro asked from Juan Gutierres Calderon, Clerk and Notary Public, a certificate and legalised copy of what had passed for the conservation of their rights, which he accordingly gave him, dated on the said day and month (31st May) of 1518.

The letter, the text of which is given in the Appendix No. iii, the original of which appears to have fallen into the hands of the Portuguese at the Moluccas, is as follows:

d

The King:

Fernando de Magallañs and Ruy Faleiro, Knights of the Order of St. James, our captains-general of the fleet, which we command to be equipped to go to discover, and the other separate captains of the said fleet, and pilots, masters, quarter-masters, and seamen of the said fleet: Inasmuch as I know for certain, according to the much information which I have obtained from persons who have seen it by experience, that there are spices in the islands of Maluco; and, chiefly, you are going to seek them with this said fleet, and my will is that you should straightway follow the voyage to the said islands in the form and guise which I have said and commanded to you, the said Ferdinand de Magallañs; moreover, I command you all and each one of you that in the navigation of the said voyage you follow the opinion and determination of the said Ferdinand de Magallañs, in order that first and foremost, before any other part, you should go to the said islands of Maluco, without there being any shortcoming in this, because thus it is fitting for our service, and after this done, the rest that may be convenient may be sought for according to what you have been commanded, and one and all neither do nor let them do anything else in anywise, under pain of losing their goods and their persons, at our discretion. Done in Barcelona, nineteenth day of April, year of one thousand five hundred and nineteen.

I, the King.

By order of the King,

Fr^{co} de los Covos.

(*Docket*).—In order that those of the fleet may follow the opinion and determination of Magallañs, in order that first and before anything else they go to the spices.

Letter of Alvaro da Costa, giving an Account to the King Dom Manuel of what passed with the King of Castile, to dissuade him from the discovery which he determined to order the execution of, by Fernan de Magalhães.

Torre do Tombo.   Gav. 18, Maço 8, No. 38.

Sire,

With respect to the business of Fernam de Magalhaes, I have done and laboured very much, as God knows, as I have written to you at length ; and now, Xebres being ill, I have spoken on this matter very firmly to the king, laying before him all the objections that there were in it, and besides other matters, setting forth how ill-seeming and unusual a matter it was for a king to receive the vassals of another king his friend, against his will; which was a thing which was not usual amongst knights, and was held to be a great fault, and a very ill-looking thing: also that I had just before offered to him in Valladolid the services of your royal self, and kingdom and lordships, while he was already receiving these men against your pleasure; and I begged him to look well that this was not a time for causing discontent to your Highness, especially in a matter of such little importance to him, and of such little certainty, and that he had many vassals and men for making discoveries when the time came, without making use of those who came away from your Highness discontented, and that your Highness could not fail to suspect that these men would labour more to do you a dis-service than for anything else ; and that his Highness had now so much to do with discovering his own kingdoms and lordships, and settling them, that such novelties ought hardly to come into his recollection, from which scandals might follow, and other things which might well be dispensed with.   I also laid before him

d 2

how ill this appeared in the year and period of the marriage, and increase of family duty and affection, and that it seemed to me that your Highness would feel deeply the knowledge that these men asked his leave to return, and that he did not give it; which would be two evils, the receiving them against your will, and the retaining them against their own wills : and I begged him on account of what was fitting for his service, and for that of your Highness that of two things he should do one, either give them leave to go, or lay aside this business for this year, by which much would not be lost, and such means might be taken that he might be served without your Highness receiving displeasure from the manner in which this should be done.

He, Sire, remained so surprised at what I said to him, that I was amazed; and he replied to me with the best words in the world, and that on no account did he desire that anything should be done, by which your Highness should be displeased, and many other good words; and he told me to speak to the Cardinal, and to relate everything to him. I, Sire, had already talked it all well over with the Cardinal, who is the best thing here, and this business does not seem good to him, and he promised me to labour as much as he could to avoid speaking to the king; and for this purpose they summoned the Bishop of Burgos, who is the person who upholds this business, and so two of the Council again made the king believe that in this he was not in fault towards your Highness, because he was not sending to make discoveries except within his limit, and very far off from the affairs of your Highness; and that your Highness ought not to take it ill that he made use of two of your vassals, men of little substance, while your Highness was making use of the services of many natives of Castile; and they alleged many other arguments : lastly, the Cardinal told me that the Bishop and those men used so much urgency in this, that at present the king could not take any other determination.

As long as Xebres was well I continued to set this busi-

ness before him, as I have said, and much more. He puts
the blame upon these Castilians who lead the king into
this matter, and withal that, he will speak to the king.
Some days past I entreated him much about this business,
and he never took a determination, and I think that he will
do likewise now. It appears to me, Sire, that your Highness might get back Fernam de Magalhāes, which would
be a great buffet to these people. I do not reckon the
bachelor [Ruy Faleiro] for much, for he is almost out of his
mind. I took steps with Dom Jorge[1] with respect to the
going there of his alcaide, and he says that he will go at
any rate; so, Sire, as this is in this manner, for all that, I
will never desist from striving in this to the extent of my
power.

Let not your Highness consider that I said much to the
king in what I did say to him, because, besides what I said
being all true, these people, as I say, do not feel anything,
neither has the king liberty up to this time to do anything
of himself, and on this account what he does (*his affairs*)
need to be felt less. The Lord increase the life and State
of your Highness for His holy service. From Saragoça,
Tuesday at night, the twenty-eighth of September [1518].[2]

I kiss the hands of your Highness.

ALVARO DA COSTA.

[1] D. Jorge of Portugal, Bishop of Siguenza.

[2] The date of the year is not given; however, as the despatch
mentions this year as the year of the marriage, it must be assumed
to have been written in 1518. D. Manuel married the daughter
of Philip I, Da. Leonor, in Villa do Crato, 24th November, 1518.
The treaty of the marriage was made at Saragossa 22nd May,
1518, and ratified in Saragossa 16th July, 1518.

*Letter from Sebastian Alvarez, Factor of Dom Manuel, to
the King, dated Seville, July* 18, 1519.

(Torre do Tombo.   Corp. Chronol., Part I.   Maço 13,
Doc. 20.)

Sire,

On the 15th of this July I received through Chavascas, the equerry, two letters from your Highness, one
of the 18th and the other of the 29th of last month, which
I understood, and without recapitulating the second one, I
answer your Highness.

There have now arrived together in this city, Christopher
de Haro and Juan de Cartagena, the chief factor of the
fleet and captain of a ship, and the treasurer and clerk of
this fleet; and in the regulations which they bring there
are clauses contrary to the instructions of Fernan de Magalhães; these having been seen by the accountant and factors
of the House of Trade, they seek how they can embroil
the affairs of Magellan, and they were at once of the opinion
of those who have recently arrived.

Together, they sent to summon Fernan de Magalhães,
and requested to know from him the order of this fleet, and
the cause why there was no captain going in the fourth
ship, but only Carvalho, who was a pilot and not a captain.
He replied, that he wished to take the ship thus for it to
carry the lantern, and for him to pass over to it from time
to time.

And they said to him that he carried many Portuguese,
and that it was not well that he should take so many.   He
answered, that he would do what he chose in the fleet without giving them any account, and that they could not do
it without rendering account to him.   There passed between them so many and such evil words, that the factors
ordered pay to be issued to the seamen and men-at-arms,
but not to any of the Portuguese whom Magellan and Ruy
Faleiro have got to take with them : and at the same time
a courier was sent to the Court of Castile.

As I saw the matter was begun and the season convenient for saying that which your Highness bade me say, I went to the lodgings of Magellan, where I found him arranging baskets and boxes with victuals of conserves and other things. I pressed him, feigning, that as I found him thus occupied, it seemed to me that the undertaking of his evil design was settled, and that, as this would be the last conversation I should have with him, I wished to recall to his memory how many times, as a good Portuguese and his friend, I had spoken to him, and opposed the great error which he was committing.

After begging his pardon, if he should receive from me any offence in the conversation, I called to his recollection how often I had spoken to him, and how well he had always answered me, and that, according to his replies, I had always hoped that at the end he would not go to the so great dis-service of your Highness; and that what I always told him was that he should see that this road had as many dangers as Saint Catharine's wheel, and that he ought to leave it and take the straight road,[1] and return to his native country and the favour of your Highness, where he would always receive benefits. In this conversation I introduced all the dangers which appeared to me, and the faults which he was committing. He said to me, that now he could do nothing else, for his honour's sake, except follow his path. I said to him, that to acquire honour unduly, and when acquired by such infamy, was neither wisdom nor honour, but rather deprivation of wisdom and honour, for he might be certain that the chief Castilians of this city, when speaking of him, held him to be a vile man, of low blood, since to the dis-service of his true king and lord he accepted such an enterprise; and so much the more since it was prepared, concerted, and requested by him, that he might be sure that he was held to be a traitor in going against the State of your Highness. Here he answered me that he saw the fault he was committing, but that he hoped to observe

---

[1] Literally, the road to Coimbra.

the service of your Highness, and to do you great service
by his going.   I told him that whoever should praise such
a speech, did not understand the matter, because, supposing
that he did not touch any of the conquest of your Highness,
how was he going to discover what he talked of; moreover,
it was to the great detriment of the revenues of your Highness, and this would be sustained by the whole realm and
by all sorts of persons : and that thought of his had been
a more virtuous one which he had when he said to me that,
if your Highness ordered him to return to Portugal, he
would do so without any other assurance of favours, and
that should your Highness not confer them, there was
always Serradossa and seven ells of serge, and some beads
of acorns.[1]   It seemed to me then that his heart was true
as to what befitted his honour and conscience ; that which
was said was so much that it is not possible to write it.

Here, Sire, he began to give a sign, telling me to tell
him more, that this did not come from myself, and that if
your Highness had bidden me say it, that I should tell him,
and the favour which you would confer upon him.   I told
him that I was not of so much tonnage as that your Highness should put me into such a business; but I said it to
him as I had done on many other occasions.   Here he
wished to do me honour, saying that if what I had begun
with him, went forward, without other persons intervening,
that your Highness would be served; but that Nuño Ribeiro
had told him one thing, and that it was of no importance;
and Joam Mendez, another, and that these did not agree;
and he told me the favour which they promised on behalf
of your Highness.   Here he made a great lamentation, and
said that he felt it all, but that he did not know of anything
by means of which he could reasonably leave a king who
had shown him so much favour.   I told him that to do that
which he ought and not to lose his honour, and the favour
which your Highness would confer upon him, would be
more certain and accompanied by truer honour : and that

---

[1] Meaning, he could become a hermit.

he should weigh his coming from Portugal, which had been for a hundred reals, more or less, of allowances,[1] which your Highness had not granted him, so as not to break your ordinance, and that two regulations had arrived contrary to his, and that which he had contracted with the King Don Carlos, and he would see whether that neglect weighed more, for him to go and do what he ought to do, or come here for that which he had come for.

He wondered much at my knowing so much, and here he told me the truth, and that the courier had left: all which I knew. And he told me that certainly there would be no reason for his throwing over the undertaking, unless they deprived him of anything which had been assigned him by the contract. But first he had to see what your Highness would do. I said to him, what more did he want to see than the instructions, and Ruy Faleiro, who said openly that he was not going to follow his lantern, and that he would navigate to the south, or would not go in the fleet? also, that he thought he was going as captain-major, whilst I knew that others were sent in opposition, whom he would not know of except at a time when he could not remedy his honour; and that he should not pay attention to the honey, which the Bishop of Burgos put to his lips, and that now was the fit time for him to see whether he would do it, and that he should give me a letter for your Highness, and that I from affection for him would go to your Highness to act on his behalf, because I had no message[2] from your Highness to occupy myself with the like, but that I only spoke what I thought as at other times I had done. He said to me that he would not say anything to me until he saw the

---

[1] This contemporary document confirms Osorio as to the cause of Magellan's being disgusted with the King of Portugal; some historians have represented the quarrel as arising from a distribution of plundered cattle. Gaspar Correa uses a similar phrase to that in this despatch, " a hundred reis, more or less".

[2] Compare this statement with that in the second line of the fifth paragraph of this despatch.

message which the courier brought: and with this we concluded. I will watch the service of your Highness to the full extent of my power.

At this juncture, it seems to me well that your Highness should know that it is certain that the navigation which these men hope to perform is known to the King Don Carlos, and Fernan Magellan has told me as much, and there might be some one to undertake the enterprise who would do more harm. I spoke to Ruy Faleiro on two occasions. He never answered me anything else than, how could he do anything against the king his lord, who did him such favour. To all that I said to him, he did not reply anything else. It seems to me that he is like a man deranged in his senses, and that this familiar of his has deprived him of whatever knowledge there was in him. It seems to me that, if Fernan Magellan were removed, that Ruy Faleiro would follow whatever Magellan did.

The ships of Magellan's fleet, Sire, are five; that is to say, one of a hundred and ten tons, two of eighty tons each, and the other two of sixty tons each, a little more or less. They are very old and patched up; for I saw them when they were beached for repairs. It is eleven months since they were repaired, and they are now afloat, and they are caulking them in the water. I went on board of them a few times, and I assure your Highness that I should be ill inclined to sail in them to the Canaries, because their knees are of touchwood.

The artillery which they all carry are eighty guns, of a very small size; only in the largest ship, in which Magellan is going, there are four very good iron cannon. All the crews whom they take in all the five vessels are two hundred and thirty men. The greater number have already received their pay; only the Portuguese, who will not accept a thousand reis, and who are waiting for the courier to arrive, because Magellan told them that he would get their pay increased, and they carry provisions for two years.

The captain of the first ship is Fernan Magellan, and of

the second, Ruy Faleiro ; of the third, Juan de Cartagena, who is the chief factor of the fleet; of the fourth, Quesada, a dependant of the Archbishop of Seville ; the fifth goes without any known captain,—Carvalho, a Portuguese, goes in her as pilot. Here it is said that, as soon as they are out of the mouth of the river, he will put into her, as captain, Alvaro da Mesquita of Estremoz, who is here.

The Portuguese who have come here to sail are,

—— Carvalho, pilot.

Estevan Gomez, pilot.

—— Serrão, pilot.

Vasco Galego, pilot ; he has been living here for some time.

Alvaro de Mesquita of Estremoz.

Martin da Mesquita of Estremoz.

Francisco d'Afonseca, son of the Corregidor of Rosmaninhal.

Christopher Ferreira, son of the Corregidor of Castelejo.

Martin Gil, son of the Judge for the Orphans of Lisbon.

Pero d'Abreu, a dependent of the Bishop of Zafy.

Duarte Barbosa, nephew of Diogo Barbosa, a dependent of the Bishop of Siguenza.

Antonio Fernandez, who lived in the Moorish quarter of Lisbon.

Luis Affonso of Beja, who was a dependent of the Lady Infanta, whom may God have in His keeping.

Juan da Silva, son of Nuno da Silva, of the island of Madeira. This man has always told me that he would not go unless, if your Highness held it to be for your service, and he behaves as a concealed friend.

Faleiro has got here his father and mother, and brothers, one of whom he takes with him.

Other small people of the servants of these also say that they are going, of which I will make a report to your Highness, if you command it, when they go.

The fifth part of this armament is from Cristoval de Haro,· who has spent on it four thousand ducats. They say here that your Highness had ordered to take from him there [in Portugal] twenty thousand cruzados of property. He gives here information about the fleets of your Highness, both of what is done, and of what is to be done. I learned that by a servant of his whom he has got there; by obtaining from him the letters, your Highness might be able to know by what means he learns these secrets.

The goods which they take are copper, quicksilver, common cloths of colours, common coloured silks, and jackets made of these silks.

It is assured that this fleet will start down the river at the end of this July; but it does not seem so to me, nor before the middle of August, even though the courier should come more quickly.

The course which it is said they are to take is straight to Cape Frio, Brasil remaining on their right hand, until they reach the line of the demarcation; from thence they are to navigate to the west and west-north-west, straight to Maluco, which land of Maluco I have seen laid down on the sphere and map, which the son of Reynell made here, which was not completed when his father came here for him; and his father finished it all, and placed these lands of Maluco; and after this pattern all the maps are made, which Diogo Ribeiro makes, and he makes the compasses, quadrants, and globes, but he does not go in the fleet, nor does he wish to do more than gain his living by his skill.[1]

From this Cape Frio, until the islands of Maluco throughout this navigation, there are no lands laid down in the maps which they carry with them. Please God the Almighty that they may make such a voyage as did the Cortereals,[2]

---

[1] . Diego Ribeiro was, later, the cosmographer of Charles V, and, with Martin Centurion in 1524, he translated into Spanish the Book of Duarte Barbosa and Magellan on the coasts of the Indian Ocean.

[2] *Id est*, never be heard of again. See Major's *Pce. Henry*, p. 374.

and that your Highness may be at rest, and for ever be envied, as you are, by all princes.

Sire, another fleet is being prepared of three small rotten ships, in which Andres Niño goes as captain; he takes out, inside these old ships, two other small vessels built in pieces; he goes to the mainland which Pedre Ayres discovered, to the port of Larym, and from thence he is to go by land twenty leagues to the South Sea, whither he is to carry by land the newly-built ships, with the rigging of the old ones, and to fit them out on that South Sea, and with these vessels he is to discover for a thousand leagues, and not more, towards the west of the coasts of the land which is named Gataio; and in these Gil Gonzalez, the accountant of the Island of Hispaniola, is to go as captain-major, and they are going for two years. When these fleets have sailed, another of four ships will then be made to go, as it is said, on the track of Magellan; but, as this is not yet put into gear for performance, nothing certain is known: and this is arranged by Christoval de Haro. Whatever more may occur, I will make known to your Highness.

As to the news of the fleet which the King Don Carlos orders to be built to defend himself from, or to attack France, or to go to the Empire, as it is said, I excuse myself from writing of it to your Highness, since your Highness will obtain them with more certainty from Nuno Ribeiro, who is in Cartagena. But there is certain news in this city by letters, that the King of France announces that the King Don Carlos is not going to be emperor, and that he will be it. The Pope assists the King of France in an honest way. He grants to him four cardinal's hats for him to give to whomsoever he pleases. It is said that the King of France keeps them to give to those whom the electors of the empire might wish. There it is assured that either the King of France will be emperor or else the person he may choose. I will take especial care to inform your Highness of what more happens with these fleets, although I had become cool in this matter, because it seemed to me that your Highness wished to learn it from some one else; for I saw here Nuno Ribeiro and other persons who spoke to me in a dissembling manner, and seeking to learn about me. I kiss the hands of your Highness.   From Seville, the 18th of July, of 1519.   SEBASTIAN ALVAREZ.

The long interval which elapsed before the example set by Magellan was followed by Drake and Van Noort (for the expedition of the Comendador Loaysa in 1527, and two others having failed, this voyage was not again attempted in those times by the Spaniards) is a proof that greater hardihood was displayed in Magellan's voyage than in those of Columbus and Gama; and the fortitude and constancy of Magellan appear strongly from the foregoing despatches, since in addition to the physical difficulties of his enterprise, he had to struggle against intrigues, jealousy, and the alternate upbraiding and cajolery of the King of Portugal's agents.   The despatch of Sebastian Alvarez to Dom Manuel, though biassed as it naturally is, shows that whatever he and the Portuguese of that day thought of Magellan's design, he himself did not consider that he was doing anything injurious to his king or country, and Camoens, though he repeats the hackneyed accusation of disloyalty against Magellan, yet boasts of his achievements as a lasting honour to Portugal, in the following lines :

> " Fired by thy fame,[1] and with his king in ire,
> To match thy deeds shall Magalhaens aspire :
> In all but loyalty, of Lusian soul,
> No fear, no danger shall his toils controul.
> Along these regions from the burning zone
> To deepest south he dares the course unknown.

[1] The fame of Vasco da Gama.

While to the kingdoms of the rising day,
To rival thee he holds the western way,
A land of giants shall his eyes behold,
Of camel strength, surpassing human mould :
And onward still, thy fame, his proud heart's guide,
Haunting him unappeased, the dreary tide
Beneath the southern star's cold gleam he braves,
And stems the whirls of land-surrounded waves.
FOR EVER SACRED TO THE HERO'S FAME
THESE FOAMING STRAITS SHALL BEAR HIS DEATHLESS NAME.
Through these dread jaws of rock he presses on ;
Another ocean's breast, immense, unknown,
Beneath the south's cold wings, unmeasured, wide,
Receives his vessels ; through the dreary tide
In darkling shades where never man before
Heard the waves howl, he dares the nameless shore.
Thus far, O favoured Lusians, bounteous heaven
Your nation's glories to your view has given.
What ensigns, blazing to the morn, pursue
The path of heroes, opened first by you !
Still be it your's the first in fame to shine :
Thus shall your brides[1] new chaplets still entwine,
With laurels ever new your brows enfold,
And braid your wavy locks with radiant gold."[2]

The poet of the Lusiad, who had said that the Muses
sang of Gama unwillingly, here concludes his praises
of Magellan with a promise to the Portuguese of ever
renewed praise—a promise which will be fulfilled by
posterity whenever the character and enterprise of Magellan are compared with those of his contemporaries;
for whilst the cruelty and violence of Gama, and the
difficulty his companions had in restraining him, were
very serious defects in his character, Magellan gave

---

[1] The nymphs of the *Ilha namorada*, or Fame.
[2] From the rather free translation of *Mickle*.

many noble examples of the opposite virtues and of
other qualities of a very high order. His conduct
on the occasion of the shipwreck near the Maldive
Islands has been already described; the clemency with
which he tempered justice when he put ,down the
mutiny in Port St. Julian—a mutiny which Sebastian
Alvarez, the King of Portugal's agent, would appear
to have been privy to, if indeed he did not prepare it,
shows great self-restraint, and the whole of his conduct in the islands of Sebu and Matan, where he fell,
defending the retreat of his companions, is more like
that of the knights errant of an earlier date, than that
of his contemporaries. Pigafetta, who was with him
at his death, was deeply affected by it, and recounts
his many virtues and qualities in an appeal to the
Grand Master of Rhodes not to allow Magellan's
memory to be lost.

Most of the captains of ships at this time, and long
afterwards, were soldiers put into naval commands;
but Magellan, besides being a military officer, was
also an experienced and learned navigator, and Pigafetta's Treatise of Navigation may be taken as the
result of Magellan's instruction in that art.[1] The

---

[1] A fuller treatise of navigation, as then practised, is contained
in a book written by Francisco Faleiro, probably a brother of Ruy
Faleiro, thus described by Barbosa Machado, in his *Biblioteca
Lusitana:*—"Francisco Faleiro, who was equally well versed in
astronomy and navigation, gave a clear statement of his science
in those arts in the following work: *Tratado de la Esfera y del
Arte de Marear, con el Regimento de las Alturas.* Sevilla, por Juan
Cronberger, 1535. 4to." This book is very rare; there is a copy
in the Hydrographer's office at Madrid.

voyage of Columbus, which employed only thirty-three days out and twenty-eight homeward-bound, cannot be compared with that of Magellan, and if Columbus was as good a seaman and navigator as Magellan, yet a certain superiority must be allowed to the latter on account of his numerous military exploits in India and Africa.

I have not been able to ascertain who was Juan Serrano, who remained in the hands of the Sebu islanders after the massacre of Duarte Barbosa and his companions, and in Navarrete he is sometimes spoken of as an inhabitant of Seville and sometimes as a Portuguese. Pigafetta speaks of him as a Spaniard, but the despatch of Sebastian Alvarez leaves no doubt as to his being Portuguese, which otherwise might have been inferred from his being a *compadre* of Joan Carvalho. It is probable that he was a relation of Francisco Serrano, the friend and correspondent of Magellan, who died in Ternate about eight months before the arrival at Tidore of Magellan's ships : it is also probable that he was the same Juan Serrano whose voyage with Francisco Serrano in 1512 from Malacca to the Java Seas is related in the book of Duarte Barbosa on the coasts of East Africa and Malabar (Hakluyt Society).

Sebastian de Elcano, a native of Guetaria in Biscay, had the good fortune to be in command of the *Victoria* on her return to Seville, and though his name is not mentioned during the voyage in any of the narratives, he reaped the principal rewards of the expedition, and on his arrival at Court, received from

e

Charles V a pension of five hundred gold crowns, and
was authorised to take for arms a globe, with the
motto "Primus me circumdedisti". Amongst other
· sonnets to his memory, are the following :

> Por tierra y por mar profundo
> Con iman y derrotero,
> Un Vascongado, el primero
> Dió la vuelta á todo el mundo.
>
> *Conchita.*

> Entraba en el breado y hueco pino,
> Tomando el dulce y suspirado puerto,
> Juan Sebastian del Cano, Vizcaino,
> Piloto de este mundo el mas esperto,
> Despues de haber andado en su camino
> Cuanto del mar se halla descubierto,
> En una nave dicha la Victoria :
> Hazaña digna de inmortal memoria.
>
> *Mosquera.*

This volume contains six contemporary accounts of
Magellan's voyage for the circumnavigation of the
globe: one was written by a Genoese pilot of the fleet;
the second by a Portuguese companion of Duarte
Barbosa, which has been preserved by Ramusio ; the
third by Antonio Pigafetta of Vicenza ; and the fourth
is a letter of Maximilian Transylvanus, a Secretary of
the Emperor Charles V; the fifth a log book of a pilot
named Francisco Albo or Alvaro ; the sixth is taken
from Gaspar Correa's *Lendas da India.*

Of Pigafetta's account, four manuscripts are known,
three of them are in French, and one in Italian.
Two of the French manuscripts are in the Bibliothèque Impériale of Paris ; one of these, numbered

5,650, is on paper; the other, numbered 68, of
the Lavallière collection, is on vellum, and is richly
illuminated; it does not contain the Brazilian and
Patagonian vocabularies given in No. 5,650, and some
rather indecent details are omitted or softened down,
which leads to the conclusion that this copy was the
one presented by Pigafetta to the Regent, Louise of
Savoy. The third French manuscript, and the most
complete, was in the possession of M. Beaupré of Nancy
till 1855, it then passed into the Solar collection, and
in 1861 was sold for 1,650 francs to a London book-
seller, and, later, was bought by Sir Thomas Phillipps
at Libri's sale.

M. Rd. Thomassy published a memoir in the *Bulletin de la Société de Géographie* of Paris, September
1843, in which he examines the question whether Pigafetta composed his account of his voyage in French.
He has come to a conclusion (which M. Ferdinand
Denis has also adopted) in favour of the French manuscript having been originally composed by Pigafetta,
and not translated from the Italian, on the grounds of
its being addressed to the grand master of Rhodes,
Villiers de l'Ile-Adam, who was himself a Frenchman,
and that Pigafetta had recently been made a Knight
of Rhodes; and that Pigafetta used the French language
for the device which he set up over his paternal house
in the street of la Luna in Vicenza, "Il n'y a pas de
roses sans épines"; that other Italians of the time had
written in French; that the Italian MS. of the Ambrosian Library of Milan, published in 1800 by Amoretti, is in bad Italian, mixed with Venetian and

Spanish, so that M. Amoretti saw in it rather a copy than the original of the relation presented to the Pope or to the Grand Master; these defects M. Amoretti removed by translating them into good Italian : also that the French edition of Fabre, though stated to be a translation from the Italian, was used in 1536 to publish an Italian edition ; whereas if an Italian edition had existed before, that of Fabre would not have been required. Fabre's edition, moreover, is very imperfect; and he puts what Pigafetta says in the third person. M. Thomassy concludes, therefore, that the version of Fabre was made from some Italian *resumé*.

In addition to the motives urged by M. Thomassy for believing that Pigafetta himself composed the French manuscripts, there is evidence of it in the phraseology of the MSS.; had these been translations from the Italian, every word would have been translated into French, whereas, instead of that, we find a great many Italian words used, especially in the vocabularies, also some Italian idioms. It was natural that Pigafetta, if he had not the French word at command, should write down an Italian one, such as "calcagno" for " talon".

For the same reason, I should be inclined to believe that the Ambrosian MS., with its mixture of Spanish words, was composed by Pigafetta himself, in whom such a mixture of words would be more natural after so long a voyage in a Spanish ship, than in an Italian scribe.

That Pigafetta did compose a work in Italian appears

from a document in the archives of Venice, containing a petition of Pigafetta to the Doge and Council of Venice, dated August 5th, 1524, applying for leave to print his account of his circumnavigation of the globe, and to have a privilege for twenty years. This is followed by a statement that the prayer of the petition was granted by the Doge and 152 of the Council, six members of which voted against Pigafetta. The text of this document is given in the Appendix ; it was communicated to me by the Geographical Society of Paris, which has published a translation of it in its bulletin of February 1869.

Until M. Amoretti published his edition of Pigafetta from the Ambrosian MS. in 1800, there never was a complete or an original Italian edition of Pigafetta ; for the quarto edition of 1536 (Grenville, 6,977), without name of author or printer, is, as is mentioned in the address to the reader, a translation from the edition of Jacques Fabre. This edition of 1536 had a privilege for fourteen years ; it must be by Ramusio, for the address to the reader is almost the same as his more abridged " discourse" in his collection of travels of Venice, 1550, and Venice, 1613, folio, 346 v. In Ramusio's collection, and in the edition of 1536, Pigafetta's voyage is preceded by the letter of Maximilian Transylvanus, Secretary of the Emperor Charles V, to the Cardinal of Salzburg. This letter of Maximilian's is not quite the same in the two books in the division of the paragraphs ; in Pigafetta's voyage there is greater similarity, and the paragraphs are numbered

identically in the edition of 1536 and in Fabre's French ∨
edition. Ramusio says :

"Magellan's voyage was written, with details, by Don
Pietro Martire, of the Council of the Indies of the Emperor, and that he had examined all those who had survived
the voyage, and returned to Seville in the year 1522 ; but,
having sent it to be printed at Rome, in the miserable sack
of that town it was lost, and it is not yet known where it
is. One who saw it and read it gives testimony of it, and
amongst the other things worthy of recollection which the
above-named Don Pietro noted in this voyage, was that the
Spaniards having navigated about three years and a month,
and the greater part of them (as is the custom of those who
navigate on the ocean) having noted down each day of each
month, when they rejoined Spain they found they had lost
one day ; that is, when they reached the port of Seville,
which was on the 7th of September, by the account which
they had kept it was the 6th. Don Pietro having related
this particularity to an excellent and rare man, Sig. Gasparo
Contarino,[1] a Venetian senator, who was then in Spain as
ambassador to his Majesty from his Republic, and having
asked him how it could be, he, as a very great philosopher,
shewed him that it could not be otherwise, as they had
navigated three years, always accompanying the sun, which
was going westwards ; and he said that the ancients had
observed that those who navigated to the west greatly
lengthened their day."

This book of Don Pietro's having been lost, says
Ramusio, he thought of translating the Latin letter of
Maximilian, and of adding to it the summary of a book
which was written by the valiant knight of Rhodes,
Messer Antonio Pigafetta, a Vicentine ; and this said
book was abridged and translated into French by a

---

[1] This name is omitted in the prologue of the edition of 1536.

very learned philosopher, named Messer Jacopo Fabri, of Paris, at the instance of the most serene mother of the most Christain King Francis, Madame Louisa the Regent, to whom the aforesaid knight had made a present of one [of his books].

This French epitome by Fabre is a small octavo of seventy-six leaves, in Gothic type (Grenville, 7,065) ; it is without date ; the title is as follows :

"Le Voyage et Navigation, faict par les Espaignolz es Isles de Mollucques, des isles quilz ont trouue audict voyage, des Roys dicelles, de leur gouuernment 't maniere de viure, auec plusieurs aultres choses.

"Cum Priuilegio, ⁋ on les vend a Paris en la maison de Simon de Colines, libraire iure de luniuersite de Paris, demeurāt en la rue sainct Jehan de Beauluais, a lenseigne du Soleil Dor."

Simon de Colines, the printer, issued his last work in 1546, and his heirs are mentioned on a work of 1550.[1]

In 1801, a French translation of Amoretti's edition of Pigafetta was published by H. J. Jansen, who added a translation from the German of M. de Murr's Notice on the Chevalier M. Behaim. In this translation, some liberties have been taken with the text ; and it is to be regretted that this translation was published instead of the French text contained in the two MSS. of the Bibliothèque Impériale ; these, even were they not Pigafetta's own composition, possess a philological interest of their own.

An English translation of Pigafetta by Richard

---

[1] Greswell, *A View of the Early Parisian Greek Press*, vol. i, p. 94.

Wren, London, 1625, is mentioned in *l'Art de Vérifier les Dates, depuis* 1770, folio, vol. iii, p. 333. There is no copy of this in the British Museum Library.

The other contemporaneous account of Magellan's voyage, a translation of which precedes that of Pigafetta's account, is by a Genoese pilot. This pilot probably was named Mestre Bautista, since Barros mentions him as a Genoese who, on the death of the pilot Joan Carvalho, was charged with piloting the *Trinidad*, which got as far as Ternate. Correa (tom. ii, p. 632) also mentions that Mestre Joan Bautista was made captain instead of Carvalho, after he had allowed the son of the King of Luzon to escape at Borneo. Of this account, three manuscripts exist; all three are in Portuguese. From two of these MSS. a printed edition was published in the *Noticias Ultramarinas*, No. ii, by the Academy of History of Lisbon. The text which served for this publication was a MS. which belonged to the library of the monks of S. Bento da Saude; and it has been supplemented and annotated from another manuscript, which is in the Bibliothèque Impériale at Paris, numbered $\frac{7158}{33}$, a copy of which was made by Dr. Antonio Nunes de Carvalho in 1831. A third manuscript of this pilot's narrative exists in the library of the Academy of History of Madrid, No. 30, Est. 11a, grada 2a.

After the Genoese pilot's narrative follows that of an anonymous Portuguese taken from Ramusio.

The letter of Maximilian, the Transylvanian, follows Pigafetta's account; this has been translated from the Latin by Mr. James Baynes, of the Printed Book

Department of the British Museum. After that comes the log-book of Francisco Albo or Alvaro, translated from a MS. in the British Museum, which is a copy from a document in Simancas. This log-book has been printed, in Navarrete's collection, apparently from the British Museum MS., and it appears to have escaped the notice of Captain Burney. It is especially valuable because it helps to fix the position of the "Unfortunate Islands", and because it establishes that the Island of Amsterdam in the Southern Indian Ocean to the North of St. Paul's Island, the discovery of which is usually attributed to the Dutch navigator Vlaming, in 1696, was discovered March 18th, 1522, by the *Victoria*, the first ship which went round the world.

There is a confusion as to the names of these two islands, which are rightly named in the Admiralty and other sea charts, but which are wrongly named in common English maps, which place St. Paul to the north of Amsterdam. The southern island is bare and arid, and the northern island has bushes and a high peak visible eighteen or twenty leagues off. Francisco Albo says this Island had no trees; but the *Victoria* may not have approached near enough to see the bushes, which, from the views of the island, appear to be near its base; it is clear that the *Victoria* approached the northern island, or Amsterdam, because not only does the latitude given by F. Albo differ from that of modern observation by only eight miles, but also because from the course steered by the *Victoria* on leaving this island, she must have sighted the northern island had the one discovered by her been the southern one. Plates are given of these two islands, taken from Valentyn's Dutch work on the East Indies. A French Geographical Dictionary sets up a claim to these islands as belonging to the government of the Isle of France or Mauritius ; it does not say on what grounds ; but if ever they were dependencies of Mauritius, they will have passed with that island into the possession of Great Britain.

Correa's narrative contains two details not given in any of the other accounts, viz., the warning given to Magellan at Tenerife by Diogo Barbosa of the intended mutiny ; and the incident of the Portuguese ship speaking the *Victoria* off the Cape of Good Hope. Correa's having been in India at the time, and relating what he heard from the Portuguese, would account for his misplacing the death of Magellan as having happened at the same time as that of Duarte Barbosa. His narrative also contains additional evidence of the violent animosity of the Portuguese against Magellan, though he himself is more favourable than other Portuguese historians to him who is one of the most renowned of their countrymen, as he undoubtedly is the greatest of ancient and modern navigators.

September 1874.

CHRONOLOGY

OF THE

FIRST VOYAGE ROUND THE WORLD.

Magellan arrives at Seville   -   - October 20,   1518

Magellan's fleet sails from Seville   Monday,[1] August 10,   1519

Magellan sails from San Lucar de Barrameda,

                Tuesday, September 20,   ,,

    ,,   arrives at Tenerife   -   - September 26,   ,,

    ,,   sails from Tenerife   -   Monday, October 3,   ,,

    ,,   arrives at Rio de Janeiro   - December 13,   ,,

    ,,   sails from Rio   -   - December 26,   ,,

    ,,   sails from Rio de la Plata   - February 2,   1520

    ,,   arrives at Port St. Julian   - March 31,

Eclipse of Sun   - April 17,

Loss of *Santiago*

Magellan sails from Port St. Julian   - August 24,   ,,

    ,,   sails from river of Santa Cruz   - October 18,   ,,

    ,,   makes Cape of the Virgins, entrance

        of Straits -   -   - October 21,   ,,

Desertion of *San Antonio*   -   - November

Magellan issues from Straits into the Pacific,

              Wednesday, November 28,   ,,

---

[1] The 10th of August was a Wednesday, and Monday was the 8th of August: all the other dates of the week and month agree and are consistent with each other.

Magellan fetches San Pablo Island   - January 24,   1521

   „   fetches Tiburones Island   - February 4,   „.

   „   reaches   the   Ladrone   Islands,
                  Wednesday, March 6,

   „   reaches Samar Island of the Philip-
       pines   -   - Saturday, March 16,

   „   reaches Mazzava Island, Thursday, March 28,

   „   arrives at Sebu Island -   - April 7,

Death of Magellan at Matan   - Saturday, April 27,

Burning of *Conception*   -   - May,

Arrival of *San Antonio* at Seville   - May 6,   „

Arrival of *Victoria* and *Trinity* at Tidore,
                  Friday, November 8,   „

Victoria sails from Tidore   -   - December 21,   „

   „   discovers Amsterdam Island, Tues-
                  day, March 18,   1522

   „   doubles the Cape of Good Hope   - May 18,[1]

   „   arrives   at   Cape   Verde   Islands,
                  Wednesday,[2] July 9,

   „   arrives at San Lucar   Saturday,[2] September 6,   „

   „   casts anchor at Seville   - Monday,[2] September 8,   „

Thanksgiving at Church of Our Lady of
       Victory   -   Tuesday,[2] September 9,   „

---

[1] According to Albo's Log-Book ; according to Pigafetta, May 6.
[2] These dates are according to the ship's time, which differed by a day from the time at the Cape Verde Islands and Seville.

CH E

Mag alh

Facsimile of the signature of Fernam de Magalhãe son of Pero de Magalhães, to a receipt in the book Moradias signed apparently in 1525, and by som erroneously supposed to be that of the navigator.

Facsimile of the signature of Duarte Barbos taken from his letter to D. Manuel, dated Canano January 12th 1513, (printed in the Appendix "Vasco da Gama", Hakluyt Society.)

Facsimile of the signature of the navigator Fernam de Magalhães, at a Council of War, at Cochim, 1510.

Magellan's signature to a letter to the Emperor Charles V, dated, Seville, October 24th 1518.

NAVIGATION AND VOYAGE WHICH FERNANDO DE MAGALHĀES MADE FROM SEVILLE TO MALUCO IN THE YEAR 1519.

(BY A GENOESE PILOT.)

HE sailed from Seville on the 10th day of August of the said year, and remained at the bar until the 21st day of September, and as soon as he got outside, he steered to the south-west to make the island of Tenerife, and they reached the said island on the day of St. Michael, which was the 29th of September.[1] Thence he made his course to fetch the Cape Verde islands, and they passed between the islands and the Cape without sighting either the one or the other.   Having got as far as this neighbourhood, he shaped his course so as to make for Brazil, and as soon as they sighted the other coast of Brazil, he steered to the south-east[2] along the coast as far as Cabo-frio, which is in twenty-three degrees south latitude ; and from this cape he steered to the west, a matter of thirty leagues, to make the Rio de Janeiro, which is in the same latitude as Cabo-frio, and they entered the said Rio on the day of St. Lucy, which was the 13th December, in which place they took in wood, and they remained there until the first octave of Christmas, which was the 26th of December of the same year.

[1] Pigafetta says the fleet went out of Seville on the 10th of August, 1519 ; that it sailed from S. Lucar on the 20th of September, and reached Tenerife on the 26th, and continued its voyage thence on the 3rd of October, navigating to the South. *Lisbon Academy note.*

[2] The Paris MS. has "south-west." This must be the true reading *Lisbon Ac. note.*   The Madrid MS. also has south-west.

They sailed from this Rio de Janeiro on the 26th December, and navigated along the coast to make the Cape of St. Mary, which is in thirty-four degrees and two-thirds; as soon as they sighted it, they made their course west-north-west, thinking they would find a passage for their voyage, and they found that they had got into a great river of fresh water, to which they gave the name of river of St. Christopher, and it is in thirty-four degrees, and they remained in it till the 2nd of February, 1520.[1]

He sailed from this river of St. Christopher on the 2nd of the said month of February; they navigated along the said coast, and further on to the south they discovered a point which is in the same river more to the south, to which they gave the name of Point St. Antony; it is in thirty-six degrees, hence they ran to the south-west, a matter of twenty-five leagues, and made another cape which they named Cape St. Apelonia, which is in thirty-six degrees; thence they navigated to the west-south-west to some shoals,[2] which they named Shoals of the Currents, which are in thirty-nine degrees; and thence they navigated out to sea, and lost sight of land for a matter of two or three days, when they again made for the land, and they came to a bay, which they entered, and ran within it the whole day, thinking that there was an outlet for Maluco, and when night came they found that it was quite closed up, and in the same night they again stood out by the way which they had come in. This bay is in thirty-four degrees;[3] they name it the island[4] of St. Matthew. They navigated from this island of St.

[1] Pigafetta mentions this river, which is the Plata, in 34 deg. 20 min. *Lisbon Ac. note.*

[2] Paris MS. "And they found themselves amongst some shoals." *Lisbon Ac. note.* The Madrid MS. is the same.

[3] Paris MS. "is in 24 degrees," which seems clearly an error of the copyists. *Lisbon Ac. note.* The Madrid MS. is in this case similar to the Paris MS.

[4] Paris MS. "the bay." *Lisbon Ac. note.* Madrid MS. "the bay."

Matthew along the coast until they reached another bay, where they caught many sea-wolves and birds; to this they gave the name of "Bay of Labours;"[1] it is in thirty-seven degrees; here they were near losing the flag-ship in a storm. Thence they navigated along the said coast, and arrived on the last day of March of the year 1520 at the Port of St. Julian, which is in forty-nine and one-third degrees,[2] and here they wintered, and found the day a little more or less than seven hours.[3]

In this port three of the ships rose up against the Captain-major, their captains saying that they intended to take him to Castile in arrest, as he was taking them all to destruction. Here, through the exertions of the said Captain-major, and the assistance and favour of the foreigners whom he carried with him, the Captain-major went to the said three ships which were already mentioned, and there the captain of one of them was killed, who was treasurer of the whole fleet, and named Luis de Mendoça; he was killed in his own ship[4] by stabs with a dagger by the chief constable of the fleet, who was sent to do this by Fernando de Magalhães in a boat with certain men. The said three ships having thus been recovered, five days later Fernando de Magalhães ordered Gaspar de Queixada to be decapitated and quartered; he was captain of one of the ships,[5] and was one of those who had mutinied.

In this port they refitted the ship. Here the captain-major made Alvaro de Mesquita, a Portuguese,[6] captain of

---

[1] We have not found mention of this name of "Bahia dos trabalhos" in any other writer. *Lisbon Ac. note.*

[2] Pigafetta puts this port in 49 deg. 30 min. The Transylvan in 49 and $\frac{1}{3}$; Barros in 50 deg., and says they arrived there on the 2nd of April. *Lisbon Ac. note.*

[3] Paris MS. "eight hours." *Lisbon Ac. note.* The Madrid MS. has "seven hours."

[4] The ship *Victoria.*   [5] The ship *Conception.*

[6] Alvaro de Mesquita was a cousin of Magellan.

one of the ships the captain of which had been killed. There
sailed from this port on the 24th of August four ships, for
the smallest of the ships had been already lost;[1] he had sent
it to reconnoitre, and the weather had been heavy, and had
cast it ashore, where all the crew had been recovered along
with the merchandise, artillery and fittings of the ship. They
remained in this port, in which they wintered, five months
and twenty-four days,[2] and they were seventy degrees less
ten minutes to the southward.[3]

They sailed on the 24th day of the month of August of
the said year from this port of St. Julian and navigated a
matter of twenty leagues along the coast, and so they entered
a river which was called Santa Cruz, which is in fifty degrees,[4]
where they took in goods and as much as they could obtain:
the crew of the lost ship were already distributed among the
other ships, for they had returned by land to where Fernando
de Magalhães was, and they continued collecting the goods
which had remained there during August and up to the 18th
September, and there they took in water and much fish
which they caught in this river; and in the other, where

---

[1] The ship which was here lost was the *Santiago*, the captain of
which was João Serrão. *Lisbon Ac. note.*

[2] There seems to be some mistake here or transcriber's error. It is
seen by the narrative that the navigators, having arrived at Port St.
Julian at the end of March, or beginning of April, and going out of it
on the 24th of August, they wintered there for the space of four months
and twenty-four days, and this is what Pigafetta says : "they passed
there nearly five months." *Lisbon Ac. note.*

[3] "E havia delles ao sull 73 gr. menos 10 minutos." It has been
impossible for us to understand the calculations of the writer in this
place. *Lisbon Ac. note.* A possible explanation of this passage may be
found in a passage of Castanheda, lib. 6, cap. 13, which describes
St. Julian as distant from Seville 71 deg. from North to South, and this
calculation would refer to the distance from Seville.

[4] The anonymous Portuguese, the companion of Duarte Barbosa,
says they gave it the name of "Santa Cruz," because they arrived there
the 14th of September, the day of the Exaltation of the Holy Cross.
Lisbon Ac. note.

they wintered, there were people like savages, and the men
are from nine to ten spans in height, very well made; they
have not got houses, they only go about from one place to
another with their flocks, and eat meat nearly raw: they are
all of them archers and kill many animals with arrows, and
with the skins they make clothes, that is to say, they make
the skins very supple, and fashion them after the shape of
the body, as well as they can, then they cover themselves
with them, and fasten them by a belt round the waist.
When they do not wish to be clothed from the waist upwards, they let that half fall which is above the waist, and
the garment remains hanging down from the belt which they
have girt round them.[1] They wear shoes which cover them
four inches above the ankle, full of straw inside to keep their
feet warm. They do not possess any iron, nor any other
ingenuity of weapons, only they make the points of their
arrows with flints, and so also the knives with which they
cut, and the adze and awls with which they cut and stitch
their shoes and clothes. They are very agile people, and
do no harm, and thus they follow their flocks: wherever
night finds them there they sleep; they carry their wives
along with them with all the chattels which they possess.
The women are very small and carry heavy burdens on their
backs; they wear shoes and clothes just like the men. Of
these men they obtained three or four and brought them in
the ships, and they all died except one, who went to Castile
in a ship which went thither.[2]

They sailed from this river of Santa Cruz on the 18th of
October:[3] they continued navigating along the coast until

[1] In the *Illustrated News* of March 27th, 1869, there is a drawing of
some Patagonians: these are represented almost exactly as they are described in the text, for some of them have their shoulders bare, and the
skins let down below the waist as here described.

[2] Probably in the ship which fled away, as will be mentioned later.
Lisbon Ac. note.

[3] Amoretti, the editor of Pigafetta, observes, that whilst the fleet was
in the river of Santa Cruz, between 50 deg. and 40 deg. South latitude,

the 21st day of the same month, October, when they discovered a cape, to which they gave the name of Cape of
the Virgins, because they sighted it on the day of the
eleven thousand virgins; it is in fifty-two degrees, a little
more or less, and from this cape a matter of two or three
leagues distance, we found ourselves at the mouth of a strait.[1]
We sailed along the said coast within that strait which they
had reached the mouth of: they entered in it a little and
anchored. Fernando de Magalhães sent to discover what
there was further in, and they found three channels, that is
to say, two more in a southerly direction, and one traversing
the country in the direction of Maluco, but at that time

there was, on the 11th of October, an eclipse of the Sun, "*which* (he
says) *the Portuguese and Spanish writers mention, and which is registered
in the astronomical tables :*" and he judges it to be an error of Castanheda putting this phenomenon on the 17th of April, and his attributing
to Magellan the calculation of longitude of which he speaks. Barros
also mentions an eclipse of the sun in April. It is noteworthy that
neither our pilot's narrative nor Pigafetta mentions a phenomenon which
still in those times did not happen without causing some impression on
men's minds, or at least without exciting public curiosity. *Lisbon
Ac. note.*

I am indebted to the courtesy of the Astronomer Royal, Mr. G. B.
Airy, for the following information, which confirms Castanheda and
Barros: "1520, April 17. There was certainly (from our own calculations) a total solar eclipse about 1 20 P.M. Greenwich time. But in the
Art de verifier les dates, in which the extreme Southern eclipses are not
included, none is mentioned for April 17 : consequently the eclipse was
a Southern eclipse, crossing the South Atlantic."

[1] This is the famous strait which till this day is named the Strait of
Magellan, for the eternal and glorious memory of the famous Portuguese
who discovered it. Castanheda says that Magellan, on account of
arriving there on the 1st of November, gave it the name of All Saints'
bay, and in the answer which André de S. Martin gave to the inquiries
made to him about that navigation, he also names the channel that of
All Saints' (Barros, Dec. 3, liv. 5, cap. 9). The anonymous Portuguese,
the companion of Duarte Barbosa, whom we have quoted above, and
who sailed in the "Victoria," says that at first the navigators called it
the Strait of the Victoria, because that ship was the first which sighted
it. (Ramusio, 3rd edition, tom. i. page 370). *Lisbon Ac. note.*

this was not yet known, only the three mouths were seen. The boats went thither, and brought back word, and they set sail and anchored at these mouths of the channels, and Fernando de Magalhāes sent two ships to learn what there was within, and these ships went: one returned to the Captain-major, and the other, of which Alvaro de Mesquita was captain, entered into one of the bays which was to the south, and did not return any more. Fernan de Magalhāes seeing that it did not come back, set sail,[1] and the next day he did not choose to make for the bays, and went to the south, and took another which runs north-west and south-east, and a quarter west and east. He left letters in the place from which he sailed, so that if the other ship returned, it might make the course which he left prescribed. After this they entered into the channel, which at some places has a width of three leagues, and two, and one, and in some places half a league, and he went through it as long as it was daylight, and anchored when it was night: and he sent the boats, and the ships went after the boats, and they brought news that there was an outlet, for they already saw the great sea on the other side ; on which account Fernando

---

[1] Alvaro de Mesquita, a Portuguese, and cousin of Magellan, was captain of this ship which went to explore the passages of the Straits, and did not return, and its pilot was Estevan Gomes, also a Portuguese. This Estevan Gomes had been requesting the Emperor Charles V. to confide to him a few caravels to go and discover new lands ; but as the proposal and enterprise of Mazellan then interposed itself, and was preferred and accepted, Estevan Gomes continued after that to be a great enemy of the illustrious captain, and now profited by the opportunity to revenge himself on him, and to give vent to his rabid envy. He conspired, therefore, with others against the captain of his ship, Alvaro de Mesquita ; they put him in irons, and brought him thus to Spain with the ship, telling the Emperor *that Magellan was crazy, and had lied to His Majesty, because he did not know where Banda was, nor Maluco.* Besides this, they brought accusations against Mesquita of having counselled and persuaded Magellan to use the severity and cruelty with which he punished the first conspirators, etc. (V. the Letter of Transylvanus and Castanheda, liv. 6, cap. 8). *Lisbon Ac. note.*

de Magalhāes ordered much artillery to be fired for rejoicing ;[1] and before they went forth from this strait they found two islands, the first one larger, and the other nearer towards the outlet is the smaller one : and they went out between these islands and the coast on the southern side, as it was deeper than on the other side. This strait is a hundred leagues in length to the outlet ; that outlet and the entrance are in fifty-two degrees latitude.[2] They made a stay in this strait from the 21st October to the 26th of November,[3]

---

[1] The ships *S. Antonio* and *Conception* were sent on this exploration of the Straits ; they were with difficulty able to double the Cape Possession, named thus in Bougainville's map, and in others. They at length entered a narrow opening, which in the maps is named the first gut, and they proceeded thence to another bay, which is named Boucant bay, or Boucam. At the end of this they entered into another strait, named the second gut, and having passed that, they came out into another bay larger than the former ones. Then, seeing that the strait was prolonged and offered an outlet to the ships, they returned with the good news to Magellan, who was waiting for them, and on seeing him, they fired off all their artillery and shouted for joy. The fleet then sailed together as far as the third bay, and as they found two channels, Magellan despatched the two vessels, *S. Antonio* and *Conception*, to examine whether the channel, which took the S.W. direction, would issue into the Pacific sea. Here it was that the ship *S. Antonio* deserted, going ahead of its companion for that purpose. The other two ships, *Victoria* and *Trinity*, meanwhile entered the third channel, where they waited four days for the explorers. During this interval, Magellan despatched a well equipped boat to discover the cape with which the strait ought to terminate : this having been sighted, and the boat returning with the news, all shed tears of consolation, and they gave to this cape the name of Cape Desire ; it is that which is at the outlet of the strait on the South side. They then turned back to seek for the ships *Conception* and *S. Antonio*,. and leaving marks by which this one might steer, in case of its having lost the way (for they were still ignorant of its desertion), they sailed forward until they came out into the Pacific Ocean. *Lisbon Ac. note.*

[2] The Paris Manuscript has "fully in 52 degrees." *Lisbon Ac. note.*

[3] Pigafetta remarks : In the strait in which they were, in the month of October, the night was only of three hours ; and Transylvan says that, in November the navigators found the night of little more than five hours ; and that on one night they saw to the left hand many fires. It

which makes thirty-six days of the said year of 1520, and as soon as they went out from the strait to sea, they made their course, for the most part, to west-north-west, when they found that their needles varied to the north-west almost two-fourths, and after they had navigated thus for many days, they found an island in a little more or less than eighteen degrees, or nineteen degrees, and also another, which was in from thirteen to fourteen degrees, and this in south latitude ;[1] they are uninhabited. They ran on until they reached the line, when Fernan de Magalhães said that now they were in the neighbourhood of Maluco, as he had information that there were no provisions at Maluco, he said that he would go in a northerly direction as far as ten or twelve degrees, and they reached to as far as thirteen degrees north, and in this latitude they navigated to the west, and a quarter south-west, a matter of a hundred leagues, where on the 6th of March, 1521, they fetched two islands inhabited by many people, and they anchored at one of them, which is in twelve degrees north ; and the inhabitants are people of little truth, and they did not take precautions against them until they saw that they were taking away the skiff of the flagship, and they cut the rope with which it was made fast, and took it ashore without their being able to prevent it. They gave this island the name of Thieves' Island *(dos ladrões)*.[2]

is from this that that country came to be called *Terra do fogo*. *Lisbon Ac. note.*

[1] The Paris MS. has, and also others which were, &c. Pigafetta places these two islands in 15 deg. and 9 deg. South latitude. See Amoretti's note, p. 45, upon their situation, in which he supposes them to be in the archipelago of the Society Islands. In some maps they are designated by the name of *Infortunadas*. *Lisbon Ac. note.*

[2] Some writers remark that Magellan gave to these islands the name of *Ilhas das velas*, on account of the many vessels with sails which he observed in that neighbourhood. But they continued to be commonly called *Ladrones* ; later they took the name of *Mariannas*, in honour of the Queen D. Marianna of Austria, widow of Philip IV, and Regent during the minority of D. Carlos II. of Castile. *Lisbon Ac. note.*

Fernando de Magalhães seeing that the skiff was lost, set sail, as it was already night, tacking about until the next day; as soon as it was morning they anchored at the place where they had seen the skiff carried off to, and he ordered two boats to be got ready with a matter of fifty or sixty men, and he went ashore in person, and burned the whole village, and they killed seven or eight persons, between men and women, and recovered the skiff, and returned to the ships; and while they were there they saw forty or fifty paros[1] come, which came from the same land, and brought much refreshments.[2]

Fernan de Magalhães would not make any further stay, and at once set sail, and ordered the course to be steered west, and a quarter south-west; and so they made land, which is in barely eleven degrees. This land is an island, but he would not touch at this one, and they went to touch at another further on which appeared first.[3] Fernando de Magalhães sent a boat ashore to observe the nature of the island; when the boat reached land, they saw from the ships two *paráos* come out from behind the point; then they called back their boat. The people of the paraos seeing that the boat was returning to the ships, turned back the paraos, and the boat reached the ships, which at once set sail for another island very near to this island, which is in ten degrees, and they gave it the name of the island of Good Signs, because they found some gold in it.[4] Whilst

---

[1] *Parós:* so our manuscripts always write it. In the edition of Pigafetta it is constantly written *praós*. It is the same kind of vessel that our writers of the affairs of Asia name *paraó*, which is of various sizes, and is much used in the South Sea Islands. Pigafetta says it is a kind of fusta or galliot. *Lisbon Ac. note.*

[2] The Paris manuscript has "much refreshments of fruit." *Lisbon Ac. note.*

[3] "A primeira;" the Paris manuscript has "da primeira;" this means, which was first sighted. See the *Relation of Pigafetta, Amoretti*, p. 54, March 16, 1521. *Lisbon Ac. note.*

[4] Pigafetta says: "We named the watering place of *Good Signs,*

they were thus anchored at this island, there came to them two paráos, and brought them fowls and cocoa nuts, and told them that they had already seen there other men like them, from which they presumed that these might be *Lequios* or *Mogores*;[1] a nation of people who have this name, or *Chiis*;[2] and thence they set sail, and navigated further on amongst many islands, to which they gave the name of the *Valley Without Peril,* and also St. Lazarus,[3] and they ran on to another island twenty leagues from that[4] from which they sailed, which is in ten degrees,[5] and came to anchor at another island, which is named Macangor,[6] which is in nine degrees; and in this island they were very well received, and they placed a cross in it.[7] This king conducted them thence a matter of thirty leagues to another island named Cabo,[8]

because here we found two springs of excellent water, and the first signs of there being gold in the country." *Lisbon Ac. note.*

[1] Paris MS. *Guoroos. Lisbon Ac. note.*

[2] Paris, "Chinas."

[3] Paris MS. : "To which they gave the name of Archipelago of St. Lazarus." We suspect there is some error of the copyist here in our text, not only on account of the novelty of the name *Vall Sem Periguo,* but also on account of its impropriety. The Paris MS. says simply Archipelago of St. Lazarus. Pigafetta also says, "They gave the name of Archipelago of St. Lazarus," as they arrived there on the 5th Sunday of Lent, which is named of Lazarus. Now, these islands are named Philippines, which was given them in the year 1542, in honour of D. Philip of Austria, son of Charles V, and afterwards King of Castile. They are between 225 deg. and 235 deg. W long. of Ferro, consequently between 195 deg. and 205 deg. from the line of demarcation. *Lisbon Ac. note.*

[4] Paris MS.; "They ran a matter of 25 leagues from that."

[5] Madrid MS., 9 degrees.

[6] Paris MS., Maçaguoa. Madrid MS., Maquamguoa.

[7] It appears this cross was set up in the island of Massana, where Mass was celebrated on the last day of March, which in this year was Easter Sunday. The island is set down by Pigafetta in 9 deg. 40 min., and the editor puts it in 192 deg. W. long. from the line of demarcation.

[8] This island, which is named and written Cabo in both MSS., is the island Zebu, one of the Philippines, which others write Cabu, Zabu, Subsuth, Zubut, Cubo, Subo, and Zubo, for it is found in all these forms in different writings. *Lisbon Ac. note.*

which is in ten degrees, and in this island Fernando de
Magalhães did what he pleased with the consent of the
country, and in one day eight hundred people became
Christian, on which account Fernan de Magalhães desired
that the other kings, neighbours to this one, should become
subject to this who had become Christian: and these did not
choose to yield such obedience. Fernan de Magalhães seeing
that, got ready one night with his boats, and burned the
villages of those who would not yield the said obedience ;[1]
and a matter of ten or twelve days after this was done he
sent to a village about half a league from that which he had
burned, which is named Matam, and which is also an island,
and ordered them to send him at once three goats, three pigs,
three loads of rice, and three loads of millet for provisions
for the ships; they replied that of each article which he sent
to ask them three of, they would send to him by twos, and
if he was satisfied with this they would at once comply, if
not, it might be as he pleased, but that they would not give
it. Because they did not choose to grant what he demanded
of them, Fernan de Magalhães ordered three boats to be
equipped with a matter of fifty or sixty men,[2] and went
against the said place, which was on the 28th day of April,
in the morning ;[3] there they found many people, who might
well be as many as three thousand or four thousand men,
who fought with such a good will that the said Fernan de
Magalhães was killed there, with six of his men,[4] in the
year 1521.

[1] Paris MS.: "And burned a village of those who would not yield
the said obedience." The narrative of Pigafetta states: "He burned
twenty or thirty houses of the village." *Lisbon Ac. note.*

[2] Pigafetta says: "We were 60 armed men, 48 went on shore with
Magellan; the 11 remained to guard the boats. *Lisbon Ac. note.*

[3] Paris MS.: "And went against the said place, and it was on the
27th day of April." Pigafetta also places this event on the 27th of
April, and observes that it was on *Saturday*, which in truth took place
that year on the 27th, and not on the 28th of April. *Lisbon Ac. note.*

[4] Pigafetta says: "With eight of our men there perished four Indians

When Fernan de Magalhães was dead the Christians got back to the ships, where they thought fit to make two captains and governors whom they should obey ;[1] and having done this, they took counsel [and decided] that the two captains should go ashore where the people had turned Christians to ask for pilots to take them to Borneo, and this was on the first day of May of the said year; when the two captains went, being agreed upon what had been said, the same people of the country who had become Christians, armed themselves against them, and whilst they reached the shore let them land in security as they had done before. Then they attacked them, and killed the two captains and twenty-six gentlemen,[2] and the other people who remained got back to the boats, and returned to the ships, and finding themselves again without captains they agreed, inasmuch as the principal persons were killed, that one Joam Lopez,[3] who was the chief treasurer, should be captain-major of the fleet, and the chief

of those who had become Christians, and we had many wounded, I being one of them; of the enemy there fell only fifteen men." *Lisbon Ac. note.*

[1] Pigafetta says: "We then chose instead of the captain, Duarte Barbosa, a Portuguese, his relation, and John Serrano, a Spaniard. The first commanded the flagship."

[2] Paris MS.: "They killed the two captains, and also 26 men with them." It was on this occasion that Duarte Barbosa, a Portuguese, and brother-in-law of Magellan, was killed. He was one of the captains here mentioned. Some of our writers have said, or conjectured, that Duarte Barbosa was killed by poison; but this is a mistake. The barbarians, indeed, drew the Castilians ashore under the pretext of giving them a banquet, but it does not follow from that that they poisoned them. The Transylvan says: *inter epulandum, ab iis, qui in insidiis collocati fuerant, opprimuntur. Fit clamor undique : nuntiatur protinus in navibus nostros occisos.* See Barros, 3, 5, 10. The other captain, who was John Serrano, was not killed, but remained alive in the hands of the barbarians at the time the boats made off, because, notwithstanding the most mournful supplications which he made from the shore for rescue, Joan Lopes de Carvalho feared further treachery, and ordered the anchor to be weighed. *Lisbon Ac. note.*

[3] Paris MS.: "One Yoam Lopez de Carvalho." *Lisbon Ac. note.*

constable of the fleet should be captain of one of the ships ; he was named Gonzalo Vaz Despinosa.[1]

Having done this they set sail, and ran about twenty-five leagues with three ships, which they still possessed ; they then mustered, and found that they were altogether one hundred and eight men[2] in all these three ships, and many of them were wounded and sick, on which account they did not venture to navigate the three ships, and thought it would be well to burn one of them—the one that should be most suitable for that purpose[3]—and to take into the two ships those that remained : this they did out at sea, out of sight of any land. While they did this many paraos came to speak to them ; and navigating amongst the islands, for in that neighbourhood there are a great many, they did not understand one another, for they had no interpreter, for he had been killed with Fernan de Magalhães. Sailing further on amongst islets they came to anchor at an island which is named Carpyam,[4] where there is gold enough, and this island is in fully eight degrees.

Whilst at anchor in this port of Capyam,[4] they had speech with the inhabitants of the island, and made peace with them, and Carvalho, who was captain-major, gave them the boat of the ship which had been burnt : this island has three[5] islets in the offing ; here they took in some refreshments, and sailed further on to west south-west, and fell in with another island, which is named Caram, and is in eleven degrees ; from this they went on further to west south-west,[6]

---

[1] Paris MS.: " Gonzalo Gomez Despinosa." *Lisbon Ac. note.*

[2] Barros says 180 men, and this seems more probable, considering the number of the men who sailed in the fleet and of those who might then have been lost, and those who were lost later, and also of those who at last reached Ternate and Europe. *Lisbon Ac. note.* The Madrid MS. has 180 men, written in full, " Semte he oytēta homēs."

[3] Pigafetta says they burned the ship *Conception.*

[4] Paris MS., " Quype." *Lisbon Ac. note.*

[5] Paris MS. has "two islets." *Lisbon Ac. note.*

[6] Paris MS. : "which is named Cagujam, and is in seven degrees ;

and fell in with a large island, and ran along the coast of
this island to the north-east,[1] and reached as far as nine
degrees and a half,[2] where they went ashore one day, with
the boats equipped to seek for provisions, for in the ships
there was now not more than for eight days. On reaching
shore the inhabitants would not suffer them to land, and
shot at them with arrows of cane hardened in the fire, so
that they returned to the ships.

Seeing this, they agreed to go to another island, where
they had had some dealings, to see if they could get some
provisions. Then they met with a contrary wind, and going
about a league in the direction in which they wished to go,
they anchored, and whilst at anchor they saw that people on
shore were hailing them to go thither; they went there with
the boats, and as they were speaking to those people by
signs, for they did not understand each other otherwise, a
man at arms, named Joam de Campos, told them to let him
go on shore, since there were no provisions in the ships, and
it might be that they would obtain some means of getting
provisions; and that if the people killed him, they would
not lose much with him, for God would take thought of his
soul; and also if he found provisions, and if they did not kill
him, he would find means for bringing them to the ships:
and they thought well of this. So he went on shore, and as
soon as he reached it, the inhabitants received him, and took
him into the interior the distance of a league, and when he
was in the village all the people came to see him, and they
gave him food, and entertained him well, especially when

from this they went on further to the West North-west." *Lisbon
Ac. note.*   Madrid MS. seven degrees.

[1] Paris MS., "to the North-east. Madrid MS., "North-east." The
Lisbon Academy copyist has North-west, and has mistaken the Paris MS.
on this point.

[2] This position seems to indicate the island of Palavan, which Pigafetta
places in 9 deg. 20 min. *Lisbon Ac. note.*

they saw that he ate pig's flesh ; because in this island they had dealings with the Moors of Borneo, and because the country and people were greedy, they made them neither eat pigs nor bring them up in the country. This country is called Dyguasam,[1] and is in nine degrees.

The said Christian seeing that he was favoured and well treated by the inhabitants, gave them to understand by his signs that they should carry provisions to the ships, which would be well paid for. In the country there was nothing except rice not pounded. Then the people set to pounding rice all the night, and when it was morning they took the rice and the said Christian, and came to the ships, where they did them great honour, and took in the rice and paid them, and they returned on shore. This man being already set on shore, inhabitants of another village, a little further on, came to the ships and told them to go to their village, and that they would give them much provisions for their money; and as soon as the said man whom they had sent arrived, they set sail and went to anchor at the village of those who had come to call them, which was named Vay Palay Cucara Canbam,[2] where Carvalho made peace with the king of the country, and they settled the price of the rice, and they gave them two measures of rice which weighed one hundred and fourteen pounds[3] for three fathoms of linen stuff of Britanny ; they took there as much rice as they wanted, and goats and pigs, and whilst they were at this place there came a Moor, who had been in the village

---

[1] Paris MS., "Degameão." *Lisbon Ac. note.* Madrid MS., "Dygamçam."

[2] Paris MS., "ypalajra cara canão." *Lisbon Ac. note.* I read this, "y palay cu cara canão:" the Madrid MS. has "fulay cucara cabam." The word *palay*, Tagal for rice, and the next sentence in the text seem to indicate that an offer to trade was mistaken for the name of this island.

[3] Paris MS., "one hundredweight and fourteen pounds." *Lisbon Ac. note.*

of Dyguaçam,[1] which belongs to the Moors of Borneo, as has been said above, and after that he went to his country.

While they were at anchor near this village of Diguaçam,[1] there came to them a parao in which there was a negro named Bastiam, who asked for a flag and a passport for the governor of Diguaçam, and they gave him all this and other things as a present. They asked the said Bastiam, who spoke Portuguese sufficiently well, since he had been in Maluco, where he became a Christian, if he would go with them and shew them Borneo; he said he would very willingly, and when the departure arrived he hid himself, and seeing that he did not come, they set sail from this port of Diguaçam on the 21st day of July[2] to seek for Borneo. As they set sail there came to them a parao, which was coming to the port of Diguaçam, and they took it, and in it they took three Moors, who said they were pilots, and that they would take them to Borneo.

Having got these Moors, they steered along this island to the south-west, and fell in with two islands at its extremity, and passed between them; that on the north side is named Bolyna, and that on the south Bamdym.[3] Sailing to the west south-west a matter of fourteen leagues, they fell in with a white bottom, which was a shoal below the water, and the black men they carried with them told them to draw near to the coast of the island, as it was deeper there, and that was more in the direction of Borneo, for from that neighbourhood the island of Borneo could already be sighted. This same day they reached and anchored at some islands, to which they gave the name of islets of St. Paul, which

[1] Paris MŚ., "Digação;" it is also written Digamcä and Digäçä. *Lisbon Ac. note.*

[2] Paris MS., "21st day of June." *Lisbon Ac. note.* Madrid MS., "21st day of June."

[3] Paris MS. "The island to the North is named Bolava, and that to the South Bamdill." *Lisbon Ac. note.* Madrid MS., "Bolina and Bamdill.'

C

was a matter of two and a half or three leagues from the great island of Borneo, and they were in about seven degrees at the south side of these islands. In the island of Borneo there is an exceedingly great mountain, to which they gave the name of Mount St. Paul; and from thence they navigated along the coast of Borneo to the south-west, beween an island and the island of Borneo itself; and they went forward on the same course and reached the neighbourhood of Borneo,[1] and the Moors whom they had with them told them that there was Borneo, and the wind did not suffer them to arrive thither, as it was contrary. They anchored at an island which is there, and which may be eight leagues from Borneo.

Close to this island is another which has many myrobolans, and the next day they set sail for the other island, which is nearer to the port of Borneo; and going along thus they saw so many shoals that they anchored, and sent the boats ashore in Borneo, and they took the aforesaid Moorish pilots on shore, and there went a Christian with them; and the boats went to set them on land, from whence they had to go to the city of Borneo, which was three leagues off, and there they were taken before the Shahbender of Borneo, and he asked what people they were, and for what they came in the ships; and they were presented to the King of Borneo with the Christian. As soon as the boats had set the said men on shore, they sounded in order to see if the ships could come in closer: and during this they saw three junks which were coming from the port of Borneo from the said city out to sea, and as soon as they saw the ships they returned inshore: continuing to sound, they found the channel by which the port is entered; they then set sail, and entered this channel, and being within the channel they anchored, and would not go further in until they received a message from

[1] Paris MS., "the neighbourhood of the port of Borneo." *Lisbon Ac. note.*

the shore, which arrived next day with two paraos: these carried certain swivel guns of metal, and a hundred men in each parao, and they brought goats and fowls, and two cows, and figs, and other fruit, and told them to enter further in opposite the islands which were near there, which was the true berth; and from this position to the city there might be three or four leagues. Whilst thus at anchor they established peace, and settled that they should trade in what there was in the country, especially wax, to which they answered that they would willingly sell all that there was in the country for their money. This port of Borneo is in eight degrees.

For the answer thus received from the King they sent him a present by Gonzalo Mendes Despinosa,[1] captain of the ship Victoria, and the King accepted the present, and gave to all of them China stuffs: and when there had passed twenty or twenty-three days that they were there trading with the people of the island, and had got five men on shore in the city itself, there came to anchor at the bar, close to them, five junks, at the hour of vespers, and they remained there that evening and the night until next day in the morning, when they saw coming from the city two hundred paraos, some under sail, others rowing. Seeing in this manner the five junks and the paraos, it seemed to them that there might be treachery, and they set sail for the junks, and as soon as the crews of the junks saw them under sail, they also set sail and made off where the wind best served them; and they overhauled one of the junks with the boats, and took it with twenty-seven men;[2] and the ships went and anchored abreast of the island of the Myrololans, with the junk made fast to the poop of the flagship, and the paraos returned to shore, and when night came there came on a squall from the

[1] Paris MS., "Gonzalo Gomez Despinosa."
[2] Paris MS., "with seventeen men." *Lisbon Ac. note.* I read twenty-seven in the Paris MS.

west in which the said junk went to the bottom alongside
the flagship, without being able to receive any assistance
from it.[1]

Next day in the morning they saw a sail, and went to it
and took it; this was a great junk in which the son of the
King of Lucam came as captain, and had with him ninety
men, and as soon as they took them they sent some of them
to the King of Borneo; and they sent him word by these
men to send the Christians whom they had got there, who
were seven men, and they would give him all the people
whom they had taken in the junk; on which account the
King sent two men of the seven whom he had got there in
a parao, and they again sent him word to send the five men
who still remained, and they would send all the people whom
they had got from the junk.　They waited two days for the
answer, and there came no message; then they took thirty
men from the junk, and put them into a parao belonging to
the junk, and sent them to the King of Borneo, and set sail
with fourteen men of those they had taken and three women;
and they steered along the coast of the said island to the
north-east, returning backwards; and they again passed
between the islands and the great island of Borneo, where
the flagship grounded on a point of the island, and so remained more than four hours, and the tide turned and it
got off, by which it was seen clearly that the tide was of
twenty-four hours.[2]

Whilst making the aforesaid course the wind shifted to
north-east, and they stood out to sea, and they saw a sail
coming, and the ships anchored, and the boats went to
it and took it; it was a small junk and carried nothing but

---

[1] *Sem se aproveitar nada delle*, or, without their having made any
use of it.

[2] Paris MS. "And so remained a matter of fourteen hours, for it
was low water, by which it was clearly seen that the tide was of fourteen
hours." *Lisbon Ac. note.*

cocoa-nuts; and they took in water and wood, and set sail along the coast of the island to the north-east, until they reached the extremity of the said island, and met with another small island, where they overhauled the ships. They arrived at this island on the day of our Lady of August, and in it they found a very good point for beaching the ships, and they gave it the name of Port St. Mary of August, ánd it is in fully seven degrees.

As soon as they had taken these precautions they set sail and steered to the south-west until they sighted the island which is named Fagajam,[1] and this is a course of thirty-eight to forty leagues : and as soon as they sighted this island they steered to the south-west, and again made an island which is called Seloque,[2] and they had information that there were many pearls there : and when they had already sighted that island the wind shifted to a head-wind, and they could not fetch it by the course they were sailing, and it seemed to them that it might be in six degrees. This same night they arrived at the island of Quipe, and ran along it to the south-east, and passed between it and another island called Tamgym,[3] and always running along the coast of the said island, and going thus, they fell in with a parao laden with sago in loaves, which is bread made of a tree which is named cajare,[4] which the people of that country eat as bread. This parao carried twenty-one men, and the chief of them had been in Maluco in the house of Francisco Serram, and having gone further along this island they arrived in sight of some islands which are named Semrryn ;[5] they are in five degrees, a little more or less. The inhabitants of this land came to see the ships, and so they had speech of one another, and an old man of these people told them that he would conduct them to Maluco.

[1] Paris MS., "Cagamja." *Lisbon Ac. note.*
[2] Paris MS., "Solloque." *Ibid.*
[3] Paris MS., "Tamgyma." *Ibid.*
[4] Paris MS., "Sagu." *Ibid.*
[5] Paris MS., "Samyns." *Ibid.*

In this manner, having fixed a time with the old man, an agreement was made with him, and they gave him a certain price for this; and when the next day came, and they were to depart, the old man intended to escape, and they understood it, and took him and others who were with him, and who also said that they knew pilot's work, and they set sail; and as soon as the inhabitants saw them go they fitted out to go after them: and of these paraos there did not reach the ships more than two, and these reached so near that they shot arrows into the ships, and the wind was fresh[1] and they could not come up with them. At midnight of that day they sighted some islands, and they steered more towards them; and next day they saw land, which was an island; and at night following that day they found themselves very close to it, and when night fell the wind calmed and the currents drew them very much inshore; there the old pilot cast himself into the sea, and betook himself to land.

Sailing thus forward, after one of the pilots had fled, they sighted another island and arrived close to it, and another Moorish pilot said that Maluco was still further on, and navigating thus, the next day in the morning they sighted three high mountains, which belonged to a nation of people whom they called the Salabos;[2] and then they saw a small island where they anchored to take in some water, and because they feared that in Maluco they would not be allowed to take it in; and they omitted doing so, because the Moorish pilot told them that there were some four hundred[3] men in that island, and that they were all very bad, and might do them some injury, as they were men of little faith; and that he would give them no such advice as to go to that island; and also because Maluco, which they were seeking, was now

[1] Paris MS., "light." *Lisbon Ac. note.* The Paris MS. seems to me to have "fresquo," and not "ffraquo."
[2] Paris MS., "Calibes." *Lisbon Ac. note.*
[3] Paris MS., "five hundred." *Lisbon Ac. note.*

near, and that its kings were good men, who gave a good reception to all sorts of men in their country; and while still in this neighbourhood[1] they saw the islands themselves of Maluco, and for rejoicing they fired all the artillery, and they arrived at the island[2] on the 8th of November of 1521, so that they spent from Seville to Maluco two years, two months and twenty-eight days, for they sailed on the 10th of August of 1519.[3]

As soon as they arrived at the island of Tydor,[4] which is in half a degree, the King thereof did them great honour, which could not be exceeded : there they treated with the King for their cargo, and the King engaged to give them a cargo and whatever there was in the country for their money, and they settled to give for the bahar of cloves fourteen ells of yellow cloth of twenty-seven tem,[5] which are worth in Castile a ducat the ell; of red cloth of the same kind ten ells; they also gave thirty ells of Brittany linen cloth, and for each of these quantities they received a bahar of cloves, likewise for thirty knives eight bahars :[6] having thus settled all the above mentioned prices, the inhabitants of the country gave them information that further on, in another island near, there was a Portuguese man. This island might be two leagues distant, and it was named Targatell ;[7] this man was the chief person of Maluco ; *there we now have got a fortress*.[8] They then wrote letters to the said Portuguese, to come and speak with them, to which he answered that he did not dare,

[1] Paris MS., "in these discussions." *Lisbon Ac. note.*

[2] Paris MS. "of Tidore." *Lisbon Ac. note.*

[3] Pigafetta says: " On Friday, 8th of November, 1521, three hours before sunset, we entered the port of an island called Tadore . . . 27 months less two days had passed that we had been seeking Maluco. *Lisbon Ac. note.*

[4] Pigafetta puts this island in 0 deg. 27 min. *Lisbon Ac. note.*

[5] In the Paris MS. this word *tem* is wanting. *Lisbon Ac. note.*

[6] Paris MS., "another bahar." *Lisbon Ac. note.*

[7] Paris MS., "Tarnate." *Lisbon Ac. note.*

[8] This clause seems to have been added to the text by the copyist;

because the King of the country forbade it; that if they obtained permission from the King he would come at once;
this permission they soon got, and the Portuguese came to
speak with them.[1] They gave him an account of the prices
which they had settled, at which he was amazed, and said
that on that account the King had ordered him not to come,
as they did not know the truth about the prices of the
country; and whilst they were thus taking in cargo there
arrived the King of Baraham,[2] which is near there, and said
that he wished to be a vassal of the King of Castile, and
also that he had got four hundred bahars of cloves, and that
he had sold it to the King of Portugal, and that they had
bought it, but that he had not yet delivered it, and if they
wished for it, he would give it all to them; to which the
captains answered that if he brought it to them, and came
with it, they would buy it, but otherwise not. The King,
seeing that they did not wish to take the cloves, asked them
for a flag and a letter of safe conduct, which they gave him,
signed by the captains of the ships.

While they were thus waiting for the cargo, it seemed to
them, from the delay in the delivery, that the King was preparing some treachery against them, and the greater part of
the ships' crews made an uproar and told the captains to go,
as the delays which the King made were for nothing else
than treachery: as it seemed to them all that it might be so,
they were abandoning everything, and were intending to
depart; and being about to unfurl the sails, the King, who

because the fortress of Ternate was only begun in the year 1522, on
St. John's day, when Antonio de Brito was captain. (Castanheda, l. 6,
cap. 12). *Lisbon Ac. note.* This clause may belong to the writer, the
pilot, since he mentions the fortress and Antonio de Brito later, subse-
quent to July of 1522.

[1] The Portuguese here mentioned seems to be Pedro Affonso de Lourosa,
who betrayed the Portuguese and passed over to the Castilians, according to Pigafetta's account. *Lisbon Ac. note.*

[2] Paris MS., " Bargão." *Lisbon Ac. note.* I read this Bachão; this
is the correct spelling.

had made the agreement with them, came to the flagship and asked the captain why he wanted to go, because that which he had agreed upon with him he intended to fulfil it as had been settled. The captain replied that the ships' crews said they should go and not remain any longer, as it was only treachery that was being prepared against them. To this the King answered that it was not so, and on that account he at once sent for his Koran, upon which he wished to make oath that nothing such should be done to them. They at once brought him this Koran, and upon it he made oath, and told them to rest at ease with that. At this the crews were set at rest, and he promised them that he would give them their cargo by the 15th December 1521, which he fulfilled within the said time without being wanting in anything.

When the two ships were already laden and about to unfurl their sails, the flagship[1] sprung a large leak, and the King of the country learning this, he sent them twenty-five divers[2] to stop the leak, which they were unable to do. They settled that the other ship should depart, and that this one should again discharge all its cargo, and unload it; and as they could not stop the leak, that they [the people of the country] should give them all that they might be in need of. This was done, and they discharged the cargo of the flagship; and when the said ship was repaired, they took in her cargo, and decided on making for the country of the Antilles, and the course from Maluco to it was 2,000 leagues a little more or less. The other ship, which set sail first, left on the 21st of December of the said year, and went out to sea for Timor, and made its course behind Java, 2,055 leagues to the Cape of-Good Hope.[3]

---

[1] The flagship was the *Trinidade*. *Lisbon Ac. note.*

[2] Pigafetta says the King sent five divers, and afterwards three more, who could not stop the water. *Lisbon Ac. note.*

[3] Pigafetta sailed in this ship the *Victoria*. The *Trinidade*, after

They refitted the ship, and took in the cargo in four months and sixteen days : they sailed on the 6th of April of the year 1522, and took their course for the mainland of the Antilles by the strait through which they had come; and at first they navigated to the North, until they came out from the islands of Ternate and Tymor;[1] afterwards they navigated along the island of Betachina, ten or eleven leagues to the North-east;[2] after that they steered about twenty leagues to the North-east, and so arrived at an island, which is named Doyz,[3] and is in three and a half degrees South latitude at its South-eastern side : from this place they navigated three or four leagues eastwards, and sighted two islands, one large and the other small; the large one was named Porquenampello,[4] and passed between it and Batechina, which lay on their starboard side. They reached a cape, to which they gave the name Cape of Palms, because they sighted it on the vigil of Palms. This cape is in two and a half degrees : thence they steered to the South to make Quimar,[5] which is land belonging to the King of Tydor, and the said King had ordered that they should receive whatever there was in the country for their money, and there they took pigs and goats, and fowls and cocoanuts aud *hava :*[6] they remained in this port eight or nine days. This port of Camarfya[7] is in one and a quarter degree.

refitting, took the opposite course and sailed for Yucatan and the isthmus of Darien, which is here called *land* of *the Antilles;* but it found itself obliged to put back to the Moluccas, and whilst about to discharge its cargo at Ternate, was cast on shore. *Lisbon Ac. note.*

[1] Paris MS., "Tydore." *Lisbon Ac. note.* The correct reading.

[2] Paris MS., "North-north-east." *Lisbon Ac. note.*

[3] Paris MS., "Domy." *Lisbon Ac. note.*

[4] Paris MS. "The large one is named Chãol, and the small one Pyliom." *Lisbon Ac. note.*

[5] Paris MS., " Quemarre." *Lisbon Ac. note.*

[6] Paris MS., " *agoa*," water, but *hava* or *ava* is a drink used in those countries. *Lisbon Ac. note.*

[7] Paris MS., " Camarro." *Lisbon Ac. note.*

They sailed from this port on the 20th[1] of April, and steered for about seventeen leagues,[2] and came out of the channel of the island of Batechina and the island Charam ;[3] and as soon as they were outside, they saw that the said island of Charam[4] ran to the South-east a good eighteen or twenty leagues, and it was not their course, for their direction was to the East[5] and a quarter North-east ; and they navigated in the said course some days, and always found the winds very contrary for their course. On the 3rd of May they made two small islands, which might be in five degrees more or less, to which they gave the name of islands of St. Antony.[6] Thence they navigated further on to the North-east, and arrived at an island which is named Cyco,[7] which is in fully nineteen degrees, and they made this island on the 11th of July.[8] From this island they took a man, whom they carried away with them, and they navigated further on, tacking about with contrary winds, until they reached forty-two degrees North latitude.

When they were in this neighbourhood, they were short of bread, wine, meat, and oil ; they had nothing to eat only water and rice, without other provisions ; and the cold was great, and they had not sufficient covering, the crews began to die, and seeing themselves in this state, they decided on putting back in the direction of Maluco, which they at once carried into effect. When at a distance of five hundred leagues from it, they desired to make the island which is

---

[1] Paris MS., " 25th." *Lisbon Ac. note.*

[2] Paris MS., " steered seventeen leagues eastwards." *Lisbon Academy note.*

[3] Paris MS., " Chao." *Lisbon Ac. note.*

[4] Paris MS., " Batechina." *Lisbon Ac. note.*

[5] Paris MS., " West." *Lisbon Ac. note.*

[6] Paris MS., " islands of St. John :" it also says they made them on the 6th. *Lisbon Ac. note.*

[7] Paris MS., " Chyquom." *Lisbon Ac. note.*

[8] Paris MS., " 11th of June." *Lisbon Ac. note.* July will be the correct reading.

named Quamgragam,[1] and as they sighted it at night, they did not choose to make it; they waited thus till it dawned next day, and they were unable to fetch the said island; and the man whom they carried with them; and whom before they had taken from that island, told them to go further on, and they would make three islands, where there was a good port, and this which the black man said, was in order to run away at them, as indeed he did run away. On arriving at these three islands, they fetched them with some danger, and anchored in the middle of them in fifteen fathoms. Of these islands, the largest was inhabited by twenty persons between men and women : this island is named Pamo ;[2] it is in twenty degrees more or less : here they took in rain-water, as there was no other in the country. In this island the black man[3] ran away. Thence they sailed to make the land of Camafo, and as soon as they sighted it they had calms, and the currents carried them away from the land; and afterwards they had a little wind, and they made for the land, but could not fetch it; they then went to anchor between the islands of Domi and Batechina, and while at anchor, a parao passed by them with some men who belonged to the King of an island named Geilôlo,[4] and they gave them news that the Portuguese were in Maluco making a fortress. Learning this, they at once sent the clerk of the ship with certain men[5] to the captain-major of those Portuguese, who was named Antonio de Bryto, to ask him to come and bring the ship to the place where they were; because the crew of the ship had mostly died, and the rest were sick, and could not navigate the ship. As soon as Antonio de Bryto saw the

[1] Paris MS., "Magregua." *Lisbon Ac. note.*
[2] Paris MS., "Mão." *Ibid.*
[3] Paris MS., " the black man and three Christians." *Ibid.*
[4] Paris MS., " Gelolo." *Ibid.*
[5] Paris MS., " certain men with letters." *Ibid.*

letter and message, he sent down Dom Gonzalo[1] Amriquiz, captain of the ship Sam Jorge,[2] and also a fusta with some country paraos, and they went thus in search of the ship, and having found it, they brought it to the fortress, and whilst they were discharging its cargo, there came a squall from the north,[3] which cast it on shore. Where this ship turned to put back to Maluco was a little more or less than 1050 or 1100 leagues from the island.

This was transcribed from the paper-book of a Genoese pilot, who came in the said ship, who wrote all the voyage as it is here. He went to Portugal in the year 1524 with Dom Amriqui de Menezes.[4] Thanks be to God.

[1] Paris MS, "Dom Garcia." Garcia, and not Gonzalo, was the name of this gentleman. See Barros and Castanheda. *Lisbon Ac. note.*

[2] Paris MS., "Sam Joze." *Lisbon Ac. note.* I read this "Sam Jorge."

[3] Paris MS., "a squall at night." *Lisbon Ac. note.* I read this "do norte" from the north, and not "de noite."

[4] It is easily seen that this note does not belong to the *Roteiro*, and that it was added by the copyist: we have already noticed the difference which there is between it and another similar note of the Paris MS. It seems that the person who wrote it made some mistake, owing to there having been many gentlemen of the name of Menezes at that time in India . . . . D. Henrique de Menezes succeeded Vasco da Gama, in 1524, as Governor of India, and therefore could not be the D. Amrique de Menezes who came to the kingdom in 1524, as the note says. This deserving Governor died at Cananor on the day of the Purification of 1526. *Lisbon Ac. note.*

NARRATIVE OF A PORTUGUESE, COMPANION OF
ODOARDO BARBOSA, IN THE SHIP *VICTORIA*,
IN THE YEAR 1519. (FROM "RAMUSIO".)

IN the name of God and of good salvation. We departed
from Seville with five ships on the tenth of August, in the
year 1519, to go and discover the Molucca Islands. We
commenced our voyage from San Lucar for the Canary
Islands, and sailed south-west 960 miles, where we found
ourselves at the island of Tenerife, in which is the harbour
of Santa Cruz in twenty-eight degrees of north latitude.
And from the island of Tenerife we sailed southwards
1680 miles, when we found ourselves in four degrees of
north latitude. From these four degrees of north latitude
we sailed south-west, until we found ourselves at the Cape
of Saint Augustin, which is in eight degrees of south latitude, having accomplished 1200 miles. And from Cape
Saint Augustin we sailed south and by south-west 864
miles, where we found ourselves in twenty degrees of south
latitude. From twenty degrees of south latitude, being at
sea, we sailed 1500 miles south-west, when we found ourselves near the river, whose mouth is 108 miles wide, and
lies in thirty-five degrees of the said south latitude. We
named it the river of Saint Christopher. From this river
we sailed 1638 miles south-west by west, where we found
ourselves at the point of the Lupi Marini, which is in forty-
eight degrees of south latitude. And from the point of the
Lupi Marini we sailed south-west 350 miles, where we
found ourselves in the harbour of Saint Julian, and stayed
there five months waiting for the sun to return towards us,
because in June and July it appeared for only four hours
each day. From this harbour of Saint Julian, which is in
fifty degrees, we departed on the 24th of August, 1520, and
sailed westward a hundred miles, where we found a river to

which we gave the name of River of Santa Cruz, and there
we remained until the 18th of October. This river is in
fifty degrees. We departed thence on the 18th of October,
and sailed along the coast 378 miles south-west by west,
where we found ourselves in a strait, to which we gave the
name Strait of Victoria, because the ship *Victoria* was the
first that had seen it: some called it the Strait of Magal-
haens, because our captain was named Fernando de Ma-
galhaens. The mouth of this strait is in fifty-three degrees
and a half, and we sailed through it 400 miles to the other
mouth, which is in the same latitude of fifty-three degrees
and a half. We emerged from this strait on the 27th of
November, 1520, and sailed between west and north-west
9858 miles, until we found ourselves upon the equinoctial
line. In this course we found two uninhabited islands, the
one of which was distant from the other 800 miles. To the
first we gave the name of Saint Peter, and to the other the
island of the Tiburones. Saint Peter is in eighteen degrees,
the island of the Tiburones in fourteen degrees of south
latitude. From the equinoctial line we sailed between west
and north-west 2046 miles, and discovered several islands
between ten and twelve degrees of north latitude. In these
islands there were many naked people as well men as women,
we gave the islands the name of the Ladrones, because the
people had robbed our ship: but it cost them very dear. I
shall not relate further the course that we made, because we
lengthened it not a little. But I will tell you that to go
direct from these islands of the Ladrones to the Moluccas it
is necessary to sail south-west a 1000 miles, and there occur many islands, to which we gave the name of the Archipelago of Saint Lazarus. A little further there are the
islands of the Moluccas, of which there are five, namely,
Ternate, Tidor, Molir, Machiam, Bachian. In Ternate the
Portuguese had built a very strong castle before I left.
From the Molucca Islands to the islands of Banda there are
three hundred miles, and one goes thither by different

courses, because there are many islands in between, and
one must sail by sight. In these islands until you reach the
islands of Banda, which are in four degrees and a half of
south latitude, there are collected from thirty to forty thou-
send cantaros of nutmegs annually, and there is likewise collected much mastic; and if you wish to go to Calicut you
must always sail amidst the islands as far as Malacca, which
is distant from the Moluccas 2000 miles, and from Malacca
to Calicut are 2000 miles more. From Calicut to Portugal
there are 14,000 miles. If from the islands of Banda you
wish to round the Cape of Good Hope, you must sail between west and south-west until you find yourself in thirty-
four degrees and a half of south latitude, and from there
you sail westward, always keeping a good look-out at the
prow not to run aground on the said Cape of Good Hope or
its neighbourhood. From this Cape of Good Hope one sails
north-west by west 2400 miles, and there finds the island of
Saint Helena, where Portuguese ships go to take in water
and wood, and other things. This island is in sixteen degrees south latitude, and there is no habitation except that
of a Portuguese man, who has but one hand and one foot,
no nose, and no ears, and is called Fornam-lopem.

Sailing 1600 miles north-west from this island of Saint
Helena you will find yourself upon the equinoctial line:
from which line you will sail 3534 miles north-west by
north, until you find yourself in thirty-nine degrees north
latitude. And if you wish to go from these thirty-nine degrees to Lisbon you will sail 950 miles eastward, where you
will find the islands of the Azores, of which there are seven,
namely, Terceira, San Jorge, Pico, Fayal, Graciosa, on the
east, the island of Saint Michael, and the island of Saint
Mary, all are between thirty-seven and forty degrees of
north latitude. From the island of Terceira you will then
sail eastward 1100 miles, where you will find yourself on
the land of Lisbon.

NAVIGATION ET DESCOUUREMENT DE LA INDIE SUPÉRIEURE FAICTE PAR MOY ANTHOYNE PIGAPHETA, VINCENTIN, CHEVALLIER DE RHODES.

D

ANTHONY PIGAPHETA, *Patrician of Vicenza, and Knight of
Rhodes, to the very illustrious and very excellent*
LORD PHILIP DE VILLERS LISLEADEN, *the famous
Grand Master of Rhodes, his most
respected Lord.*[1]

SINCE there are several curious persons (very illustrious and
very reverend lord) who not only are pleased to listen to and
learn the great and wonderful things which God has permitted me to see and suffer in the long and perilous navigation, which I have performed (and which is written hereafter),
but also they desire to learn the methods and fashions of the
road which I have taken in order to go thither, [and who do]
not grant firm belief to the end unless they are first well advised and assured of the commencement. Therefore, my lord,
it will please you to hear that finding myself in Spain in the
year of the Nativity of our Lord, one thousand five hundred
and nineteen, at the court of the most serene king[2] of the
Romans, with the reverend lord, Mons. Francis Cheregato,[3]
then apostolic proto-notary, and ambassador of the Pope
Leon the Tenth, who, through his virtue, afterwards arrived
at the bishoprick of Aprutino and the principality of
Theramo, and knowing both by the reading of many books
and by the report of many lettered and well-informed persons
who conversed with the said proto-notary, the very great
and awful things of the ocean, I deliberated, with the favour

---

[1] Son Seigneur osservatissime.
[2] Charles V was elected Emperor the 28th June, 1519.
[3] Chiericato.   Milan edition.

of the Emperor and the above-named lord, to experiment and go and see with my eyes a part of those things. By which means I could satisfy the desire of the said lords, and mine own also. So that it might be said that I had performed the said voyage, and seen well with my eyes the things hereafter written.

Now in order to decypher the commencement of my voyage (very illustrious lord) ; having heard that there was in the city of Seville, a small armade to the number of five ships, ready to perform this long voyage, that is to say, to find the islands of Maluco, from whence the spices come: of which armade the captain-general was Fernand de Magaglianes, a Portuguese gentleman, commander of *St. James of the Sword*, who had performed several voyages in the ocean sea (in which he had behaved very honourably as a good man), I set out with many others in my favour from Barcelona, where at the time the Emperor was, and came by sea as far as Malaga, and thence I went away by land until I arrived at the said city of Seville. There I remained for the space of three months, waiting till the said armade was in order and readiness to perform its voyage. And because (very illustrious lord) that on the return from the said voyage, on going to Rome towards the holiness of our Holy Father,[1] I found your lordship at Monterosa,[2] where of your favour you gave me a good reception, and afterwards gave me to understand that you desired to have in writing the things which God of His grace had permitted me to see in my said voyage ; therefore to satisfy and accede to your desire,[3] I have reduced into this small book the principal things, in the best manner that I have been able.

Finally (very illustrious lord), after all provisions had been made, and the vessels were in order, the captain-general, a

---

[1] Clement VII (Medici) was elected Pontiff in 1523, and died in 1534.
[2] Monterosi. Milan edition.
[3] The Milan edition attributes this desire to the Pope.

discreet and virtuous man, careful of his honour, would not
commence his voyage without first making some good and
wholesome ordinances, such as it is the good custom to make
for those who go to sea. Nevertheless he did not entirely
declare the voyage which he was going to make, so that his
men should not from amazement and fear be unwilling to accompany him on so long a voyage, as he had undertaken in
his intention. Considering the great and impetuous storms[1]
which are on the ocean sea, where I wished to go; and for
another reason also, that is to say that the masters and
captains of the other ships of his company did not love him :
of this I do not know the reason, except by cause of his,
the captain-general, being Portuguese, and they were
Spaniards or Castilians, who for a long time have been in
rivalry and ill will with one another. Notwithstanding this
all were obedient to him. He made his ordinances such as
those which follow, so that during the storms at sea, which
often come on by night and day, his ships should not go
away and separate from one another. These ordinances he
published and made over in writing to each master of the
ships, and commanded them to be observed and inviolably
kept, unless there were great and legitimate excuses, and
appearance of not having been able to do otherwise.

Firstly, the said captain-general willed that the vessel in
which he himself was should go before the other vessels,
and that the others should follow it; therefore he carried by
night on the poop of his ship a torch or faggot of burning
wood, which they called farol, which burned all the night,
so that his ships should not lose sight of him. Sometimes
he set a lantern, sometimes a thick cord of reeds[2] was
lighted, which was called trenche.[3] This is made of reeds
well soaked in the water, and much beaten, then they are
dried in the sun or in the smoke, and it is a thing very suitable for such a matter. When the captain had made one of

---

[1] Fortunes.　　　[2] Jonq.　　　[3] Estrenque, made of esparta.

his signals to his people, they answered in the same way. In that manner they knew whether the ships were following and keeping together or not. And when he wished to take a tack on account of the change of weather, or if the wind was contrary, or if he wished to make less way, he had two lights shown; and if he wished the others to lower their small sail,[1] which was a part of the sail attached to the great sail, he showed three lights. Also by the three lights, notwithstanding that the wind was fair for going faster, he signalled that the studding sail should be lowered; so that the great sail might be quicker and more easily struck and furled when bad weather should suddenly set in, on account of some squall[2] or otherwise. Likewise when the captain wished the other ships to lower the sail he had four lights shown, which shortly after he had put out and then showed a single one, which was a signal that he wished to stop there and turn, so that the other ships might do as he did. Withal, when he discovered any land, or shoal, that is to say, a rock at sea, he made several lights be shown or had a bombard fired off. If he wished to make sail, he signalled to the other ships with four lights, so that they should do as he did, and follow him. He always carried this said lantern suspended to the poop of his vessel. Also when he wished the studding sail to be replaced with the great sail, he showed three lights. And to know whether all the ships followed him and were coming together, he showed one light only besides the fanol, and then each of the ships showed another light, which was an answering signal.

Besides the above-mentioned ordinances for carrying on seamanship as is fitting, and to avoid the dangers which may come upon those who do not keep watch, the said captain, who was expert in the things required for navigation, ordered that three watches should be kept at night. The

[1] Bonnette=stun sail, formerly added below the square sail.
[2] Groupade.

first was at the beginning of the night, the second at midnight, and the third towards break of day, which is commonly
called *La diane*, otherwise the star of the break of day.
Every night these watches were changed; that is to say, he
who had kept the first watch, on the following day kept the
second, and he who had kept the second kept the third;
and so on they changed continually every night. The said
captain commanded that his regulations both for the signals
and the watches should be well observed, so that their
voyage should be made with greater security. The crews
of this fleet were divided into three companies; the first
belonged to the captain, the second to the pilot or *nochier*,
and the third to the master. These regulations having
been made, the captain-general deliberated on sailing, as
follows.

Monday, the day of St. Laurence, the 10th of August, in
the year above mentioned, the fleet, provided with what was
necessary for it, and carrying crews of different nations, to
the number of two hundred and thirty-seven men in all the
five ships, was ready to set sail from the mole of Seville; and
firing all the artillery, we made sail only on the foremast,
and came to the end of a river named Betis, which is now
called Guadalcavir. In going along this river we passed
by a place named Gioan de Farax, where there was[1] a large
population of Moors, and there there was a bridge over the
river by which one went to Seville. This bridge was ruined,
however there had remained two columns which are at the
bottom of the water, on which account it is necessary to
have people of the country of experience and knowledge to
point out the convenient spot for safely passing between
these two columns, from fear of striking against them.
Besides that, it is necessary in order to pass safely by this
bridge and by other places on this river, that the water
should be rather high. After having passed the two

_____

[1] Milan edition adds here, *formerly*.

columns we came to another place named Coria, and passing by many little villages lying along the said river, at last we arrived at a castle, which belongs to the Duke of Medina Sidonia, named St. Lucar, where there is a port from which to enter the ocean sea. It is entered by the east wind and you go out by the west wind. Near there is the cape of St. Vincent, which, according to cosmography, is in thirty-seven degrees of latitude, at twenty miles distance from the said port; and from the aforesaid town to this port by the river there are thirty-five or forty miles. A few days afterwards the captain-general came along the said river with his boat, and the masters of the other ships with him, and we remained some days in this port to supply the fleet with some necessary things. We went every day to hear mass on shore, at a church named Our Lady of Barrameda, towards St. Lucar. There the captain commanded that all the men of the fleet should confess before going on any further, in which he himself showed the way to the others. Besides he did not choose that anyone should bring any married woman, or others to the ships, for several good considerations.

Tuesday, the 20th September of the said year,[1] we set sail from St. Lucar, making the course of the south-west otherwise named Labeiche;[2] and on the twenty-sixth of the said month we arrived at an island of great Canaria, named Teneriphe, which is in twenty-eight degrees latitude; there we remained three days and a half to take in provisions and other things which were wanted. After that we set sail thence and came to a port named Monterose, where we sojourned two days to supply ourselves with pitch, which is a thing necessary for ships. It is to be known that among the other isles which are at the said great Canaria, there is one, where not a drop of water is to be found proceeding from a fountain or a river, only once a day at the hour of

---

[1] 1519.　　　　　　　　　　[2] Garbin and Libeccio.

midday, there descends a cloud from the sky which envelops a large tree which is in this island, and it falls upon the leaves of the tree, and a great abundance of water distils from these leaves, so that at the foot of the tree there is so large a quantity of water that it seems as if there was an ever-running fountain. The men who inhabit this place are satisfied with this water; also the animals, both domestic and wild, drink of it.

Monday, the third of October of the said year, at the hour of midnight, we set sail, making the course auster, which the levantine mariners call Siroc,[1] entering into the ocean sea. We passed the Cape Verd and the neighbouring islands in fourteen-and-a-half degrees, and we navigated for several days by the coast of Guinea or Ethiopia; where there is a mountain called Sierra Leona, which is in eight degrees latitude according to the art and science of cosmography and astrology. Sometimes we had the wind contrary and at other times sufficiently good, and rains without wind. In this manner we navigated with rain for the space of sixty days until the equinoctial line, which was a thing very strange and unaccustomed to be seen, according to the saying of some old men and those who had navigated here several times. Nevertheless, before reaching this equinoctial line we had in fourteen degrees a variety of weather and bad winds, as much on account of squalls as for the head winds and currents which came in such a manner that we could no longer advance. In order that our ships might not perish nor broach to[2] (as it often happens when the squalls come together), we struck our sails, and in that manner we went about the sea hither and thither until the fair weather came. During the calm there came large fishes near the ships which they called *Tiburoni* (sharks), which have teeth of a terrible kind, and eat people when they find them in the sea either alive or dead. These fishes are caught with a device which

---

[1] South-east. [2] Donnassent à travers.

the mariners call hamc, which is a hook of iron. Of these,
some were caught by our men. However, they are worth
nothing to eat when they are large ; and even the small ones
are worth but little. During these storms the body of St.
Anselme appeared to us several times ; amongst others, one
night that it was very dark on account of the bad weather,
the said saint appeared in the form of a fire lighted at the
summit of the mainmast,[1] and remained there near two hours
and a half, which comforted us greatly, for we were in tears,
only expecting the hour of perishing ; and when that holy
light was going away from us it gave out so great a brilliancy
in the eyes of each, that we were near a quarter-of-an-hour like
people blinded, and calling out for mercy. For without any
doubt nobody hoped to escape from that storm. It is to be
noted that all and as many times as that light which represents the said St. Anselme shows itself and descends upon a
vessel which is in a storm at sea, that vessel never is lost.
Immediately that this light had departed the sea grew
calmer, and then we saw divers sorts of birds, amongst
others there were some which had no fundament.[2] There
is also another kind of bird of such a nature that when the
female wishes to lay her eggs she goes and lays them on the
back of the male, and there it is that the eggs are hatched.
This last kind have no feet and are always in the sea.
There is another kind of bird which only lives on the
droppings of the other birds, this is a true thing, and they
are named Cagaselo, for I have seen them follow the other
birds until they had done what nature ordered them to do ;
and after it has eat this dirty diet it does not follow any
other bird until hunger returns to it ; it always does the
same thing.[3] There are also fish which fly, and we saw a

---

[1] La grande gabbe.   [2] N'avoyent point de fondement.
[3] In reality this bird swallows the fish which it forces the fishing
bird to disgorge.

great quantity of them together, so many that it seemed that it was an island in the sea.

After that we had passed the equinoctial line, towards the south, we lost the star of the tramontana, and we navigated between the south and Garbin, which is the collateral wind [or point] between south and west; and we crossed as far as a country named Verzin, which is in twenty-four degrees and a half of the antarctic sky. This country is from the cape St. Augustine, which is in eight degrees in the antarctic sky. At this place we had refreshments of victuals, like fowls and meat of calves,[1] also a variety of fruits, called battate, pigne (pine-apples), sweet, of singular goodness, and many other things, which I have omitted mentioning, not to be too long. The people of the said place gave, in order to have a knife, or a hook[2] for catching fish, five or six fowls, and for a comb they gave two geese, and for a small mirror, or a pair of scissors, they gave so much fish that ten men could have eaten of it. And for a bell (or hawk's-bell)[3] they gave a full basket[4] of the fruit named battate; this has the taste of a chestnut, and is of the length of a shuttle.[5] For a king of cards, of that kind which they used to play with in Italy, they gave me five fowls, and thought they had cheated me. We entered into this port the day of Saint Lucy[6] [13th December], before Christmas, on which day we had the sun on the zenith,[7] which is a term of astrology. This zenith is a point in the sky, according to astrologers, and only in imagination, and it answers to over our head in a straight line, as may be seen by the treatise of the sphere,[8] and by Aristotle, in the first book, *De Cœlo et Mondo*. On the day that we had the sun in the zenith

[1] The Milan edition has "flesh of the Anta, like that of a cow"; and a note says the anta is the tapir.   [2] Haim.

[3] Aigueillette, same as esquillette.   [4] Coffin.

[5] Naveau, for navette.

[6] Le jour de Saincte Lucie aux auantz de Noël.

[7] Par zenit.   [8] Or of Lespere.

we felt greater heat, as much as when we were on the equinoctial line.

The said country of Verzin is very abundant in all good things, and is larger than France, Spain, and Italy together. It is one of the countries which the King of Portugal has conquered [acquired]. Its inhabitants are not Christians, and adore nothing, but live according to the usage of nature, rather bestially than otherwise. Some of these people live a hundred, or a hundred and twenty, or a hundred and forty years, and more ; they go naked, both men and women. Their dwellings are houses that are rather long, and which they call " boy"; they sleep upon cotton nets, which they call, in their language, " amache." These nets are fastened to large timbers from one end of their house to the other. They make the fire to warm themselves right under their bed. It is to be known that in each of these houses, which they call " boy," there dwells a family of a hundred persons, who make a great noise. In this place they have boats, which are made of a tree, all in one piece, which they call " canoo." These are not made with iron instruments, for they have not got any, but with stones, like pebbles, and with these they plane[1] and dig out these boats. Into these thirty or forty men enter, and their oars are made like iron shovels : and those who row these oars are black people, quite naked and shaven, and look like enemies of hell. The men and women of this said place are well made in their bodies. They eat the flesh of their enemies, not as good meat, but because they have adopted this custom. Now this custom arose as follows : an old woman of this place of Verzim had an only son, who was killed by his enemies, and, some days afterwards, the friends of this woman captured one of the said enemies who had put her son to death, and brought him to where she was. Immediately the said old woman, seeing the

---

[1] Rabotent.

man who was captured, and recollecting the death of her child, rushed upon him like a mad dog, and bit him on the shoulder. However, this man who had been taken prisoner found means to run away, and told how they had wished to eat him, showing the bite which the said old woman had made in his shoulder. After that those who were caught on one side or other were eaten. Through that arose this custom in this place of eating the enemies of each other. But they do not eat up the whole body of the man whom they take prisoner; they eat him bit by bit, and for fear that he should be spoiled, they cut him up into pieces, which they set to dry in the chimney, and every day they cut a small piece, and eat it with their ordinary victuals in memory of their enemies. I was assured that this custom was true by a pilot, named John Carvagio, who was in our company, and had remained four years in this place; it is also to be observed that the inhabitants of this place, both men and women, are accustomed to paint themselves with fire, all over the body, and also the face. The men are shaven, and wear no beard, because they pluck it out themselves, and for all clothing they wear a circle surrounded with the largest feathers of parrots,[1] and they only cover their posterior parts, which is a cause of laughter and mockery. The people of this place, almost all, excepting[2] women and children, have three holes in the lower lip, and carry, hanging in them, small round stones, about a finger in length. These kind of people, both men and women, are not very black, but rather brown,[3] and they openly show their shame, and have no hair on the whole of their bodies. The king of this country is called

---

[1] Papegaulx.

[2] Fabre's French printed edition, and the Italian edition of 1536, both *include* the women and children:—

"Quasi tous tant homes que femmes que enfants ont trois pertuis en la levre dembas," etc. "Tutti gli huomini donne et fanciulli hanno tre buchi," etc.   [3] Tané.

Cacich, and there are here an infinite number of parrots, of which they give eight or ten for a looking-glass ; there are also some little cat-monkeys[1] having almost the appearance of a lion ; they are yellow, and handsome, and agreeable to look at.   The people of this place make bread, which is of a round shape, and they take the marrow of certain trees which are there, between the bark and the tree, but it is not at all good, and resembles fresh cheese. There are also some pigs which have their navel on the back,[2] and large birds which have their beak like a spoon, and they have no tongue.   For a hatchet or for a knife they used to give us one or two of their daughters as slaves, but their wives they would not give up for anything in the world.   According to what they say the women of this place never render duty to their husbands by day, but only at night; they attend to business out of doors, and carry all that they require for their husband's victuals inside small baskets on their heads, or fastened to their heads.   Their husbands go with them, and carry a bow of vergin,[3] or of black palm, with a handful of arrows of cane. They do this because they are very jealous of their wives. These carry their children fastened to their neck, and they are inside a thing made of cotton in the manner of a net. I omit relating many other strange things, not to be too prolix ; however, I will not forget to say that mass was said twice on shore, where there were many people of the said country, who remained on their knees, and their hands joined in great reverence, during the mass, so that it was a pleasure and a subject of compassion to see them.   In a short time they built a house for us, as they imagined that we should remain a long time with them, and, at our departure thence, they gave us a large quantity of verzin.   It is a colour which proceeds from the trees which are in this country,

---

[1] De petites chattes maymounes.

[2] Leur lombric sur leschine.

[3] Milan edition calls it wood of Brasile.

and they are in such quantity that the country is called from it Verzin.

It is to be known that it happened that it had not rained for two months before we came there, and the day that we arrived it began to rain, on which account the people of the said place said that we came from heaven, and had brought the rain with us, which was great simplicity, and these people were easily converted to the Christian faith. Besides the above-mentioned things which were rather simple, the people of this country showed us another, very simple ; for they imagined that the small ships' boats were the children of the ships, and that the said ships brought them forth when the boats were hoisted out to send the men hither and thither; and when the boats were along-side the ship they thought that the ships were giving them suck.

A beautiful young girl came one day inside the ship of our captain, where I was, and did not come except to seek for her luck : however, she directed her looks to the cabin of the master, and saw a nail of a finger's length, *and went and took it as something valuable and new, and hid it in her hair, for otherwise she would not have been able to conceal[1] it, because she was naked,* and, bending forwards, she went away ; and the captain and I saw this mystery.[2]

[1] Musser.

- This passage is from MS. No. 68, the Regent Louisa's copy, for whom it appears to have been adapted ; that in No. 5650, and in Amoretti and Fabre's editions, is less fit for publication: the words from * to [2] are omitted in No. 68.

[2] The 1536 edition omits the story of the girl, and instead says :—

" Nella prima costa di terra che ariuammo, ad alcune femine schiave che haueuamo leuate ne le naui d'altri paesi, & erano grauide vennero le doglie del parto, per il che loro sole si uscirono di naue, & smontorono in terra, & partorito che hebbero con li figluoli in braccio se ne ritorna-rono subito in nave."

Fabre says :—

" En la première coste que passerent aulcunes esclaves enfanterent et

SOME WORDS OF THIS PEOPLE OF VERZIN.

Milan Edition.

Millet	-	- Au mil	- Maize.	
Flour	-	- Farine -	- Huy.	
A hook	-	- Ung haim	- Pinda.	
A knife	-	- Ung coutteau	- Taesse	- Tarse.
A comb	-	- Ung peigne	- Chignap	- Chipag.
A fork	-	- Une forcette	- Pirame.	
A bell	-	- Une sonnette	- Itemnaraca	- Hanmaraca.

Good, more than good - Bon, plus que bon tum maraghatom.

We remained thirteen days in this country of Verzin, and, departing from it and following our course, we went as far as thirty-four degrees and a third towards the antarctic pole ; there we found, near a river, men whom they call " cannibals,"[1] who eat human flesh, and one of these men, great as a giant, came to the captain's ship to ascertain and ask if the others might come. This man had a voice like a bull, and whilst this man was at the ship his companions carried off all their goods which they had to a castle further off, from fear of us. Seeing that, we landed a hundred men from the ships, and went after them to try and catch some others ; however they gained in running away. This kind of people did more with one step than we could do at a bound. In this same river there were seven little islands, and in the largest of them precious stones are found. This place was formerly called the Cape of St. Mary, and it was thought there that from thence there was a passage to the Sea of Sur ; that is to say, the South Sea. And it is not found that any ship has ever discovered anything more, having passed beyond the said

quant estoient en traveil se mirent hors du basteau et après retournerent au basteau et nourrirent leurs enfans."

This story is improbable, as women were not allowed to come on board ship. Fabre then relates the story of the young girl.

[1] Canibali.

cape. And now it is no longer a cape, but it is a river which has a mouth seventeen leagues in width, by which it enters into the sea. In past time, in this river, these great men named Canibali ate a Spanish captain, named John de Sola,[1] and sixty men who had gone to discover land, as we were doing, and trusted too much to them.

Afterwards following the same course towards the Antarctic pole, going along the land, we found two islands full of geese and goslings, and sea wolves, of which geese the large number could not be reckoned; for we loaded all the five ships with them in an hour. These geese are black, and have their feathers all over the body of the same size and shape, and they do not fly, and live upon fish; and they were so fat that they did not pluck them, but skinned them. They have beaks like that of a crow. The sea wolves of these two islands are of many colours, and of the size and thickness of a calf, and have a head like that of a calf, and the ears small and round. They have large teeth, and have no legs, but feet joining close on to the body, which resemble a human hand; they have small nails to their feet, and skin between the fingers like geese. If these animals could run they would be very bad and cruel, but they do not stir from the water, and swim and live upon fish. In this place we endured a great storm, and thought we should have been lost, but the three holy bodies, that is to say, St. Anselmo, St. Nicolas, and Sta. Clara, appeared to us, and immediately the storm ceased.

Departing thence as far as forty nine degrees and a half in the Antarctic heavens (as we were in the winter), we entered into a port to pass the winter, and remained there two whole months without ever seeing anybody. However, one day, without anyone expecting it, we saw a giant, who was on the shore of the sea, quite naked, and was dancing and leaping, and singing, and whilst singing he put the

[1] Solis.

E

sand and dust on his head. Our captain sent one of his
men towards him, whom he charged to sing and leap like
the other to reassure him, and show him friendship. This
he did, and immediately the sailor led this giant to a little
island where the captain was waiting for him; and when he
was before us he began to be astonished, and to be afraid,
and he raised one finger on high,[1] thinking that we came
from heaven. He was so tall that the tallest of us only
came up to his waist;[2] however[3] he was well built. He had
a large face, painted red all round, and his eyes also were
painted yellow around them, and he had two hearts painted
on his cheeks; he had but little hair on his head, and it
was painted white. When he was brought before the captain he was clothed with the skin of a certain beast, which
skin was very skilfully sewed. This beast[4] has its head and
ears of the size of a mule, and the neck and body of the
fashion of a camel, the legs of a deer, and the tail like
that of a horse, and it neighs like a horse. There is a
great quantity of these animals in this same place. This
giant had his feet covered with the skin of this animal in
the form of shoes, and he carried in his hand a short and
thick bow, with a thick cord made of the gut of the said
beast, with a bundle of cane arrows, which were not very
long, and were feathered like ours,[5] but they had no iron at
the end, though they had at the end some small white and
black cut stones, and these arrows were like those which the
Turks use. The captain caused food and drink to be given
to this giant, then they showed him some things, amongst
others, a steel mirror. When the giant saw his likeness in
it, he was greatly terrified, leaping backwards, and made
three or four of our men fall down.

---

[1] "Contremont."

[2] Falkner (1774, Hereford) in his account of Patagonia, says he saw
men among the Puelches seven feet six inches high.   [3] "Combien."

[4] The guanaco, a kind of Lama.   [5] "Empanées."

After that the captain gave him two bells, a mirror, a comb, and a chaplet of beads, and sent him back on shore, having him accompanied by four armed men. One of the companions of this giant, who would never come to the ship, on seeing the other coming back with our people, came forward and ran to where the other giants dwelled. These came one after the other all naked, and began to leap and sing, raising one finger to heaven, and showing to our people a certain white powder made of the roots of herbs, which they kept in earthen pots, and they made signs that they lived on that, and that they had nothing else to eat than this powder. Therefore our people made them signs to come to the ship and that they would help them to carry their bundles.[1] Then these men came, who carried only their bows in their hands; but their wives came after them laden like donkeys, and carried their goods. These women are not as tall as the men, but they are very sufficiently large. When we saw them we were all amazed and astonished, for they had the breasts half an ell[2] long, and had their faces painted, and were dressed like the men. But they wore a small skin before them to cover themselves. They brought with them four of those little beasts of which they make their clothing, and they led them with a cord in the manner of dogs coupled together. When these people wish to catch these animals with which they clothe themselves, they fasten one of the young ones to a bush, and afterwards the large ones come to play with the little one, and the giants are hid behind some hedge, and by shooting their arrows they kill the large ones. Our men brought eighteen of these giants, both men and women, whom they placed in two divisions, half on one side of the port, and the other half at the other, to hunt the said animals. Six days after, our people on going to cut wood, saw another giant, with his face painted and clothed like the above-

---

[1] " Besongnes."   [2] " Brasse."

mentioned, he had in his hand a bow and arrows, and approaching our people he made some touches on his head and then on his body, and afterwards did the same to our people.   And this being done he raised both his hands to heaven.   When the captain-general knew all this, he sent to fetch him with his ship's boat, and brought him to one of the little islands which are in the port, where the ships were.   In this island the captain had caused a house to be made for putting some of the ships' things in whilst he remained there.   This giant was of a still better disposition than the others, and was a gracious and amiable person, who liked to dance and leap.   When he leapt he caused the earth to sink in a palm depth at the place where his feet touched.   He was a long time with us, and at the end we baptised him, and gave him the name of John.   This giant pronounced the name of Jesus, the Pater noster, Ave Maria, and his name as clearly as we did: but he had a terribly strong and loud voice.   The captain gave him a shirt and a tunic[1] of cloth, and seaman's breeches,[2] a cap, a comb, some bells, and other things, and sent him back to where he had come from.   He went away very joyous and satisfied.   The next day this giant returned, and brought one of those large animals before mentioned, for which the captain gave him some other things, so that he should bring more.   But afterwards he did not return, and it is to be presumed that the other giants killed him because he had come to us.

Fifteen days later we saw four other giants, who carried no arrows, for they had hid them in the bushes, as two of them showed us, for we took them all four, and each of them was painted in a different way.   The captain retained the two younger ones to take them to Spain on his return; but it was done by gentle and cunning means, for otherwise they would have done a hurt to some of our men.   The manner in which he retained them was that he gave them

<hr/>
[1] " Sayon."   [2] " Bragues marinicres."

many knives, forks, mirrors, bells, and glass, and they held all these things in their hands. Then the captain had some irons brought, such as are put on the feet of malefactors: these giants took pleasure in seeing the irons, but they did not know where to put them, and it grieved them that they could not take them with their hands, because they were hindered by the other things which they held in them. The other two giants were there, and were desirous of helping the other two, but the captain would not let them, and made a sign to the two whom he wished to detain that they would put those irons on their feet, and then they would go away: at this they made a sign with their heads that they were content. Immediately the captain had the irons put on the feet of both of them, and when they saw that they were striking with a hammer on the bolt which crosses the said irons to rivet them, and prevent them from being opened, these giants were afraid, but the captain made them a sign not to doubt of anything. Nevertheless when they saw the trick which had been played them, they began to be enraged,[1] and to foam like bulls, crying out very loud Setebos,[2] that is to say, the great devil, that he should help them. The hands of the other two giants were bound, but it was with great difficulty; then the captain sent them back on shore, with nine of his men to conduct them, and to bring the wife of one of those who had remained in irons, because he regretted her greatly, as we saw by signs. But in going away one of those two who were sent away, untied his hands and escaped, running with such lightness that our men lost sight of him, and he went away where his companions were staying; but he found nobody of those

---

[1] "Bouffer", to be angry, also to blow, to puff.

[2] Setebos, though represented by the Spaniards as a demon, would, no doubt, be the Patagonian name of the Deity. Shakespeare has twice brought in Setebos in the *Tempest*, as invoked by Caliban. There can be no doubt of his having got the name of Setebos from the account of Magellan's voyage.

that he had left with the women because they had gone to
hunt.   However he went to look for them, and found them,
and related to them all that had been done to them.   The
other giant whose hands were tied struggled as much as he
could to unfasten himself, and to prevent his doing so, one
of our men struck him, and hurt him on the head, at which
he got very angry; however he led our people there where
their wives were.   Then John Cavagio,[1] the pilot who was
the chief conductor of these two giants, would not bring
away the wife of one of the giants who had remained in
irons on that evening, but was of opinion that they should
sleep there, because it was almost night.   During this time
the one of the giants who had untied his hands came back
from where he had been, with another giant, and they seeing their companion wounded on the head, said nothing at
that moment, but next morning they spoke in their language to the women, and immediately all ran away together,
and the smallest ran faster than the biggest, and they left
all their chattels.   Two of these giants being rather a long
way off shot arrows at our men, and fighting thus, one of
the giants pierced with an arrow the thigh of one of our
men, of which he died immediately.   Then seeing that he
was dead, all ran away.   Our men had cross-bows and
guns,[2] but they never could hit one of these giants, because
they did not stand still in one place, but leaped hither and
thither.   After that, our men buried the man who had been
killed, and set fire to the place where those giants had left
their chattels.   Certainly these giants run faster than a
horse, and they are very jealous of their wives.

When these giants have a stomach-ache, instead of taking
medicine they put down their throats an arrow about two
feet long ; then they vomit a green bile[3] mixed with blood :
and the reason why they throw up this green matter is because they sometimes eat thistles.   When they have head-

---

[1] " Carvalho."   [2] " Escouppetes."   [3] " Collère."

aches they make a cut across the forehead, and also on the arms and legs, to draw blood from several parts of their bodies. One of the two we had taken, and who was in our ship, said that the blood did not choose to remain in the place and spot of the body where pain was felt. These people have their hair cut short and clipped in the manner of monks with a tonsure : they wear a cord of cotton round their head, to this they hang their arrows when they go a-hunting. . . .[1]

When one of them dies, ten or twelve devils appear and dance all round the dead man. It seems that these are painted, and one of these enemies is taller than the others, and makes a greater noise, and more mirth than the others: that is whence these people have taken the custom of painting their faces and bodies, as has been said. The greatest of these devils is called in their language Setebos, and the others Cheleule. Besides the above-mentioned things, this one who was in the ship with us, told us by signs that he had seen devils with two horns on their heads, and long hair down to their feet, and who threw out fire from their mouths and rumps. The captain named this kind of people Pataghom,[2] who have no houses, but have huts made of the skins of the animals with which they clothe themselves, and go hither and thither with these huts of theirs, as the gypsies[3] do; they live on raw meat, and eat a certain sweet root, which they call Capac. These two giants that we had in the ship ate a large basketful[4] of biscuit, and rats without skinning them, and they drank half a bucket of water at each time.

We remained in this port, which was called the port of St. Julian, about five months, during which there happened to us many strange things, of which I will tell a part. One was, that immediately that we entered into this port, the

---

[1] " Et lient leur membre dedans le corps pour le très grand froid."
[2] On account of their large feet.   [3] " Egiptiens."   [4] Coffin.

masters of the other four ships plotted treason against the captain-general, in order to put him to death. These were thus named : John of Carthagine, conductor[1] of the fleet ; the treasurer, Loys de Mendoza ; the conductor,[2] Anthony Cocha ; and Gaspar de Casada.[3] However, the treason was discovered, for which the treasurer was killed with stabs of a dagger, and then quartered. This Gaspar de Casada had his head cut off, and afterwards was cut into quarters ; and the conductor having a few days later attempted another treason, was banished with a priest, and was put in that country called Pattagonia.[4] The captain-general would not put this conductor to death, because the Emperor Charles had made him captain of one of the ships. One of our ships, named St. James, was lost in going to discover the coast ; all the men, however, were saved by a miracle, for they were hardly wet at all. Two men of these, who were saved, came to us and told us all that had passed and happened, on which the captain at once sent some men with sacks full of biscuit for two months. So, each day we found something of the ship of the other men who had escaped from the ship which was lost ; and the place where these men were was twenty-five leagues from us, and the road bad and full of thorns, and it required four days to go there, and no water to drink was to be found on the road, but only ice, and of that little. In this port of St. Julian there were a great quantity of long capres,[5] called Missiglione ; these had pearls in the midst. In this place they found incense, and ostriches, foxes, sparrows, and rabbits[6]

---

[1] Milan edition calls him "vehadore", overseer or purveyor.

[2] "Contador." Milan edition.   [3] "Quesada."

[4] Maximilian, the Transylvanian, relates that when Gomez abandoned Magellan in the Straits, he returned by this spot and picked up these two men.

"Capres," mussels or oysters ; the Milan edition adds, that they were not eatable.   [6] "Connins.

a good deal smaller than ours.[1]   We set up at the top of
the highest mountain which was there a very large cross, as
a sign that this country belonged to the King of Spain;
and we gave to this mountain the name of Mount of Christ.

Departing thence, we found in fifty-one degrees less one-
third (50° 40′ S.), in the Antarctic, a river of fresh water,
which was near causing us to be lost, from the great winds
which it sent out; but God, of his favour, aided us.   We
were about two months in this river, as it supplied fresh
water and a kind of fish an ell long, and very scaly,[2] which
is good to eat.   Before going away, the captain chose that
all should confess and receive the body of our Lord like
good Christians.

CHAPTER.[3]

After going and taking the course to the fifty-second
degree of the said Antarctic sky, on the day of the Eleven
Thousand Virgins [October 21], we found, by a miracle, a
strait which we called the Cape of the Eleven Thousand
Virgins, this strait is a hundred and ten leagues long,
which are four hundred and forty miles, and almost as
wide as less than half a league,[4] and it issues in another
sea, which is called the peaceful sea;[5] it is surrounded by
very great and high mountains covered with snow.   In
this place it was not possible to anchor[6] with the anchors,
because no bottom was found, on which account they were
forced to put the moorings[7] of twenty-five or thirty fathoms

---

[1] "Plus petites assez que les notres:" "assai piu piccoli". Milan edition.
[2] "Seameux."
[3] The MS. is thus divided, but without numbers to the chapters.
[4] "Et quasi autant de largeur moins de demye lieue."
[5] "La mer paisible."   [6] "Surgir."
[7] "De mettre les proysses en terre."

length on shore. This strait was a round place surrounded
by mountains, as I have said, and the greater number of
the sailors thought that there was no place by which to go
out thence to enter into the peaceful sea. But the captain-
general said that there was another strait for going out, and
said that he knew it well, because he had seen it by a marine
chart of the King of Portugal, which map had been made
by a great pilot and mariner named Martin of Bohemia.[1]
The captain sent on before two of his ships, one named *St.
Anthony* and the other the *Conception*, to seek for and discover the outlet of this strait, which was called the Cape de
la Baya. And we, with the other two ships, that is to say,
the flagship named *Trinitate*, and the other the *Victory*,
remained waiting for them within the Bay, where in the
night we had a great storm, which lasted till the next
day at midday, and during which we were forced to weigh
the anchors and let the ships go hither and thither about
the bay. The other two ships met with such a head wind[2]
that they could not weather[3] a cape which the bay made
almost at its extremity; wishing to come to us, they were
near being driven to beach the ships.[4] But, on approaching
the extremity of the bay, and whilst expecting to be lost,
they saw a small mouth, which did not resemble a mouth
but a corner,[5] and (like people giving up hope[6]) they threw
themselves into it, so that by force they discovered the
strait. Seeing that it was not a corner, but a strait of land,
they went further on and found a bay, then going still
further they found another strait and another bay larger

---

[1] Martin Behaim, who lived at Fayal and Nuremberg. A globe was
constructed at Nuremberg under the instructions of Martin Behaim in
1492, and given by him to the town of Nuremberg. This globe dis-
proves the idea that Martin Behaim or his maps had indicated to
Magellan any straits, for the whole continent of America is absent
from it.

[2] " Trauerse."   [3] " Chevaucher."   [4] " Entrer à sec."
[5] " Canton."   [6] (" Comme abandonnans.")

than the first two, at which, being very joyous, they suddenly returned backwards to tell it to the captain-general. Amongst us we thought that they had perished: first, because of the great storm; next, because two days had passed that we had not seen them. And being thus in doubt[1] we saw the two ships under all sail, with ensigns spread, come towards us : these, when near us, suddenly discharged much artillery, at which we, very joyous, saluted them with artillery and shouts. Afterwards, all together, thanking God and the Virgin Mary, we went to seek further on.

After having entered inside this strait we found that there were two mouths, of which one trended to the Sirocco (S.E.), and the other to the Garbin (S.W.). On that account the captain again sent the two ships, *St. Anthony* and *Conception*, to see if the mouth which was towards Sirocco had an outlet beyond into the said peaceful sea. One of these two ships, named *St. Anthony*, would not wait for the other ship, because those who were inside wished to return to Spain : this they did, and the principal reason was on account of the pilot[2] of the said ship being previously discontented with the said captain-general, because that before this armament was made, this pilot had gone to the Emperor to talk about having some ships to discover countries. But, on account of the arrival of the captain-general, the Emperor did not give them to this pilot, on account of which he agreed with some Spaniards, and the following night they took prisoner the captain of their ship, who was a brother[3] of the captain-general, and who was named Alvar de Meschite; they wounded him, and put him in irons. So they carried him off to Spain. And in this ship, which went away and returned, was one of the two above-mentioned giants whom we had taken, and when he felt the heat he

[1] " Souspecon."
[2] His name was Estevan Gomez.   [3] Cousin.

died. The other ship, named the *Conception*, not being able
to follow that one, was always waiting for it, and fluttered
hither and thither. But it lost its time, for the other took
the road by night for returning. When this happened, at
night the ship of the captain and the other ship went together to discover the other mouth to Garbin (S.W.), where,
on always holding on our course, we found the same strait.
But at the end[1] we arrived at a river which we named the
River of Sardines, because we found a great quantity of
them. So we remained there four days to wait for the
other two ships. A short time after we sent a boat well
supplied with men and provisions to discover the cape of
the other sea: these remained three days in going and
coming. They told us that they had found the cape, and
the sea great and wide. At the joy which the captain-
general had at this he began to cry, and he gave the name
of Cape of Desire to this cape, as a thing which had been
much desired for a long time. Having done that we turned
back to find the two ships which were at the other side, but
we only found the *Conception*, of which ship we asked what
had become of her companion. To this the captain of the
said ship, named John Serrano (who was pilot of the first
ship which was lost) as has been related), replied that he
knew nothing of her, and that he had never seen her since
she entered the mouth. However, we sought for her through
all the strait, as far as the said mouth, by which she had
taken her course to return. Besides that, the Captain-
General sent back the ship named the *Victory* as far as the
entrance of the strait to see if the ship was there, and he
told the people of this ship that if they did not find the ship
they were looking for, they were to place an ensign on the
summit of a small hill, with a letter inside a pot placed in
the ground near the ensign, so that if the ship should by
chance return, it might see that ensign, and also find the

[1] "A la fin."

letter which would give information of the course which the captain was holding. This manner of acting had been ordained by the captain from the commencement, in order to effect the junction of any ship which might be separated from the others. So the people of the said ship did what the captain had commanded them, and more, for they set two ensigns with letters; one of the ensigns was placed on a small hill at the first bay, the other on an islet in the third bay, where there were many sea wolves and large birds. The captain-general waited for them with the other ship near the river named Isles: and he caused a cross to be set upon a small island in front of that river, which was between high mountains covered with snow. This river comes and falls into the sea near the other river of the Sardines.

If we had not found this strait the captain-general had made up his mind to go as far as seventy-five degrees towards the antarctic pole; where at that height in the summer time there is no night, or very little: in a similar manner in the winter there is no day-light, or very little, and so that every one may believe this, when we were in this strait the night lasted only three hours, and this was in the month of October.

The land of this strait on the left hand side looked towards the Sirocco wind, which is the wind collateral to the Levant and South; we called this strait Pathagonico. In it we found at every half league a good port and place for anchoring, good waters, wood all of cedar, and fish like sardines, missiglioni, and a very sweet herb named appio (celery).[1] There is also some of the same kind which is bitter. This herb grows near the springs, and from not finding anything else we ate of it for several days. I think that there is not in the world a more beautiful country, or better strait than this one. In this ocean sea one sees a

[1] "Apium dulce."

very amusing chase of fish, which are of three sorts, of an ell or more in length, and they call these fish Dorades, Albacores, and Bonitos; these follow and pursue another sort of fish which flies, which they call Colondriny,[1] which are a foot long or more, and are very good to eat. When these three sorts of fish find in the water any of these flying fish, immediately they make them come out of the water, and they fly more than a cross bow-shot, as long as their wings are wet; and whilst these fishes fly the other three run after them under the water, seeing the shadow of those that fly: and the moment they fall into the water they are seized upon and eaten by the others which pursue them, which is a thing marvellous and agreeable to see.

VOCABLES DES GEANTS PATHAGONIENS.

Milan Edition.		*Milan Edition.*	
Le chef	- Her .. idem.	Les oreilles	- Sane .. id.
Yeulx	- Ather .. oter.	Les esselles	- Salischin .. id.
Le nez	- Or .. id.	La mamelle	- Othen .. oton.
Les silz	- Occhechl .. id.	La poitrine	- Ochy .. ochii.
Paupieres des yeulx	Sechechiel .. id.	Le corps	- Gechel.
Aux deux narines	Orescho .. id.	Le vit	- Scachet .. sachet.
La bouche	- Xiam .. chian.	Le couillons	- Scancos .. sachan-
Les leures	- Schiane .. schiaine.	Le con	- Isse .. id. [cos.
Les dentz	- Phor .. for.	Le foutre	- Johoi.
La langue	- Schial .. id.	Les cuisses	- Chiaue .. id.
Le menton	- Sechen .. secheri.	Le genouil	- Tepin .. id.
Les cheueulx[2]	- Ajchir .. archiz.	Le cul	- Schiachen .. schiaguen.
Le visaige	· Cogechel.	Les fesses	- Hoy .. hoii.
La gorge	- Ohumer .. ohumez.	Le braz	- Mar .. riaz.
La copa* (le cou)	Schialeschin.	Le poulse	- Ohoy .. holion.
Les epaulles	- Peles.	Les jambes	- Choss .. id.
Le coude	- Cotel.	Les piedz	- Teche .. ti.
La main	- Chene.	Alcalcagno*	- There .. tire.
La paulme de la main	Canneghin.	La cheuille du pied	Perchi .. id.

[1] Golondrina in Spanish, a swallow.
[2] In the Milan edition " Barba", the beard.

	Milan Edition.		*Milan Edition.*
Le doit	- Cori .. id.	La plante ou sole du pied	Cartschem .. caotschoni.
Les ongles	- Colim .. colmi.	Nous -	- Chen.
Le cueur	- Chol .. tol.	Si ou ouy	- Rei.
Le grater	- Ghecare .. id.	L'or -	- Pelpeli .. id.
Homo sguerzo*	- Calischen .. id.	Petre lazure[3]	- Secheghi..sechey.
Au jeune	- Calemi .. id.	Le soleil	- Calexchem .. id.
L'eau	- Oli .. holi.	Les estoilles	- Settere .. id.
Le feu	- Ghialeme..gialeme.	La mer	- Aro .. id.
La fumée	- Jaiche .. giache.	Le vent	- Om .. oni.
La fortune (storm)	Ohone .. id.	A la pignate*	- Aschame .. id.
Le poisson	- Hoi .. id.	A demander	- Ghelhe .. gheglie.
Le manger	- Mecchiere .. id.	Vien icy	- Haisi .. hai.
Une escuelle	- Elo .. etlo.	Au regarder	- Conne .. id.
A combatre .	- Oamaghei ;.. ohomagse.	A aller	- Rhei .. id.
Alle frezze*	- Sethe .. seche.	A la nef[4]	- Theu .. id.
Ung chien	- Holl .. id.	A courir[5]	- Hiam .. tiam.
Ung loup	- Ani .. id.	Al struzzo vcelo*[6]	Hoihoi.
A aller loing	- Schien.	A ses œufs[7]	- Jan.
A la guide	- Anti.	La pouldre d'herbe[7]	Qui.
Aladorer[1]	- Os .. id.	Mangent[8]	- Capac .. id.
Ung papegault[2]	- Cheche.	Le bonnet	- Aichel .. id.
La caige doyseau	Cleo .. id.	Coulernoire	- Amet .. oinel.
Al missiglion* (oyster)	- Siameni .. id.	Rouge	- Theiche .. faiche.
Drap rouge	- Terechai .. id.	Jaulne	- Peperi .. id.
Al cocinare*	- Ixecoles..irocoles.	Le diable grand,	Setebos .. id.
La ceincture	- Cathechin .. id.	Les petitz diables,	Cheleule .. id.
Une oye	- Chache .. cache.	†	

* The Italian words mixed up in the French MS. show that this MS. was written by Pigafetta, and not translated from his Italian.

† None of these words resemble those given by the Jesuit, Falkner, from the language of the Moluche tribe.

[1] " Flairer, odorat," to smell.
[2] A parrot, not in the Milan edition.
[3] " Lapis lazuli", in the Milan edition " Gemma".
[4] In the Milan edition " nieve", snow.
[5] In the Milan edition " coprire, couvrir".
[6] An ostrich, not in the Milan edition.
[7] Not in the Milan edition. [8] Food, the root used as bread.

All these words are pronounced in the throat, because they pronounce them thus.

These words were given me by that giant whom we had in the ship, because he asked me for *capac*, that is to say bread, since they thus name that root which they use for bread, and *oli* that is to say water.   When he saw me write these names after him, and ask for others he understood (what I was doing) with my pen in my hand.[1]   Another time I made a cross and kissed it in showing it to him ; but suddenly he exclaimed Setebos ! and made signs to me that if I again made the cross it would enter into my stomach and make me die.   When this giant was unwell[2] he asked for the cross, and embraced and kissed it much, and he wished to become a Christian before his death, and we named him Paul.   When these people wish to light a fire they take a pointed stick and rub it with another until they make a fire in the pith of a tree which is placed between these sticks.

(In the Milan Edition here begins Book II.)

Wednesday, the twenty-eighth of November, 1520, we came forth out of the said strait, and entered into the Pacific sea, where we remained three months and twenty days without taking in provisions or other refreshments, and we only ate old biscuit reduced to powder, and full of grubs, and stinking from the dirt which the rats had made on it when eating the good biscuit, and we drank water that was yellow and stinking.   We also ate the ox hides which were under the main-yard,[3] so that the yard should not break the rigging :[4] they were very hard on account of

---

[1] This passage is not quite clear :—" Quand il me veyt escripre ces noms après luy demandant des aultres il mentendoit auecq la plume en main."

[2] The printed edition of Milan has: " ammalato dell' infermità di cui mori."   [3] " Antena magiore."   [4] " Sartia."

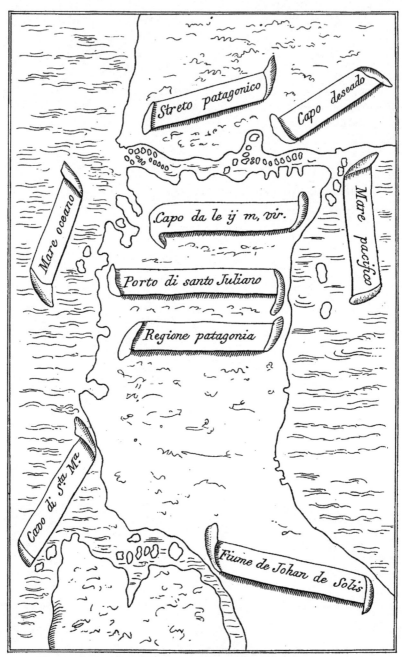

Streto patagonico

Capo deseado

Mare oceano

Capo da le ij m. vir.

Mare pacifico

Porto di santo Juliano

Regione patagonia

Capo di S.ta M.a

Fiume de Johan de Solis

PIGAFETTA'S MAP OF MAGELLAN'S STRAITS.

the sun, rain, and wind, and we left them for four or five days in the sea, and then we put them a little on the embers, and so ate them; also the sawdust of wood,[1] and rats which cost half-a-crown[2] each, moreover enough of them were not to be got. Besides the above-named evils, this misfortune which I will mention was the worst, it was that the upper and lower gums of most of our men grew so much[3] that they could not eat, and in this way so many suffered, that nineteen died, and the other giant, and an Indian from the county of Verzin. Besides those who died, twenty-five or thirty fell ill of divers sicknesses, both in the arms and legs, and other places, in such manner that very few remained healthy. However, thanks be to the Lord, I had no sickness. During those three months and twenty days we went in an open sea,[4] while we ran fully four thousand leagues in the Pacific sea. This was well named Pacific, for during this same time we met with no storm, and saw no land except two small uninhabited islands, in which we found only birds and trees. We named them the Unfortunate Islands; they are two hundred leagues apart from one another, and there is no place to anchor, as there is no bottom. There we saw many sharks, which are a kind of large fish which they call Tiburoni. The first isle is in fifteen degrees of austral latitude,[5] and the other island is in nine degrees. With the said wind we ran each day fifty or sixty leagues,[6] or more; now with the wind astern, sometimes on a wind[7] or otherwise. And if our Lord and his Mother had

---

[1] " Segature de asse." " Segature di tavole." Milan.

[2] " Escu, mezzo-ducato." Milan edition.

[3] Effects of scurvy. Gama's seamen suffered in the same way, after passing the Cape of Good Hope.   [4] " Nous allasmes en ung goulfe."

[5] " En tirant au vent haustral." For these islands, see the log book of Francisco Albo.

[6] The Milan edition has here: "According to the reckoning we made with the chain astern."

[7] " Aulcunesfoys a lorce ou autrement."

F

not aided us in giving us good weather to refresh ourselves
with provisions and other things, we should all have died of
hunger in this very vast sea, and I think that never man
will undertake to perform such a voyage.

When we had gone out of this strait, if we had always
navigated to the west we should have gone[1] without finding
any land except the Cape of the Eleven Thousand Virgins,
which is the eastern head of the strait in the ocean sea, with
the Cape of Desire at the west in the Pacific sea. These
two capes are exactly in fifty-two degrees of latitude of the
antarctic pole.

The antarctic pole is not so covered with stars as the
arctic, for there are to be seen there many small stars con-
gregated together, which are like to two clouds a little
separated from one another, and a little dimmed,[2] in the
midst of which are two stars, not very large, nor very bril-
liant, and they move but little:[3] these two stars are the
antarctic pole. Our compass needle still pointed a little to
its arctic pole; nevertheless it had not as much power as on
its own side and region.[4] Yet when we were in the open
sea,[5] the captain-general[6] asked of all the pilots, whilst still

---

[1] The Milan edition has here the words: "All round the earth,"
which makes the meaning clearer.

[2] "Car on y veoit plusieurs estoilles petites congregées ensemble qui
sont en guise de deux nuées ung peu separées l'une de l'autre, et ung
peu obfusquées." The Magellanic clouds.

[3] "Au milieu desquelles sont deux estelles non trop grandes ne moult
reluysantes, et petitement se mouvent." The Milan edition has: "Due
stelle molto grande e rilucenti, che hanno poco moto."

[4] "Nostre calamite ung peu tiroit toujours a son pol arctique. Neant-
moins navoit point tant de force comme de son coste et sa bande."
Milan edition has: "La nostra calamita volgeasi sempre al polo artico,
deviando però alcun poco dal punto del settentrione."

[5] "Goulfe, in mezzo al mare."

[6] "Le captaine-general demanda a tous les pillotz allant tousiours a
la voyle par quel chemyn nauigant on puntuast es cartes. Lesquelz
tous respondirent par sa voye punctuellement donnée. Et il respondit
quilz punctuoyent faulsement (chose qui estoit ainsi), et quil conuenoit

going under sail, in what direction they were navigating and pointing the charts. They all replied, by the course he had given, punctually [pricked in]; then he answered, that they were pointing falsely (which was so), and that it was fitting to arrange the needle of navigation, because it did not receive so much force as in its own quarter. When we were in the middle of this open sea we saw a cross of five stars, very bright, straight, in the west, and they are straight one with another.[1]

During this time of two months and twelve days we navigated between west and north-west (maestral), and a quarter west of north-west, and also north-west, until we came to the equinoctial line, which was at [a point] one hundred and twenty-two degrees distant from the line of repartition. This line of delimitation is thirty degrees distant from the meridian,[2] and the meridian[3] is three degrees distant from the Cape Verd towards the east.[4] In going by this course we passed near two very rich islands; one is in twenty degrees latitude in the antarctic pole, and is called Cipanghu; the other, in fifteen degrees of the same pole, is named Sumbdit Pradit. After we had passed the equinoctial line we navigated between west, and north-west and a quarter west, by north-west. Afterwards we made two

---

auister laigueille du nauiguer porce que ne recepuoit tant de force comme de sa part." The Milan edition has: " Cio ben sapeva il nostro capitano generale, e perciò, quando ci trovanno veleggiando in mezzo al mare, egli domando a tutti i piloti, ai quali già indicato aveva il punto a cui doveano tendere, per qual cammino puntassero nelle loro carte; risposer tutti, che puntavano al luogo da lui ordinato: ed egli disse che puntavano falso; e che conveniva ajutare l'ago calamitato, il quale in tal posizione non era attrato con tanta forza, quanto lo è dalla sua parte, cioè nell' emisfero boreale."

[1] " Et sont tres justes l'une avecques laultre." Milan: " Ed esattamente disposte in forma di croce." Dante may have heard of the S. Cross through Marco Polo.

[2] " Du vent de midy."   [3] " Le mydy."

[4] " Vers le leuant"; it should be " ponant."

hundred leagues to westwards, then changed the course to
a quarter of south-west, until in thirteen degrees north
latitude, in order to approach the land of Cape Gaticara,[1]
which cape (under correction of those who have made cosmography), (for they have never seen it), is not placed
where they think, but is towards the north, in twelve
degrees or thereabouts.

After having navigated sixty leagues[2] by the said course,
in twelve degrees latitude, and a hundred and forty-six of
longitude, on Wednesday, the 6th of March, we discovered a small island in the north-west direction,[3] and two
others lying to the south-west. One of these islands was
larger and higher than the other two. The captain-general
wished to touch at the largest of these three islands to get
refreshments of provisions; but it was not possible because
the people of these islands entered into the ships and robbed
us, in such a way that it was impossible to preserve oneself
from them. Whilst we were striking and lowering the sails
to go ashore, they stole away with much address and dili-
gence the small boat called the skiff, which was made fast
to the poop of the captain's ship, at which he was much
irritated, and went on shore with forty armed men, burned
forty or fifty houses, with several small boats, and killed
seven men of the island; they recovered their skiff. After
this we set sail suddenly, following the same course. Before
we went ashore some of our sick men begged us that if we
killed man or woman, that we should bring them their
entrails, as they would see themselves suddenly cured.

[1] Cattigara. Cape Comorin, in 8 deg. 27 min. N. latitude.
[2] The Milan edition has seventy.
" La volte du vent de maestral."

CHAPTER.

It must be known that when we wounded any of this kind of people with our arrows, which entered inside their bodies, they looked at the arrow, and then drew it forth with much astonishment, and immediately afterwards they died.[1] Immediately after we sailed from that island, following our course, and those people seeing that we were going away followed us for a league, with a hundred small boats, or more, and they approached our ships, showing to us fish, and feigning to give it to us. But they threw stones at us, and then ran away, and in their flight they passed with their little boats between the boat which is towed at the poop and the ship going under full sail; but they did this so quickly, and with such skill that it was a wonder. And we saw some of these women, who cried out and tore their hair, and I believe[2] that it was for the love of those whom we had killed.

CHAPTER.

These people live in liberty and according to their will, for they have no lord or superior; they go quite naked, and some of them wear beards, and have their hair down to the waist. They wear small hats, after the fashion of the Albanians; these hats are made of palm leaves. The people are as tall as us, and well made: they adore nothing, and when they are born they are white, later they become brown, and have their teeth black and red. The women also go naked, except that they cover their nature with a thin bark, pliable like paper, which grows between the tree and the

---

[1] The Milan edition has here: " Which did not fail to cause compassion."

[2] The Milan edition has for " I believe", "certainly".

bark of the palm. They are beautiful and delicate, and whiter than the men, and have their hair loose and flowing, very black and long, down to the earth. They do not go to work in the fields, nor stir from their houses, making cloth and baskets of palm leaves. Their provisions are certain fruits named Cochi, Battate; there are birds, figs a palm long,[1] sweet canes, and flying fish. The women anoint their bodies and their hair with oil of cocho and giongioli (sesame). Their houses are constructed of wood, covered with planks, with fig leaves, which are two ells in length: they have only one floor: their rooms and beds are furnished with mats,[2] which we call matting,[3] which are made of palm leaves, and are very beautiful, and they lie down on palm straw, which is soft and fine. These people have no arms, but use sticks,[4] which have a fish bone at the end. They are poor, but ingenious, and great thieves, and for the sake of that we called these three islands the Ladrone Islands. The pastime of the men and the women of this place, and their diversion, is to go with their little boats to catch those fish which fly, with hooks made of fish bones. The pattern of their small boats is painted here-after, they are like the fuseleres,[5] but narrower. Some of them black and white, and others red. On the opposite side to the sail, they have a large piece of wood, pointed above, with poles across, which are in the water, in order to go more securely under sail: their sails are of palm leaves, sewed together, and of the shape of a lateen sail, fore and aft. They have certain shovels like hearth shovels,[6] and there is no difference between the poop and the prow in these boats, and they are like dolphins bounding from wave to wave. These thieves thought, according to the signs they made,

---

[1] Bananas, or plantains.   [2] Stores.

[3] "Nattes."   [4] "Baston."

[5] Milan edition, "fusiniere": boats named after Fusine, from which people are ferried to Venice.   [6] For paddles.

that there were no other men in the world besides them.

Saturday, the 16th of March, 1521, we arrived at daybreak in sight of a high island, three hundred leagues distant from the before-mentioned Thieves' island. This isle is named Zamal.[1] The next day the captain-general wished to land at another uninhabited island near the first,[2] to be in greater security and to take water, also to repose there a few days. He set up there two tents on shore for the sick, and had a sow[3] killed for them.

Monday, the 18th of March, after dinner, we saw a boat come towards us with nine men in it: upon which the captain-general ordered that no one should move or speak without his permission.[4] When these people had come into this island towards us, immediately the principal[5] one amongst them went towards the captain-general with demonstrations of being very joyous at our arrival. Five of the most showy[6] of them remained with us, the others who remained with the boat went to call some men who were fishing, and afterwards all of them came together.[7] The captain seeing that these people were reasonable,[8] ordered food and drink to be given them, and he gave them some red caps, looking glasses, combs, bells, ivory, and other things. When these people saw the politeness of the captain, they presented some fish, and a vessel of palm wine, which

[1] Now called Samar, in the Philippine group.

[2] Instead of these words the Milan edition has: "Which later we learned was named Humunù." Amoretti says this island is situated near Cape Guigan of the Island of Samar.

[3] Amoretti presumes this sow was brought from the Ladrones. Desbrosses, t. ii, p. 55.

[4] "Congé."   [5] "Apparant." Milan edition, "principale".

[6] "Apparant." Milan edition, "ornati".

[7] The Milan edition adds here: "We learned that the island-which they came from was named Zuluan, and it is a small island."

[8] Milan: "Sociable."

they call in their language Uraca;[1] figs more than a foot[2] long, and others smaller and of a better savour, and two cochos.[3] At that time they had nothing to give him, and they made signs to us with their hands that in four days they would bring us Umai, which is rice, cocos, and many other victuals.

To explain the kind of fruits above-named it must be known that the one which they call cochi, is the fruit which the palm trees bear. And as we have bread, wine, oil, and vinegar, proceeding from different kinds, so these people have those things proceeding from these palm trees only. It must be said that wine proceeds from the said palm trees in the following manner. They make a hole at the summit of the tree as far as its heart, which is named palmito, from which a liquor comes out in drops down the tree, like white must, which is sweet, but with somewhat of bitter.[4] They have canes as thick as the leg, in which they draw off this liquor, and they fasten them to the tree from the evening till next morning, and from the morning to the evening, because this liquor comes little by little. This palm produces a fruit named cocho, which is as large as the head, or thereabouts: its first husk is green, and two fingers in thickness, in it they find certain threads, with which they make the cords for fastening their boats. Under this husk there is another very hard, and thicker than that of a walnut. They burn this second rind, and make with it a powder which is useful to them. Under this rind there is a white marrow of a finger's thickness, which they eat fresh with meat and fish, as we do bread, and it has the taste of an almond, and if anyone dried it[5] he might make bread of it. From the middle of this marrow there comes out a clear sweet water,

[1] Arrak.
[2] Bananas. The Milan edition has: "More than a palm in length."
[3] Cocoa-nuts.   [4] "Verdeur."
[5] Here the Milan edition adds: "And reduced it to flour."

and very cordial, which, when it has rested a little, and settled, congeals and becomes like an apple.[1]   When they wish to make oil they take this fruit, the coco, and let it get rotten, and they corrupt this marrow in the water, then they boil it, and it becomes oil in the manner[2] of butter.   When they want to make vinegar, they let the water in the cocoa-nut get bad, and they put it in the sun, when it turns to vinegar like white wine.   From this fruit milk also can be made, as we experienced, for we scraped this marrow and then put it with its water, and passed it through a cloth, and thus it was milk like that of goats.   This kind of palm tree is like the date-palm,[3] but not so rugged.   Two of these trees can maintain a family of ten persons : but they do not draw wine as above-mentioned always from one tree, but draw from one for eight days, and from the other as long.   For if they did not, otherwise the trees would dry up.   In this manner they last a hundred years.[4]

These people became very familiar and friendly with us, and explained many things to us in their language, and told us the names of some islands which we saw with our eyes before us.   *The island where they dwelt is called Zuluam, and it is not large.*[5]   As they were sufficiently agreeable and conversible we had great pleasure with them.   The captain seeing that they were of this good condition, to do them greater honour conducted them to the ship, and showed them all his goods, that is to say, cloves, cinnamon, pepper, ginger, nutmeg, mace,[6] gold, and all that was in the ship.   He also had some shots fired with his artillery, at which they were so much afraid that they wished to jump

[1] Milan edition has: " Takes the consistency of honey."

[2] Milan edition has: " Thick as butter."

[3] Here the Milan edition adds: "But its trunk, without being smooth, is less knotty."

[4] Milan edition has : " We were told that one of these trees lasts," etc.

*-[5] Here omitted in Milan edition.   [6] " Matia.

from the ship into the sea. They made signs that the things which the captain had shown them grew there where we were going. When they wished to leave us they took leave of the captain and of us with very good manners and gracefulness, promising us to come back to see us. The island we were at was named Humunu; nevertheless because we found there two springs of very fresh water we named it the Watering Place of good signs,[1] and because we found here the first signs of gold. There is much white coral to be found here, and large trees which bear fruit smaller than an almond, and which are like pines. There were also many palm trees both good and bad. In this place there were many circumjacent islands, on which account we named them the archipelago of St. Lazarus, because we stayed there on the day and feast of St. Lazarus. This region and archipelago is in ten degrees north latitude, and a hundred and sixty-one degrees longitude from the line of demarcation.

Friday, the 22nd of March, the above-mentioned people, who had promised us to return, came about midday, with two boats laden with the said fruit cochi, sweet oranges, a vessel of palm wine, and a cock, to give us to understand that they had poultry in their country, so that we bought all that they brought. The lord of these people was old, and had his face painted, and had gold rings suspended to his ears, which they name Schione,[2] and the others had many bracelets and rings of gold on their arms, with a wrapper of linen round their head. We remained at this place eight days: the captain went there every day to see his sick men, whom he had placed on this island to refresh them: and he gave them himself every day the water of this said fruit the cocho, which comforted them much. Near this isle is another where there are a kind of people who wear

---

[1] " Aquade des bons signes."

[2] This word is not in the Milan edition, nor in the Tagal Dictionary.

holes[1] in their ears so large that they can pass their arms through them; these people are Caphre, that is to say, Gentiles, and they go naked, except that round their middles they wear cloth made of the bark of trees. But there are some of the more remarkable of them who wear cotton stuff, and at the end of it there is some work of silk done with a needle. These people are tawny,[2] fat, and painted, and they anoint themselves with the oil of coco nuts and sesame,[3] to preserve them from the sun and the wind. Their hair is very black and long, reaching to the waist, and they carry small daggers and knives, ornamented with gold, and many other things, such as darts,[4] harpoons, and nets to fish, like.........,[5] and their boats are like ours.

The Monday of Passion week, the 25th of March, and feast of our Lady, in the afternoon, and being ready to depart from this place, I went to the side of our ship to fish, and putting my feet on a spar to go down to the store room,[6] my feet slipped, because it had rained, and I fell into the sea without any one seeing me, and being near drowning by luck I found at my left hand the sheet of the large sail which was in the sea, I caught hold of it and began to cry out till they came to help and pick me up with the boat. I was assisted not by my merits, but by the mercy and grace of the fountain of pity. That same day we took the course between west and southwest,[7] and passed amidst four small islands, that is to say, Cenalo, Huinanghar, Ibusson, and Abarien.

Thursday, the 28th of March, having seen the night before fire upon an island, at the morning we came to

---

[1] "Picquetez", not in Ste. Palaye's Glossary.
[2] "Tanez."   [3] "Giongioli."
[4] "Fascines," "faxina."   "Foscine," Milan edition.
[5] Milan edition: "Like our rizali."
[6] "Chambre des munitions." "Mezza de guarnigione," Milan edition.
[7] "Ponnant et le garbin."

anchor at this island; where we saw a small boat which
they call Boloto, with eight men inside, which approached
the ship of the captain-general.　Then a slave of the captain's, who was from Sumatra, otherwise named Traprobana,
spoke from afar to these people, who understood his talk,[1]
and came near to the side of the ship, but they withdrew
immediately, and would not enter the ship from fear of us.
So the captain seeing that they would not trust to us
showed them a red cap, and other things, which he had tied
and placed on a little plank,[2] and the people in the boat
took them immediately and joyously, and then returned to
advise their king.　Two hours afterwards, or thereabouts,
we saw come two long boats, which they call Ballanghai,
full of men.　In the largest of them was their king sitting
under an awning of mats; when they were near the ship of
the captain-general, the said slave spoke to the king, who
understood him well, because in these countries the kings
know more languages than the common people.　Then the
king ordered some of his people to go to the captain's ship,
whilst he would not move from his boat, which was near
enough to us.　This was done, and when his people returned
to the boat, he went away at once.　The captain gave good
entertainment to the men who came to his ship, and gave
them all sorts of things, on which account the king wished
to give the captain a rather large bar of solid gold, and a
chest[3] full of ginger.　However, the captain thanked him
very much but would not accept the present.　After that,
when it was late, we went with the ships near to the houses
and abode of the king.

The next day which was Good Friday, the captain sent
on shore the before-mentioned slave, who was our interpreter, to the king to beg him to give him for money some
provisions for his ships, sending him word that he had not

---

[1] Malay.　　　　[2] " Aez=ais." Milan edition : " Tavola."
[3] " Sporta", Milan edition : "basket."

come to his country as an enemy, but as a friend. The
king on hearing this came with seven or eight men in a
boat, and entered the ship, and embraced the captain, and
gave him three china dishes covered with leaves full of
rice, and two *dorades*, which are rather large fish, and of the
sort above-mentioned, and he gave him several other things.
The captain gave this king a robe of red and yellow cloth,
made in the Turkish fashion, and a very fine red cap, and
to his people he gave to some of them knives, and to others
mirrors. After that refreshments were served up to them.
The captain told the king, through the said interpreter,
that he wished to be with him, *cassi*[1] *cassi*, that is to say,
brothers. To which the king answered that he desired to
be the same towards him. After that the captain showed
him cloths of different colours, linen, coral, and much other
merchandise, and all the artillery, of which he had some
pieces fired before him, at which the king was much astonished; after that the captain had one of his soldiers armed
with white armour, and placed him in the midst of three
comrades, who struck him with swords and daggers. The
king thought this very strange, and the captain told him,
through the interpreter, that a man thus in white armour
was worth a hundred of his men; he answered that it was
true; he was further informed that there were in each ship
two hundred like that man. After that the captain
showed him a great number of swords, cuirasses, and
helmets, and made two of the men play with their swords
before the king; he then showed him the sea chart and the
ship compass, and informed him how he had found the
strait to come there, and of the time which he had spent in
coming; also of the time he had been without seeing any
land, at which the king was astonished. At the end the
captain asked[2] if he would be pleased that two of his people

[1] " Intimate friends," Tagal Dictionary.

[2] The Milan edition represents the King as making the request, and
the captain-general consenting to it.

should go with him to the places where they lived, to see some of the things of his country. This the king granted, and I went with another.

When I had landed, the king raised his hands to the sky, and turned to us two, and we did the same as he did; after that he took me by the hand, and one of his principal people took my companion, and led us under a place covered with canes, where there was a ballanghai, that is to say, a boat, eighty feet long or thereabouts, resembling a fusta. We sat with the king upon its poop, always conversing with him by signs, and his people stood up around us, with their swords, spears, and bucklers. Then the king ordered to be brought a dish of pig's flesh and wine.[1] Their fashion of drinking is in this wise, they first raise their hands to heaven, then take the drinking vessel in their right hand, and extend the left hand closed towards the people. This the king did, and presented to me his fist, so that I thought that he wanted to strike me; I did the same thing towards him; so with this ceremony, and other signs of friendship, we banqueted, and afterwards supped with him.

I ate flesh on Good Friday, not being able to do otherwise, and before the hour of supper, I gave several things to the king, which I had brought. There I wrote down several things as they name them in their language, and when the king and the others saw me write, and I told them their manner of speech, they were all astonished. When the hour for supper had come, they brought two large china dishes, of which one was full of rice, and the other of pig's flesh, with its broth[2] and sauce. We supped with the same signs and ceremonies, and then went to the king's palace, which was made and built like a hay grange, covered with

---

[1] The Milan edition adds here: "At each mouthful we drank a cup of wine, and whatever remained in the cup, though that rarely happened, was put into another vase."

[2] "Brouet." "Brodo," Milan edition.

fig and palm leaves. It was built on great timbers high
above the ground, and it was necessary to go up steps and
ladders to it. Then the king made us sit on a cane mat,
with our legs doubled as was the custom; after half an hour
there was brought a dish of fish roast in pieces, and ginger
fresh gathered that moment, and some wine. The eldest son
of the king, who was the prince, came where we were, and
the king told him to sit down near us, which he did; then
two dishes were brought, one of fish, with its sauce, and the
other of rice, and this was done for us to eat with the
prince. My companion enjoyed the food and drink so much
that he got drunk. They use for candles or torches the gum
of a tree which is named Animé, wrapped up in leaves of palms
or fig trees. The king made a sign that he wished to go
to rest, and left with us the prince, with whom we slept on
a cane mat, with some cushions and pillows of leaves. Next
morning the king came and took me by the hand, and so we
went to the place where we had supped, to breakfast, but the
boat came to fetch us. The king, before we went away, was
very gay, and kissed our hands, and we kissed his. There
came with us a brother of his, the king of another island,[1]
accompanied by three men. The captain-general detained
him to dine with us, and we gave him several things.

In the island belonging to the king who came to the ship
there are mines of gold, which they find in pieces as big as
a walnut or an egg, by seeking in the ground. All the
vessels which he makes use of are made of it, and also some
parts of his house, which was well fitted up according to the
custom of the country, and he was the handsomest man that
we saw among these nations. He had very black hair com-

---

[1] It will be seen further on that these brothers were kings or lords of
two cities on the coast of Mindanao, of which one was named Butuan,
the other Calagan. The first place retains its name, the other is named
Caragua. The King of Butuan was also King of the Island of Massaua,
between Mindanao and Samar. Note, Milan edition.

ing down to his shoulders, with a silk cloth on his head, and two large gold rings hanging from his ears, he had a cloth of cotton worked with silk, which covered him from the waist to the knees, at his side he wore a dagger, with a long handle which was all of gold, its sheath was of carved wood.[1] Besides he carried upon him scents of storax and benzoin. He was tawny and painted all over. The island of this king is named Zuluan and Calagan, and when these two kings wish to visit one another they come to hunt in this island where we were.[2] Of these kings the painted king is called Raia Calambu, and the other Raia Siani.[3]

On Sunday, the last day of March, and feast of Easter, the captain sent the chaplain ashore early to say mass, and the interpreter went with him to tell the king that they were not coming on shore to dine with him, but only to hear the mass. The king hearing that sent two dead pigs. When it was time for saying mass the captain went ashore with fifty men, not with their arms, but only with their swords, and dressed as well as each one was able to dress, and before the boats reached the shore our ships fired six cannon shots as a sign of peace. At our landing the two kings were there, and received our captain in a friendly manner, and placed him between them, and then we went to the place prepared for saying mass, which was not far from the shore. Before the mass began the captain threw a quantity of musk rose water on those two kings, and when the offertory of the mass came, the two kings went to kiss the cross like us, but they offered nothing, and at the elevation of the body of our Lord they were kneeling like us, and adored our Lord with joined hands. The ships fired all their artillery at the elevation of the body of our Lord. After mass had been said each one did the duty of a Chris-

---

[1] The Milan edition adds here: "On each of his teeth he had three spots of gold, so that his teeth appeared to be bound with gold."

[2] Massaua.   [3] Milan edition: "Siagu."

tian, receiving our Lord. After that the captain had some sword-play by his people, which gave great pleasure to the kings. Then he had a cross brought, with the nails and crown, to which the kings made reverence, and the captain had them told that these things which he showed them were the sign of the emperor his lord and master, from whom he had charge and commandment to place it in all places where he might go or pass by. He told them that he wished to place it in their country for their profit, because if there came afterwards any ships from Spain to those islands, on seeing this cross, they would know that we had been there, and therefore they would not cause them any displeasure to their persons nor their goods; and if they took any of their people, on showing them this sign, they would at once let them go. Besides this, the captain told them that it was necessary that this cross should be placed on the summit of the highest mountain in their country, so that seeing it every day they might adore it, and that if they did thus, neither thunder, lightning, nor the tempest could do them hurt. The kings thanked the captain, and said they would do it willingly. Then he asked whether they were Moors or Gentiles, and in what they believed. They answered that they did not perform any other adoration, but only joined their hands, looking up to heaven, and that they called their God, Aba. Hearing this, the captain was very joyful, on seeing that, the first king raised his hands to the sky and said that he wished it were possible for him to be able to show the affection which he felt towards him. The interpreter asked him for what reason there was so little to eat in that place, to which the king replied that he did not reside in that place except when he came to hunt and to see his brother, but that he lived in another island where he had all his family. Then the captain asked him if he had any enemies who made war upon him, and that if he had any he would go and defeat them with his men and ships, to

G

put them under his obedience. The king thanked him, and answered that there were two islands the inhabitants of which were his enemies; however, that for the present it was not the time to attack them. The captain therefore said to him that if God permitted him to return another time to this country, he would bring so many men that he would put them by force under his obedience. Then he bade the interpreter tell them that he was going away to dine, and after that he would return to place the cross on the summit of the mountain. The two kings said they were content, and on that they embraced the captain, and he separated from them.

After dinner we all returned in our dress coats[1], and we went together with the two kings to the middle of the highest mountain we could find, and there the cross was planted. After that the two kings and the captain rested themselves; and, while conversing, I asked where was the best port for obtaining victuals. They replied that there were three, that is to say, Ceylon, Zzubu,[2] and Calaghan, but that Zzubu was the largest and of the most traffic. Then the kings offered to give him pilots to go to those ports, for which he thanked them, and deliberated to go there, for his ill-fortune[3] would have it so. After the cross had been planted on that mountain, each one said the Paternoster and Ave Maria, and adored it, and the kings did the like. Then we went down below to where their boats were. There the kings had brought some of the fruit called cocos and other things to make a collation and to refresh us. The captain, being desirous to depart the next day in the morning, asked the king for the pilots to conduct us to the above-mentioned ports, promising him to treat them like themselves, and that he would leave one of his own men as a hostage. The first king said that he would

---

[1] "Pourpoints."

[2] Ceylon is the island of Leyte, and Zzubu is Sebu. Milan edition.

[3] "Malle adventure."

go himself and conduct him to this port, and be his pilot, but that he should wait two days, until he had had his rice gathered in and done other things which he had to do, begging him to lend him some of his men so as to get done sooner. This the captain agreed to.

This kind of people are gentle, and go naked, and are painted. They wear a piece of cloth made from a tree, like a linen cloth, round their body to cover their natural parts : they are great drinkers. The women are dressed in tree cloth from their waists downwards; their hair is black, and reaches down to the ground; they wear certain gold rings in their ears. These people chew most of their time a fruit which they call areca, which is something of the shape of a pear; they cut it in four quarters, and after they have chewed it for a long time they spit it out, from which afterwards they have their mouths very red. They find themselves the better from the use of this fruit because it refreshes them much, for this country is very hot, so that they could not live without it. In this island there is a great quantity of dogs, cats, pigs, fowls, and goats, rice, ginger, cocos, figs, oranges, lemons, millet, wax, and gold mines. This island is in nine degrees and two-thirds north latitude, and one hundred and sixty-two longitude[1] from the line of demarcation : it is twenty-five leagues distant from the other island where we found the two fountains of fresh water. This island is named Mazzava.

We remained seven days in this place; then we took the tack of Maestral, passing through the midst of five isles, that is to say, Ceylon, Bohol, Canighan, Baibai, and Satighan.[2] In this island of Satighan is a kind of bird[3] called Barbastigly, which are as large as eagles. Of these we

[1] If Massaua is the island Limassava of Bellin's map, it is in 9 deg. 40 min. N. latitude, but in 190 deg. W. longitude from the line of demarcation. Note, Milan edition.

[2] "Gatighan." Milan edition.   [3] "Pipistrelli." Milan edition.

killed only one, because it was late. We ate it, and it had
the taste of a fowl. There are also in this island doves,
tortoises, parrots, and certain black birds as large as a fowl,
with a long tail. They lay eggs as large as those of a goose.
These they put a good arm's length[1] under the sand in the
sun, where they are hatched by the great heat which the
heated sand gives out ; and when these birds are hatched
they push up[2] the sand and come out. These eggs are good
to eat. From this island of Mazzabua[3] to that of Satighan
there are twenty leagues, and on leaving Satighan we went
by the west ; but the King of Mazzabua could not follow
us ; therefore we waited for him near three islands, that is
to say, Polo, Ticobon, and Pozzon. When the king arrived
he was much astonished at our navigation, the captain-
general bade him come on board his ship with some of his
principal people, at which they were much pleased. Thus we
went to Zzubu, which is fifteen leagues off from Satighan.

Sunday, the 7th of April, about midday, we entered the
port of Zzubu, having passed by many villages. There[4] we
saw many houses which were built on trees. On approaching
the principal town the captain-general commanded all his
ships to hang out their flags. Then we lowered the sails in
the fashion in which they are struck when going to fight,
and he had all the artillery fired, at which the people of this
place were greatly frightened. The captain sent a young
man whom he had brought up,[5] with the interpreter to the
king of this island Zzubu. These having come to the town,
found a great number of people and their king with them,
all alarmed by the artillery which had been fired. But the
interpreter reassured them, saying that it was the fashion
and custom to fire artillery when they arrived at ports, to
show signs of peace and friendship ; and also, to do more
honour to the king of the country, they had fired all the ar-

---

[1] " Bien une brassée."   [2] " Haulsent."   [3] " Massava."
[4] " Illecques."   [5] " Nourry." Milan edition : " Un suo allievo."

tillery. The king and all his people were reassured. He then bade one of his principal men ask what we were seeking. The interpreter answered him that his master was captain of the greatest king in the world, and that he was going by the command of the said sovereign to discover the Molucca islands. However, on account of what he had heard where he had passed, and especially from the King of Mazzava, of his courtesy and good fame, he had wished to pass by his country to visit him, and also to obtain some refreshment of victuals for his merchandise. The king answered him that he was welcome, but that the custom was that all ships which arrived at his country or port paid tribute, and it was only four days since that a ship called the Junk of Ciama,[1] laden with gold and slaves, had paid him his tribute, and, to verify what he said, he showed them a merchant of the said Ciama, who had remained there to trade with the gold and slaves. The interpreter said to him that this captain, on account of being captain of so great a king as his was, would not pay tribute to any sovereign in the world; and that if he wished for peace he would have peace, aud if he wished for war he would have war. Then the merchant above-mentioned replied to the king in his own language, "Look well, oh king,[2] what you will do, for these people are of those who have conquered Calicut, Malacca, and all greater India; if you entertain them well and treat them well you will find yourself the better for it, and if ill, it will be so much the worse for you, as they have done at Calicut and Malacca." The interpreter, who understood all this discourse, said to them that the king, his master, was a good deal more powerful in ships and by land than the King of Portugal, and declared to him that he was the King of Spain and Emperor of all Christendom, wherefore, if he would not be his friend and treat his subjects well, he would another time send against

---

[1] Siam.   [2] "Cata Raja chita." Milan edition.

him so many men as to destroy him. Then the king answered that he would speak to his council, and give an answer the next day. Afterwards the king ordered a collation to be brought of several viands, all of meat, in porcelain dishes, with a great many vessels of wine. When the repast was over, our people returned, and related all to the captain ; and the King of Mazzabua, who was on board the captain's ship, and who was the first king after him of Zzubu, and the lord of several isles, wished to go on shore to relate to the king the politeness and courtesy of our captain.

Monday morning our clerk went with the interpreter to the town of Zzubu, and the king, accompanied by the principal men of his kingdom, came to the open space, where we made our people sit down near him, and he asked whether there was more than one captain in all those ships, and whether he wished that the king should pay tribute to the emperor, his master, to which our people answered, no, but that the captain only wished to trade with the things which he had brought with the people of his country, and not with others. Then the king said that he was content, and as a greater sign of affection he sent him a little of his blood from his right arm, and wished he should do the like. Our people answered that he would do it. Besides that, he said that all the captains who came to his country had been accustomed to make a present to him, and he to them, and therefore they should ask their captain if he would observe the custom. Our people answered that he would ; but as the king wished to keep up the custom, let him begin and make a present, and then the captain would do his duty.

Tuesday morning following the King of Mazzava, with the Moor, came to the ship, and saluted the captain on behalf of the King of Zzubu, and said that the king was preparing a quantity of provisions, as much as he could, to make a present of to him, and that after dinner he would send two of his nephews, with others of his principal people, to make

peace with him. Then the captain had one of his men armed
with his own armour, and told him that all of us would
fight armed in that manner, at which the Moorish merchant
was rather astonished; but the captain told him not to be
afraid, and that our arms were soft to our friends and rough
to our enemies; and that as a cloth wipes away the sweat
from a man, so our arms destroy the enemies of our faith.
The captain said this to the Moor, because he was more in-
telligent than the others, and for him to relate it all to the
King of Zzubu.

After dinner, the nephew of this king, who was a prince,[1]
with the King of Mazzava, the Moor, the governor, and the
chief of police,[2] and eight of the principal men, came to
the ship to make peace with us. The captain-general was
sitting in a chair of red velvet, and near him were the principal men of the ships sitting in leather chairs, and the
others on the ground on mats. Then the captain bade the
interpreter ask the above-mentioned persons if it was their
custom to speak in secret or in public, and whether the
prince who was come with them had power to conclude
peace. They answered yes, that they would speak in public,
and that they had the power to conclude peace. The captain spoke at length on the subject of peace, and prayed God
to confirm it in heaven. These people replied that they had
never heard such words as these which the captain had spoken
to them, and they took great pleasure in hearing them. The
captain, seeing then that those people listened willingly to
what was said to them, and that they gave good answers,
began to say a great many more good things to induce
them to become Christians. After many other subjects, the
captain asked them who would succeed the king in their
country after his death. They answered that the king had
no son, but several daughters, and that this prince was his

---

[1] That is the hereditary prince.

[2] " Bariselle." Milan edition : " Bargello maggiore.".

nephew, and had for a wife the king's eldest daughter, and
for the sake of that they called him prince.   They also said
that when the father and mother were old they took no further account of them, but their children commanded them.
Upon which the captain told them how God had made
heaven and earth and all other things in the world, and
that He had commanded that everyone should render
honour and obedience to his father and mother, and that
whoever did otherwise was condemned to eternal fire.   He
then pointed out to them many other things concerning our
faith.   The people heard these things willingly, and be-
sought the captain to leave them two men to teach and
show them the Christian faith, and they would entertain
them well with great honour.   To this the captain answered
that for the moment he could not leave them any of his
people, but that if they wished to be Christians that his
priest would baptise them, and that another time he would
bring priests and preachers to teach them the faith.   They
then answered that they wished first to speak to their king,
and then would become Christians.   Each of us wept for the
joy which we felt at the goodwill of these people, and the
captain told them not to become Christians from fear of
us, or to please us, but that if they wished to become Christian they must do it willingly, and for the love of God, for
even though they should not become Christian, no displeasure would be done them, but those who became Christian
would be more loved and better treated than the others.
Then they all cried out with one voice, that they did not
wish to become Christians from fear, nor from complai-
sance, but of their free will.   The captain then said that if
they became Christians he would leave them the arms which
the Christians use, and that his king had commanded him
so to do.   At last they said they did not know what more
to answer to so many good and beautiful words which he
spoke to them, but that they placed themselves in his

hands, and that he should do with them as with his own
servants. Then the captain, with tears in his eyes, embraced
them, and, taking the hand of the prince and that of the
king, said to him that by the faith he had in God, and to his
master the emperor, and by the habit of St. James which he
wore, he promised them to cause them to have perpetual
peace with the King of Spain, at which the prince and the
others promised him the same. After peace had been concluded, the captain had refreshments served to them. The
prince and the King of Mazzava, who was with him, presented to the captain on behalf of his king large baskets
full of rice, pigs, goats, and fowls, and desired the captain
to be told he should pardon them that their present was
not as fine as was fitting for him. The captain gave to
the prince some very fine cloth and a red cap, and a quantity of glass and a cup of gilt glass. Glasses are much
prized in this country. To the other people belonging to
the Prince he gave various things. Then he sent by me and
another person to the King of Zzubu a robe of yellow and
violet silk in the fashion of a Turkish jubbeh, a red cap,
very fine, and certain pieces of glass, and had all of them put
in a silver dish, and two gilt glasses.

When we came to the town we found the King of Zzubu
at his palace, sitting on the ground on a mat made of palm,
with many people about him. He was quite naked, except
that he had a cloth round his middle, and a loose wrapper
round his head, worked with silk by the needle. He had a
very heavy chain round his neck, and two gold rings hung
in his ears with precious stones. He was a small and fat
man, and his face was painted with fire in different ways.
He was eating on the ground on another palm mat, and
was then eating tortoise eggs in two china dishes, and he
had four vessels full of palm wine, which he drank with a
cane pipe.[1] We made our obeisance, and presented to him

---

[1] The usage of drinking through a tube was also observed by Van
Noort among these peoples. Note, Milan edition.

what the captain had sent him, and told him through the interpreter that it was not as a return for his present which he had sent to the captain, but for the affection which he bore him. That done, his people told him all the good words and explanations of peace and religion which he had spoken to them. The king wished to detain us to supper, but we made our excuses and took leave of him. The prince, nephew of the king, conducted us to his house, and showed us four girls who played on four instruments, which were strange and very soft, and their manner of playing is rather musical. Afterwards he made us dance with them. These girls were naked except from the waist to the knees, where they wore a wrap made of the palm tree cloth, which covered their middles, and some were quite naked. There we made a repast, and then returned to the ships.

Wednesday morning, because the night before one of our men had died, the interpreter and I, by order of the captain, went to ask the king for a place where we might bury the deceased. We found the king accompanied by a good many people, and, after paying him due honour, we told him of the death of our man, and that the captain prayed him that he might be put into the ground. He replied that if he and his people were ready to obey our master, still more reason was there for his land and country being subject to him. After that we said we wished to consecrate the grave in our fashion and place a cross on it. The sovereign said that he was content, and that he would worship that cross as we did. The deceased was buried in the middle of the open space of the town, as decently as possible, and performing the above-mentioned ceremonies to set them a good example, and in the evening we buried another. This done, we brought a good quantity of merchandise into the town of this king, and placed it in a house, and he took it under his charge and promised that no one would do harm or injury to the king. Four of our men were chosen to despatch and sell this merchandise. These people live with justice, and good weight and measure, loving peace, and are people who love ease and pleasure.[1] They have wooden scales, after the fashion of those of north of the Loire,[2] for weighing their merchandise. Their houses are made of wood and beams and canes, founded on piles, and are very high, and must be entered by means of ladders; their rooms are like ours, and underneath they keep their cattle, such as pigs, goats, and fowls. The young people sound bag-pipes,[3] made like ours, and call them Subin.[4]

In this island of the king's there is a kind of animal carrying a shell called carniolle, fine to look at, which cause the whale to die. For the whale swallows them alive; then, when they are inside its body, they come out of their shell and go and eat the whale's heart: and the people of this country find this animal alive inside the whale. These animals, the carniolles, have the teeth and skin black, and their shell is white. Their flesh is good to eat, and they call them Laghan.[5]

The following Friday we showed them a shop full of our merchandise, which was of various strange sorts, at which they were surprised. For metal, iron, and other big goods they gave us gold, and for the other small and sundry goods they gave us rice, pigs, goats, and other provisions. They gave us ten weights of gold for fourteen pounds of iron: each weight is a ducat and a half. The captain-general would not allow a large quantity of gold to be taken, so that the sailors should not sell what belonged to them too

[1] " Gens de bon temps."

[2] " Pardeça;" that is to say, "Par de ça la Loire," or "Langue d'oil." Languedoc was called " Par de la." The Milan edition describes the scales as a wooden pole suspended in the middle, with a basin suspended by three cords at one end, and a cord at the other end with a weight equal to the basin to which weights are attached.

[3] " Sonnent de zampogne."

[4] Perhaps this should be Sulin. *Vide* Marsden, *Malay Dictionary.*

[5] Lagan, a large sea snail. *Tagal Dictionary.*

cheap from thirst for gold, and lest by that means he might be constrained to do likewise with his merchandise, for he wished to sell it better.

Saturday following a scaffolding was made in the open space, fitted with tapestry and palm branches, because the king had promised our captain to become Christian on Sunday. He told him not to be afraid when our artillery fired on that day, for it was the custom to load it on those feasts without firing stones or other balls.

Sunday morning, the fourteenth day of April, we went on shore, forty men, of whom two were armed, who marched before us, following the standard of our king emperor. When we landed the ships discharged all their artillery, and from fear of it the people ran away in all directions. The captain and the king embraced one another, and then joyously we went near the scaffolding, where the captain and the king sat on two chairs, one covered with red, the other with violet velvet. The principal men sat on cushions, and the others on mats, after the fashion of the country. Then the captain began to speak to the king through the interpreter to incite him to the faith of Jesus Christ, and told him that if he wished to be a good Christian, as he had said the day before, that he must burn all the idols of his country, and, instead of them, place a cross, and that everyone should worship it every day on their knees, and their hands joined to heaven : and he showed him how he ought every day to make the sign of the cross. To that the king and all his people answered that they would obey the commands of the captain and do all that he told them. The captain took the king by the hand, and they walked about on the scaffolding, and when he was baptised he said that he would name him[1] Don Charles, as the emperor his sovereign was named ; and he named the prince Don Fernand, after the brother of the emperor, and the King of Mazzava

[1] The Milan edition says he was before named Raja Humabon.

Jehan : to the Moor he gave the name of Christopher, and to the others each a name of his fancy. Thus, before mass, there were fifty men baptised. After mass had been heard the captain invited the king and his other principal men to dine with him, but he would not. He accompanied the captain, however, to the beach, and on his arrival there the ships fired all their artillery. Then, embracing one another, they took leave.

After dinner our chaplain and some of us went on shore to baptise the queen. She came with forty ladies, and we conducted them on to the scaffolding ; then made her sit down on a cushion, and her women around her, until the priest was ready. During that time they showed her an image of our Lady, of wood, holding her little child, which was very well made, and a cross. When she saw it, she had a greater desire to be a Christian, and, asking for baptism, she was baptised and named Jehanne, like the mother of the emperor. The wife of the prince, daughter of this queen, had the name of Catherine, the Queen of Mazzava Isabella, and the others each their name. That day we baptised eight hundred persons of men, women, and children. The Queen was young and handsome, covered with a black and white sheet; she had the mouth and nails very red, and wore on her head a large hat made of leaves of palm, with a crown over it made of the same leaves, like that of the Pope. After that she begged us to give her the little wooden boy to put in the place of the idols.[1] This we did, and she went away. In the evening the king and queen, with several of their people, came to the sea beach, where the captain had some of the large artillery fired, in which they

---

[1] After the death of Magellan the image of the Infant Jesus was preserved as an idol until the year 1598, in which the Spaniards returned to that place with missionaries, who, having found it, not only placed it in veneration, but gave to the city which they founded there the name of City of Jesus, which it still preserves. Note of Milan edition.

took great pleasure.[1]   The captain and the king called one
another brother.

At last, in eight days, all the inhabitants of this island
were baptised, and some belonging to the neighbouring
islands.   In one of these we burned a village because the
inhabitants would not obey either the king or us.   There
we planted a cross because the people were Gentiles : if they
had been Moors, we should have erected a column, as a sign
of their hardness of heart, because the Moors are more difficult to convert than the Gentiles.   The captain-general went
ashore every day to hear mass, to which there came many
of the new Christians, to whom he explained various points
of our religion.   One day the queen came with all her state.
She was preceded by three damsels, who carried in their
hands three of her hats : she was dressed in black and
white, with a large silk veil with gold stripes, which covered her head and shoulders.   Very many women followed
her, with their heads covered with a small veil, and a hat
above that : the rest of their bodies and feet were naked,
except a small wrapper of palm cloth which covered their
natural parts.   Their hair fell flowing over their shoulders.
The queen, after making a bow to the altar, sat upon a
cushion of embroidered silk, and the captain sprinkled over
her and over some of her ladies rose water and musk, a
perfume which pleases the ladies of this country very much.
The captain on that occasion approved of the gift which I
had made to the queen of the image of the Infant Jesus,
and recommended her to put it in the place of her idols,
because it was a remembrancer of the Son of God.   She
promised to do all this, and to keep it with much care.

In order that the king might be more respected and
obeyed, the captain-general got him to come one day at the
hour of mass with his silk robe, and summoned his two
brothers, one named Bondara, who was the father of the

---

[1] Here ends the translation made from the French MS.; what follows
is from the Milan edition.

prince, and the other named Cadaro, and some of his chief men, whose names were Simiut, Sibuaia, Sisacai,[1] Magalibe, and others whom it is unnecessary to name separately ; and he made them all swear to be obedient to their king, whose hand they all of them kissed.   He then asked the king to swear that he would always be obedient and faithful to the King of Spain, and he took the oath.   Then the captain drew a sword before the image of the Virgin Mary, and said to the king that when such an oath had been taken by anyone, he should rather die than be wanting to his oath.   After that he himself promised to be always faithful to him, swearing by the image of our Lady, by the life of the emperor his sovereign, and by the habit which he wore.   He then made a present to the king of a velvet chair, and told him that wherever he went he should always have it carried before him by some of his attendants, and showed him the way in which it should be carried.   The king told the captain that he would do all this on account of the affection which he bore him, of which he wished to give him a token, preparing for that purpose some jewels to present to him ; these were two rather large gold rings for the ears, two others for the arms, and two for the ancles, all of them adorned with precious stones.   The finest ornaments of the kings of these countries consist in these rings, for otherwise they go naked and barefooted, with only a piece of cloth from the waist to the knees.

The captain-general, who had informed the king and all those who had been baptised of the obligation they were under of burning their idols, which they had promised to do, seeing that they retained them and made them offerings of meat, reproved them severely for it. They thought to excuse themselves sufficiently by saying that they did not do that now on their own account, but for a sick person, for the idols to restore him his health. This sick man was a brother of the prince, and was reputed to be the most valiant and

[1] " Si" is a prefix of honour to a proper name.

wise man in the island, and his illness was so severe that for
four days he had not spoken. Having heard this, the captain, seized with zeal for religion, said that if they had a
true faith in Jesus Christ, they should burn all the idols,
and the sick man should be baptised, and he would be immediately cured, of which he was so certain that he consented to lose his head if the miracle did not take place.
The king promised that all this should be done, because he
truly believed in Jesus Christ. Then we arranged, with all
the pomp that was possible, a procession from the place to
the house of the sick man. We went there, and indeed
found him unable to speak or to move. We baptised him,
with two of his wives and ten girls. The captain then
asked him how he felt, and he at once spoke, and said that
by the grace of Our Lord he was well enough. This great
miracle was done under our eyes. The captain, on hearing
him speak, gave great thanks to God. He gave him a refreshing drink to take, and afterwards sent to his house a
mattress, two sheets, a covering of yellow wool, and a
cushion, and he continued to send him, until he was quite
well, refreshing drinks of almonds, rosewater, rosoglio, and
some sweet preserves.

On the fifth day the convalescent rose from his bed, and
as soon as he could walk, he had burned, in the presence of
the king and of all the people, an idol which some old women
had concealed in his house. He also caused to be destroyed
several temples constructed on the sea shore, in which
people were accustomed to eat the meat offered to the idols.
The inhabitants applauded this, and, shouting "Castile, Castile," helped to throw them down, and declared that if God
gave them life they would burn all the idols they could find,
even if they were in the king's own house.

These idols are made of wood, they are concave or hollowed out behind, they have the arms and legs spread out,
and the feet turned upwards; they have a large face, with

four very large teeth like those of a wild boar, and they are
all painted.

Since I have spoken of the idols, it may please your
illustrious Highness to have an account of the ceremony
with which, in this island, they bless the pig.   They begin
by sounding some great drums (tamburi), they then bring
three large dishes, two are filled with cakes of rice and cooked
millet rolled up in leaves, and roast fish, in the third are
Cambay clothes, and two strips of palm cloth.   A cloth of
Cambay is spread out on the ground : then two old women
come, each of whom has in her hand a reed trumpet.   They
step upon the cloth and make an obeisance to the Sun : they
then clothe themselves with the above mentioned cloths.
The first of these puts on her head a handkerchief which
she ties on her forehead so as to make two horns, and taking another handkerchief in her hand, dances and sounds
her trumpet, and invokes the Sun.   The second old woman
takes one of the strips of palm cloth, and dances, and also
sounds her trumpet; thus they dance and sound their
trumpets for a short space of time, saying several things to
the sun.   The first old woman then drops the handkerchief
she has in her hand, and takes the other strip of cloth, and
both together sounding their trumpets, dance for a long
time round the pig which is bound on the ground.   The
first one always speaks in a low tone to the sun, and the
second answers her.   The second old woman then presents
a cup of wine to the first, who, whilst they both continue
their address to the sun, brings the cup four or five times
near her mouth as though going to drink, and meanwhile
sprinkles the wine on the heart of the pig.   She then gives
up the cup, and receives a lance which she brandishes,
whilst still dancing and reciting, and four or five times
directs the lance at the pig's heart, at last with a sudden
and well aimed blow she pierces it through and through.
She withdraws the lance from the wound, which is then

H

closed and dressed with herbs. During the ceremony a
torch is always burning, and the old woman who pierced the
pig takes and puts it out with her mouth, the other old
woman dips the end of her trumpet in the pig's blood, and
with it marks with blood the forehead of her husband, and
of her companion, and then of the rest of the people. But
they did not come and do this to us. That done the old
women took off their robes, and ate what was in the two
dishes, inviting only women to join them. After that they
get the hair off the pig with fire. Only old women are able
to consecrate the boar in this manner, and this animal is
never eaten unless it is killed in this manner.

(Here follows an account of a custom, for a description of
which see De Morga's Philippine Islands, p. 304.)

When our people went on shore by day or by night, they
always met with some one who invited them to eat and
drink. They only half cook their victuals, and salt them
very much, which makes them drink a great deal ; and they
drink much with reeds, sucking the wine from the vessels.
Their repasts always last from five to six hours.

When one of their chiefs dies they always use the following funeral ceremonies, of which I was witness. The most
respected women of the country came to the house of the
deceased, in the midst of which lay the corpse in a chest ;
round which were stretched cords after the manner of an
enclosure, and many branches of trees were tied to these
cords : a strip of cotton was fastened to each of these branches
like a pennant. Under these the women I have mentioned
sat down covered with white cotton cloth. Each of them
had a damsel who fanned her with a palm fan. The other
women sat sadly round the room. Meanwhile a woman cut
off by degrees the hair of the dead man with a knife :
another who had been his principal wife, lay extended on
him, with her mouth hands and feet on the mouth hands

and feet of the dead man. When the first woman cut off the hair, she wept, and when she stopped cutting, she sung. Round the room there were many vases of porcelain, with embers in them, on which, from time to time, they threw myrrh, storax, and benzoin, which gave out a good and strong smell in the room. These ceremonies last for five or six days, during which the corpse is kept in the house, and I believe that they anoint it with oil of camphor to preserve it. They afterwards put it in a chest, closed with wooden bolts, and place it in an enclosed place covered with logs of wood.

The islanders told us that every evening towards midnight, there used to come to the city, a black bird of the size of a crow, which perching on the houses whistled, and caused all the dogs to howl, and these double cries lasted four or five hours. They would never tell us the cause of that phenomenon, of which we also were witnesses.

Friday, the 26th of April, Zula, who was one of the principal men or chiefs of the island of Matan, sent to the captain a son of his with two goats to make a present of them, and to say that if he did not do all that he had promised, the cause of that was another chief named Silapulapu, who would not in any way obey the King of Spain, and had prevented him from doing so : but that if the captain would send him the following night one boat full of men to give him assistance, he would fight and subdue his rival. On the receipt of this message, the captain decided to go himself with three boats. We entreated him much not to go to this enterprise in person, but he as a good shepherd would not abandon his flock.

We set out from Zubu at midnight, we were sixty men armed with corslets and helmets ; there were with us the Christian king, the prince, and some of the chief men, and many others divided among twenty or thirty balangai. We arrived at Matan three hours before daylight. The captain before attacking wished to attempt gentle means, and sent on shore the Moorish merchant to tell those islanders who were of the party of Cilapulapu, that if they would recognise the Christian king as their sovereign, and obey the King of Spain, and pay us the tribute which.had been asked, the captain would become their friend, otherwise we should prove how our lances wounded. The islanders were not terrified, they replied that if we had lances, so also had they, although only of reeds, and wood hardened with fire. They asked however that we should not attack them by night, but wait for daylight, because they were expecting rein- forcements, and would be in greater number. This they said with cunning, to excite us to attack them by night, supposing that we were ready; but they wished this because they had dug ditches between their houses and the beach, and they hoped that we should fall into them.

We however waited for daylight; we then leaped into the water up to our thighs, for on account of the shallow water and the rocks the boats could not come close to the beach, and we had to cross two good crossbow shots through the water before reaching it. We were forty-nine in number, the other eleven remained in charge of the boats. When we reached land we found the islanders fifteen hundred in num- ber, drawn up in three squadrons; they came down upon us with terrible shouts, two squadrons attacking us on the flanks, and the third in front. The captain then divided his men in two bands. Our musketeers and crossbow-men fired for half an hour from a distance, but did nothing, since the bullets and arrows, though they passed through their shields made of thin wood, and perhaps wounded their arms, yet did not stop them. The captain shouted not to fire, but he was not listened to. The islanders seeing that the shots of our guns did them little or no harm would not retire, but shouted more loudly, and springing from one side to the other to avoid our shots, they at the same time drew nearer to us, throwing arrows, javelins, spears hardened in fire, stones, and even mud, so that we could hardly defend ourselves. Some of them cast lances pointed with iron at the captain-general.

He then, in order to disperse this multitude and to terrify them, sent some of our men to set fire to their houses, but this rendered them more ferocious. Some of them ran to the fire, which consumed twenty or thirty houses, and there killed two of our men. The rest came down upon us with greater fury; they perceived that our bodies were defended, but that the legs were exposed, and they aimed at them principally. The captain had his right leg pierced by a poisoned arrow, on which account he gave orders to retreat by degrees; but almost all our men took to precipitate flight, so that there remained hardly six or eight of us with him. We were oppressed by the lances and stones which the enemy hurled at us, and we could make no more resistance. The bombards which we had in the boats were of no assistance to us, for the shoal water kept them too far from the beach. We went thither, retreating little by little, and still fighting, and we had already got to the distance of a crossbow shot from the shore, having the water up to our knees, the islanders following and picking up again the spears which they had already cast, and they threw the same spear five or six times; as they knew the captain they aimed specially at him, and twice they knocked the helmet off his head. He, with a few of us, like a good knight, remained at his post without choosing to retreat further. Thus we fought for more than an hour, until an Indian succeeded in thrusting a cane lance into the captain's face. He then, being irritated, pierced the Indian's breast with his lance, and left it in his body, and trying to draw his sword he was unable to draw it more than half way, on account of a javelin wound which he had received in the right arm. The enemies seeing this all rushed against him, and one of them with a great sword, like a great scimetar[1] gave him a

---

[1] Spear, like a partisan, but larger. French MS. of Nancy.

great blow on the left leg, which brought the captain down on his face, then the Indians threw themselves upon him, and ran him through with lances and scimetars, and all the other arms which they had, so that they deprived of life our mirror, light, comfort, and true guide. Whilst the Indians were thus overpowering him, several times he turned round towards us to see if we were all in safety, as though his obstinate fight had no other object than to give an opportunity for the retreat of his men. We who fought to extremity, and who were covered with wounds, seeing that he was dead, proceeded to the boats which were on the point of going away. This fatal battle was fought on the 27th of April of 1521, on a Saturday; a day which the captain had chosen himself, because he had a special devotion to it. There perished with him eight of our men, and four of the Indians, who had become Christians; we had also many wounded, amongst whom I must reckon myself. The enemy lost only fifteen men.

He died; but I hope that your illustrious highness will not allow his memory to be lost, so much the more since I see revived in you the virtue of so great a captain, since one of his principal virtues was constance in the most adverse fortune. In the midst of the sea he was able to endure hunger better than we. Most versed in nautical charts, he knew better than any other the true art of navigation, of which it is a certain proof that he knew by his genius, and his intrepidity, without any one having given him the example, how to attempt the circuit of the globe, which he had almost completed.[1]

The Christian king could indeed have given us aid, and would have done so; but our captain far from forseeing that which happened, when he landed with his men, had charged him not to come out of his balangai, wishing that he should

---

[1] The text of this appeal has been given by M. Denis in the *Univers Pittoresque*, from the MS. of Nancy, now of Sir Thomas Phillipps' library.

stay there to see how we fought. When he knew how the captain had died he wept bitterly for him.

In the afternoon the king himself, with our consent, sent to tell the inhabitants of Matan, that if they would give up to us the body of our captain, and of our other companions who were killed in this battle, we would give them as much merchandise as they might wish for; but they answered that on no account would they ever give up that man, but they wished to preserve him as a monument of their triumph. When the death of the captain was known, those who were in the city to trade, had all the merchandise at once transported to the ships. We then elected in the place of the captain, Duarte Barbosa, a Portuguese, and a relation of the captain's, and Juan Serrano a Spaniard.

Our interpreter, who was a slave of the captain-general, and was named Henry, having been slightly wounded in the battle, would not go ashore any more for the things which we required, but remained all day idle, and wrapped up in his mat (Schiavina). Duarte Barbosa, the commander of the flag ship, found fault with him, and told him that though his master was dead, he had not become free on that account, but that when we returned to Spain he would return him to Doña Beatrice, the widow of the captain-general; at the same time he threatened to have him flogged, if he did not go on shore quickly, and do what was wanted for the service of the ships. The slave rose up, and did as though he did not care much for these affronts and threats; and having gone on shore, he informed the Christian king that we were thinking of going away soon, but that if he would follow his advice, he might become master of all our goods and of the ships themselves. The King of Zubu listened favourably to him, and they arranged to betray us. After that the slave returned on board, and showed more intelligence and attention than he had done before.

Wednesday morning, the 1st of May, the Christian king

sent to tell the two commanders that the jewels prepared as
presents for the King of Spain were ready, and he invited
them to come that same day to dine with him, with some of
his most honoured companions, and he would give them over
to them.   The commanders went with twenty-four others,
and amongst them was our astrologer named San Martin of
Seville.   I could not go because I was swelled with a
wound from a poisoned arrow in the forehead.   Juan Carvalho, with the chief of police, who also were invited, turned
back, and said that they had suspected some bad business,
because they had seen the man who had recovered from illness by a miracle, leading away the priest to his own house.
They had hardly spoken these words when we heard great
lamentations and cries.   We quickly got up the anchors
and, coming closer to the beach, we fired several shots with
the cannon at the houses.   There then appeared on the
beach Juan Serrano, in his shirt, wounded and bound, who
entreated us, as loudly as he could, not to fire any more, or
else he would be massacred.   We asked him what had become of his companions and the interpreter, and he said
that all had been slain except the interpreter.   He then
entreated us to ransom him with some merchandise; but
Juan Carvalho, although he was his gossip, joined with
some others, refused to do it, and they would not allow any
boat to go ashore, so that they might remain masters of the
ships.   Serrano continued his entreaties and lamentations,
saying, that if we departed and abandoned him there, he
would soon be killed; and after that he saw his lamentations
were useless, he added that he prayed God to ask for an
account of his life at the day of Judgment from Juan Carvalho, his gossip.[1]   Notwithstanding, we sailed immediately;
and I never heard any more news of him.

In this island of Zubu there are dogs and cats, and other
animals, whose flesh is eaten; there is also rice, millet,
panicum, and maize; there are also figs, oranges, lemons,

---

[1] " Compadre."

sugar-canes, cocos, gourds, ginger, honey, and other such things; they also make palm-wine of many qualities. Gold is abundant. The island is large, and has a good port with two entrances: one to the west, and the other to the east-north-east. It is in ten degrees north latitude and 154 east longitude from the line of demarcation.

In this island there are several towns, each of which has its principal men or chiefs. Here are the names of the towns and their chiefs:—

Cingapola: its chiefs are Cilaton, Ciguibucan, Cimaninga, Cimaticat, Cicanbul.[1]

Mandani: its chief is Aponoaan.

Lalan: its chief is Teten.

Lalutan: its chief is Japau.

Lubucin: its chief is Cilumai.

All these countries were in obedience to us, and paid a kind of tribute.

Near to Zubu there is, as we said, the island of Matan, the most considerable town of which is called Matan, and its chiefs are Zula and Cilapulapu. The village, which we burned on the occasion of the fatal battle, is named Bulaia.

In this island, before we lost our captain-general, we had news of Maluco.

(Book III of the Milan Edition.)

DEPARTURE FROM ZUBU.

When we were at a distance of eighteen leagues from the island of Zubu, near the head of another island called Bohol,[2] in the midst of that archipelago, seeing that our crews were too much reduced in number, so that they were not sufficient for managing all the three ships, we burned the *Conception* after transporting into the other two all that it con-

---

[1] See Note, p. 95.   [2] This island is still named Bohol.

tained that was serviceable. We then took the S.S.W. course, coasting along an island called Panilongon,[1] where the people were black as in Ethiopia.

We then arrived at a large island,[2] the king of which having come on board our ship, in order to show that he made alliance with us and would be friendly, drew blood from his left hand, and stained with it his breast, his face, and the tip of his tongue. We then did likewise, and when the king went away, I alone accompanied him on shore to see the island.

We entered a river[3] where we met many fishermen, who presented some of their fish to the king. He then took off the cloth which covered his middle, and some of his chief men who were with him did the same, they then all began to row and to sing. Passing near many houses, which were on the brink of the river, we arrived at two hours of the night[4] at the house of the king, which was two leagues from the mouth of the river where the ships were.

When we reached the house, people came to meet us with many torches, made of canes and palm leaves, full of the before-mentioned gum, called *anime*. Whilst supper was being got ready, the king, with two of his chiefs, and two rather handsome ladies, drank a large vase full of palm wine, without eating anything. I, excusing myself saying that I had already supped, only drank once. In drinking they use the ceremony which I have already described in speaking of the King of Massava.[5] Then the supper was brought, which consisted of rice and fish, very much salted, in porcelain dishes. Rice with them takes the place of bread. They cook it in the following manner, which is common to all these countries. They place inside an earthen

[1] Panilongon, now called Panlao.
[2] Mindanao. The French edition of the year IX calls it " Butuan".
[3] A river which comes into the Bay of Kipit.
[4] Probably two hours after nightfall.   [5] See p. 78.

pot like ours, a large leaf which lines it all round internally, then they put in the water and the rice, and cover up the pot. They let it boil until the rice has taken the consistency of bread, and then they take it out in pieces.

When the supper was over the king had brought a cane mat, and a mat of palm leaf, with a cushion of leaves, and this was to be my bed. I slept there with one of his chiefs. The king with the two ladies went to sleep in another place.

When it was day, whilst breakfast was being prepared, I went to take a turn in the island, and entered several houses, constructed like those of the neighbouring islands; I saw there a good many utensils of gold, but very little victuals. I returned to the king's house, and we breakfasted with rice and fish. I succeeded in making the king understand by signs, that I should like to see the queen; and he made a sign to me that he was content, and we set out together to the top of a hill, under which her house was placed. I entered the house and made her an obeisance, she did likewise to me. I sat down by the side of her; she was weaving a palm mat to sleep upon. Throughout her house were seen porcelain vases suspended to the walls, and four metal timbals, of which one was very large, another of middle size, and two small ones, and she amused herself by playing on them. There were many male and female slaves for her service. We asked leave and returned to the king's house, who immediately ordered a refreshment of sugar canes.

After midday, as I wished to return to the ships, the king, with the other chief men of the island, desired to accompany me in the same *balangai*, going by the same river; on its right bank I saw on an eminence three men hanging to a tree, the branches of which had been cut off. I asked of the king what those unhappy people were, he answered me that they were malefactors and thieves. These people go naked like their neighbours. In this island are found

pigs, goats, fowls, rice, ginger, and other things which
were common to the islands named before. That which is
most abundant is gold. They showed me certain valleys,
making signs that there was more gold there than hairs on
the head, but that as they had not iron to dig it out, it required great labour to acquire it, and which they did not
choose to undergo. The king is named Raja Calanao.

This part of the island called Chipit is the same land as
Butuan and Calagan, it passes above Bohol, and borders on
Massava. Its port is good enough ; it is in 8° N. latitude,
and 167° of longitude from the line of demarcation ; it is
fifty leagues distance from Zubu. Towards the North-west
is the island of Lozon,[1] which is at two days' distance ; a
large island, to which come to trade every year six or eight
junks of the people called Lequii.[2]

On leaving this place, and taking our course between
west and south-west, we touched at an almost uninhabited
island, which afterwards we learned was named Cagayan.
The few people there are Moors, who have been banished
from an island called Burné.[3] They go naked like the
others, and carry blow-pipes with small quivers at their
sides full of arrows, and a herb with which they poison
them. They have daggers, with hilts adorned with gold
and precious stones, lances, bucklers, and small cuirasses
of buffaloes' hide. These people took us for something
Divine or holy. There are some very large trees in this
island, but little victuals. It is in 7° 30′ North latitude,
and forty-three leagues from Chipit.

Continuing our voyage we changed our course to between West and North-west, and after running twenty-five
leagues, we arrived at a large island, which we found well
provided with victuals, and it was great good fortune for us

---

[1] Luçon.
[2] The author speaks of this nation further on.
[3] Borneo.

since we were so reduced by hunger and so badly supplied, that we were several times on the point of abandoning the ships, and establishing ourselves on some land, in order to live. In this island, which we learned was named Palaoan, we found pigs, goats, fowls, yams, bananas of various kinds, some of which are half a cubit long, and as thick as the arm, others are only a span long, and others are still smaller, and these are the best ; they have cocoa nuts, sugar canes, and certain roots like turnips. They cook rice under the fire in bamboo canes, or wooden vessels, and it keeps longer than that cooked in earthen pots. They draw from the rice with a kind of alembic a wine that is better and stronger than the palm wine. In short we found this island to be a promised land.

We presented ourselves to the king, who contracted alliance and friendship with us, and to assure us of it, he asked for one of our knives, with which he drew blood from his breast, with which he touched his forehead and tongue. We repeated the same ceremony.[1]

The people of Palaoan go naked like the other islanders, they almost all till their own fields. They have blow-pipes, with thick arrows more than a span in length, with a point like that of a harpoon ; some have a point made with a fish bone, and others are of reed, poisoned with a certain herb ; the arrows are not trimmed with feathers, but with a soft light wood. At the foot of the blow-pipe they bind a piece of iron, by means of which, when they have no more arrows, they wield the blow-pipe like a lance. They like to adorn themselves with rings and chains of gimp and with little bells, but above all they are fond of brass wire, with which they bind their fish hooks. They have some rather large domestic cocks, which, from some superstition, they do not eat, but they keep them for fighting ; on such occasions they

---

[1] This paragraph is not in Amoretti's edition, and is taken from the French edition of 1802.

make bets and offer prizes, which are acquired by the owner of the conquering cock.

Going from Palaoan towards the South-west, after a run of ten leagues, we reached another island.[1] Whilst coasting it, it seemed in a certain manner to go forward;[2] we coasted it for a distance of fully fifty[3] leagues, until we found a port. We had hardly reached the port when the heavens were darkened, and the lights of St. Elmo appeared on our masts.

The next day the king of that island sent a prahu to the ships; it was very handsome, with its prow and stern ornamented with gold; on the bow fluttered a white and blue flag, with a tuft of peacock's feathers at the top of the staff; there were in the prahu some people playing on pipes and drums, and many other persons. Two almadias followed the prahu; these are fishermen's boats, and a prahu is a kind of fusta. Eight old men of the chiefs of the island came into the ships, and sat down upon a carpet on the poop, and presented a painted wooden vase full of betel and areca (fruits which they constantly chew), with orange and jessamine flowers, and covered over with a cloth of yellow silk. They also gave two cages full of fowls, two goats, three vessels full of wine, distilled from rice, and some bundles of sugar cane. They did the same to the other ship; and embracing us they departed. Their rice wine is clear like water, but so strong that many of our men were intoxicated. They call it arak.

Six days later the king again sent three very ornamented prahus, which came playing pipes and drums and cymbals, and going round the ships, their crews saluted us with their

---

[1] Borneo.

[2] That is to say, "To move against the stream on account of the contrary currents." Note to Amoretti's edition.

[3] Ramusio has five leagues, but the Milan MS. has fifty, which is the real distance.

cloth caps, which hardly cover the tops of their heads. We
saluted them, firing the bombards without stones. Then
they made us a present of various victuals, but all made with
rice, either wrapped in leaves in the form of a long cylin-
der, or in the shape of a sugar loaf, or in the shape of
a cake, with eggs and honey. They then said that their
king was well pleased that we should make provisions here
of wood and water, and that we might traffic at our pleasure
with the islanders. Having heard this, seven of us entered
one of the prahus, taking with us presents for the king, and
for some of his court. The present intended for the king
consisted in a Turkish coat of green velvet, a chair of violet
coloured velvet, five ells of red cloth, a cap, a gilt goblet,
and a vase of glass, with its cover, three packets of paper,
and a gilt pen and ink case. We took for the queen three
ells of yellow cloth, a pair of slippers, ornamented with
silver, and a silver case full of pins. For the king's governor or minister three ells of red cloth, a cap, and a gilt
goblet; and for the herald who had come in the prahu, a
coat of the Turkish fashion, of red and green colours, a cap
and a packet of paper. For the other seven chief men who
had come with him, we prepared presents; for one cloth, for
another a cap, and for each a packet of paper. Having
made these preparations, we entered the prahu, and departed.

When we arrived at the city, we were obliged to wait
about two hours in the prahu, until there came thither two
elephants covered with silk, and twelve men, each of whom
carried a porcelain vase covered with silk, for conveying
and wrapping up our presents. We mounted the elephants,
and those twelve men preceded us, carrying the vases with
our presents. We went as far as the house of the governor,
who gave us supper with many sorts of viands. There we
slept through the night, on mattresses filled with cotton,
and covered with silk, with sheets of Cambay stuff.

On the following day we remained doing nothing in the house till midday, and after that we set out for the king's palace. We were again mounted upon the elephants, and the men with the presents preceded us as before. From the governor's house to that of the king, all the streets were full of men armed with swords, spears, and bucklers, the king having so commanded. We entered the palace still mounted upon the elephants; we then dismounted, and ascended a staircase, accompanied by the governor and some of the chief men, and entered a large room full of courtiers, whom we should call the barons of the kingdom; there we sat upon a carpet, and the vases with the presents were placed near us.

At the end of this hall there was another a little higher, but not so large, all hung with silk stuffs, among which were two curtains of brocade hung up, and leaving open two windows which gave light to the room.

There were placed three hundred men of the king's guard with naked daggers in their hands, which they held on their thighs. At the end of this second hall was a great opening, covered with a curtain of brocade, and on this being raised we saw the king sitting at a table, with a little child of his, chewing betel. Behind him there were only women.

Then one of the chief men informed us that we could not speak to the king, but that if we wished to convey anything to him, we were to say it to him, and he would say it to a chief or courtier of higher rank, who would lay it before a brother of the governor, who was in the smaller room, and they by means of a blow pipe placed in a fissure in the wall would communicate our thoughts to a man who was near the king, and from him the king would understand them. He taught us meanwhile to make three obeisances to the king, with the hands joined above the head, raising first one then the other foot, and then to kiss the hands to him. This is the royal obeisance.

Then by the mode which had been indicated to us, we gave him to understand that we belonged to the King of Spain, who wished to be in peace with him, and wished for nothing else than to be able to trade with his island. The king caused an answer to be given that he was most pleased that the king of Spain was his friend, and that we could take wood and water in his states, and traffic according to our pleasure. That done we offered the presents, and at each thing which they gave to him, he made a slight inclination with his head. To each of us was then given some brocade, with cloth of gold, and some silk, which they placed upon one of our shoulders, and then took away to take care of them. A collation of cloves and cinnamon was then served to us, and after that the curtains were drawn. and the windows closed. All the men who were in the palace had their middles covered with cloth of gold and silk, they carried in their hands daggers with gold hilts, adorned with pearls and precious stones, and they had many rings on their fingers.

We again mounted the elephants, and returned to the house of the governor. Seven men preceded us there, carrying the presents made to us, and when we reached the. house they gave to each one of us what was for him, putting it on our left shoulder, as had been done in the king's palace. To each of these seven men we gave a pair of knives in recompense for their trouble.

Afterwards there came nine men to the governor's house, sent by the king, with as many large wooden trays, in each of which were ten or twelve china dishes, with the flesh of various animals, such as veal, capons, fowls, peacocks, and others, with various sorts of fish, so that only of flesh there were thirty or thirty-two different viands. We supped on the ground on a palm mat; at each mouthful we drank a little china cup of the size of an egg full of the distilled liquor of rice : we then ate some rice and some things made

of sugar, using gold spoons made like ours. In the place
in which we passed the two nights there were two candles
of white wax always burning, placed on high chandeliers of
silver, and two oil lamps with four wicks each. Two men
kept watch there to take care of them. The next morning
we came upon the same elephants to the sea shore, where
there were two prahus ready, in which we were taken back
to the ships.

This city is entirely built on foundations in the salt water,
except the houses of the king and some of the princes : it
contains twenty-five thousand fires or families.[1] The houses
are all of wood, placed on great piles to raise them high up.
When the tide rises the women go in boats through the city
selling provisions and necessaries.[2] In front of the king's
house there is a wall made of great bricks, with barbicans
like forts, upon which were fifty-six bombards of metal, and
six of iron. They fired many shots from them during the
two days that we passed in the city.

The king to whom we presented ourselves is a Moor, and
is named Raja Siripada : he is about forty years of age, and
is rather corpulent. No one serves him except ladies who
are the daughters of the chiefs. No one speaks to him except
by means of the blow-pipe as has been described above. He
has ten scribes, who write down his affairs on thin bark of
trees, and are called *chiritoles*.[3] He never goes out of his
house except to go hunting.

On Monday, the 29th of July, we saw coming towards us
more than a hundred prahus, divided into three squadrons,
and as many *tungulis*, which are their smaller kind of boats.
At this sight, and fearing treachery, we hurriedly set sail,

[1] This number seems exaggerated. Now it has only two or three
thousand houses. *Hist. Générale des Voyages*, tom. xv, p. 138. Note,
Milan edition.

[2] They do likewise now at high tide. Note, Milan edition.

[3] " Cherita-tulis," writers of narratives.

and left behind an anchor in the sea. Our suspicions increased when we observed that behind us were certain junks
which had come the day before. Our first operation was to
free ourselves from the junks, against which we fired, cap-
turing four and killing many people : three or four other
junks went aground in escaping. In one of those which we
captured was a son of the king of the isle of Luzon, who was
captain-general of the King of Burné, and who was coming
with the junks from the conquest of a great city named
Laoe, situated on a headland of this island opposite Java
Major. He had made this expedition and sacked that city
because its inhabitants wished rather to obey the King of
Java than the Moorish King of Burné. The Moorish king
having heard of the ill-treatment by us of his junks, hastened to send to say, by means of one of our men who was on
shore to traffic, that those vessels had not come to do any
harm to us, but were going to make war against the Gentiles,
in proof of which they showed us some of the heads of those
they had slain.

Hearing this, we sent to tell the king that if it was so, that
he should allow two of our men who were still on shore, with
a son of our pilot, Juan Carvalho, to come to the ships :
this son of Carvalho's had been born during his first residence in the country of Brazil : but the king would not consent. Juan Carvalho was thus specially punished, for without communicating the matter to us, in order to obtain a large
sum of gold, as we learned later, he had given his liberty to
the captain of the junks. If he had detained him, the King
Siripada would have given anything to get him back, that
captain being exceedingly dreaded by the Gentiles who are
most hostile to the Moorish king.

And, with respect to that, it is well to know and understand that in that same port where we were, beyond the city
of the Moors of which I have spoken, there is another inhabited by Gentiles, larger than this one, and also built in the

salt water.   So great is the enmity between the two nations
that every day there occurs strife.   The king of the Gentiles
is as powerful as the king of the Moors, but he is not so
proud; and it seems that it would not be so difficult to in-
troduce the Christian religion into his country.[1]

As we could not get back our men, we retained on board
sixteen of the chiefs, and three ladies whom we had taken
on board the junks, to take them to Spain.   We had destined the ladies for the Queen; but Juan Carvalho kept them
for himself.

The Moors of Burné go naked like the other islanders.
They esteem quicksilver very much, and swallow it.   They
pretend that it preserves the health of those who are well,
and that it cures the sick.   They venerate Mahomed and
follow his law.   They do not eat pig's flesh. . . . .[2]   With
their right hand they wash their face, but do not wash their
teeth with their fingers.   They are circumcised like the Jews.
They never kill goats or fowls without first speaking to the
sun.[3]   They cut off the ends of the wings of fowls and the
skin under their feet, and then split them in two.   They do
not eat any animal which has not been killed by themselves.

In this island is produced camphor, a kind of balsam
which exudes from between the bark and the wood of the
tree.   These drops are small as grains of bran.   If it is left
exposed by degrees it is consumed : here it is called capor.
Here is found also cinnamon, ginger, mirabolans, oranges,
lemons, sugarcanes, melons, gourds, cucumbers, cabbage,

---

[1] The Portuguese introduced Christianity into this country, which
lasted till 1590.   Now the Gentiles have been obliged to abandon the
sea-coast, and have retired to the mountains.   *Sonnerat*, Note of Milan
edition.

[2] Here some details are omitted, which, with the whole of this paragraph, have been written by Pigafetta, because he was an Italian, and
not a Spaniard or Portuguese, in which case he would have been better
informed.

[3] An error natural enough in an Italian.

onions. There are also many animals, such as elephants, horses, buffaloes, pigs, goats, fowls, geese, crows, and others.

They say that the King of Burné has two pearls as large as a hen's eggs, and so perfectly round that if placed on a smooth table they cannot be made to stand still. When we took him the presents I made signs to him that I desired to see them, and he said that he would show them to me, but he did not do so. On the following day some of the chief men told me that they had indeed seen them.

The money which the Moors use in this country is of metal,[1] and pierced for stringing together. On one side only it has four signs, which are four letters of the great King of China : they call it *Picis*.[2] For one cathil (a weight equal to two of our pounds) of quicksilver they gave us six porcelain dishes, for a cathil of metal they gave one small porcelain vase, and a large vase for three knives. For a hand of paper they gave one hundred picis. A *bahar* of wax (which is two hundred and three cathils) for one hundred and sixty cathils of bronze : for eighty cathils a bahar of salt : for forty cathils a bahar of *anime*, a gum which they use to caulk ships, for in these countries they have no pitch. Twenty tabil make a cathil. The merchandise which is most esteemed here is bronze, quicksilver, cinnabar, glass, woollen stuffs, linens ; but above all they esteem iron and spectacles.

Since I saw such use made of porcelain, I got some information respecting it, and I learned that it is made with a kind of very white earth, which is left underground for fully fifty years to refine it, so that they are in the habit of saying that the father buries it for his son. It is said that if poison is put into a vessel of fine porcelain it breaks immediately.

The junks mentioned several times above are their largest vessels, and they are constructed in this manner. The lower part of the ships and the sides to a height of two spans above

---

[1] Brass or bronze. Note, Milan edition.

[2] " Pitis", small coin, 600 to a dollar at Achin.

water-line are built of planks joined together with wooden
bolts, and they are well enough put together. The upper
works are made of very large canes for a counterpoise.[1] One
of these junks carries as much cargo as our ships. The
masts are of bamboo, and the sails of bark of trees. This
island is so large that to sail round it with a prahu would require three months. It is in 5° 15′ north latitude and 176° 40′
of longitude from the line of demarcation.[2]

On leaving this island we returned backwards to look for
a convenient place for caulking our ships, which were leaking, and one of them, through the negligence of the pilot,
struck on a shoal near an island named Bibalon ;[3] but, by the
help of God, we got her off. We also ran another great
danger, for a sailor, in snuffing a candle, threw the lighted
wick into a chest of gunpowder; but he was so quick in
picking it out that the powder did not catch fire.

On our way we saw four prahus. We took one laden with
cocoanuts on its way to Burné; but the crew escaped to a
small island, and the other three prahus escaped behind
some other small islands.

Between the northern cape of Burné and the island named
Cimbonbon, situated in 8° 7′ N. latitude there is a very convenient port for refitting ships, and we entered it; but as
we were wanting many things necessary for our work, we
had to spend there forty-two days. Each one worked at one
thing or another according to the best of his knowledge or
ability; but our greatest labour was going to get wood in

[1] The Milan edition has added to the text, "*which project outside* for
a counterpoise"; and supposes this refers to an outrigger. Junks have
no outriggers; prahus have projecting gunwales, which widen the deck.

[2] This latitude is that of the northern point of Borneo; the longitude
is much diminished, as usual. Pigafetta has taken care to mark in his
map of the island of Borneo, his voyage of fifty leagues from the point
to the port, and has placed Laöe at the southern point of the island.
Note, Milan edition.

[3] Now named Balaba.   Note, Milan edition.

the thickets, as the ground was covered with briars and thorny shrubs, and we had no shoes.

In this island there are some very large wild boars. Whilst we were in a boat we killed one which was crossing from one island to another. Its head was two and a half spans long, and its tusks were exceedingly long.[1] Here also are crocodiles; those of the land are larger than those of the sea-coast. There are oysters and very large turtles; of these we caught two. The flesh alone of one of them weighed twenty pounds, and of the other forty-four pounds. We caught a kind of fish with a head like that of a pig, and which had two horns; its body was all covered with bone, and on its back it had a kind of saddle: this was a small one. In this island are also found certain trees, the leaves of which, when they fall, are animated, and walk. They are like the leaves of the mulberry tree, but not so long; they have the leaf stalk[2] short and pointed, and near the leaf stalk they have on each side two feet. If they are touched they escape, but if crushed they do not give out blood.[3] I kept one for nine days in a box. When I opened it the leaf went round the box. I believe they live upon air. The island in which we were is called Pulaoan.

On leaving this island—that is to say, the port which is at the extremity of it—we met a junk which was coming from Borneo. We made signals to it to strike its sails; but as it would not obey we overtook it, captured and pillaged it. It had on board the Governor of Pulaoan, with a son and a brother of his. We made them all prisoners, and put them to ransom to give within seven days four hundred measures of rice, twenty pigs, as many goats, and four hun-

---

[1] The Babi-rusa, or hog deer.　　　　[2] " Picciulo."

[3] Other travellers have seen similar leaves, and being more versed in natural history than our Pigafetta, soon knew that the motion of these leaves came from the insect which lived inside. (*Hist. Gén. des Voy.*, tom. xv, p. 58.) Note, Milan edition.

dred and fifty fowls. They caused all this to be given us, and besides added spontaneously cocoanuts, figs, sugar-canes, and vessels full of palm wine. We, in consequence of his generosity, restored to him some of his daggers and arquebuses; we also gave him a flag, a garment of yellow damask, and fifteen ells of linen. We gave to his son a cloak of blue cloth, and to his brother a garment of green cloth, and to the others other things, and we parted good friends.

We turned backwards, passing between the island of Cagayan and the port of Cipit,[1] taking a course east and a quarter south-east, to seek the islands of Maluco. We passed between certain little mountains,[2] around which we found many weeds, although there was there a great depth. Passing between these islets it seemed that we were in another sea.

Having left Cipit to the east, we saw to the west two islands called Zolo[3] and Taghima,[4] near which islands pearls are found. The two pearls of the King of Burné, of which I have spoken, were found there, and this is the manner in which he obtained them, according to the account which was given me of it. The King of Burné married a daughter of the King of Zolo, who told him that her father had these two big pearls. He desired to have them, and decided on getting them by any means, and one night he set out with five hundred prahus full of armed men, and went to Zolo, and took the king with his two sons, and brought them to Burné, and did not restore them to liberty until they gave him the two pearls.

Continuing our course east and a quarter north-east we passed near two inhabited places called Cavit and Subanin, and passed near an island called Monoripa, ten leagues dis-tant from the before-mentioned islets. The inhabitants of this island always live in their vessels, and have no houses

---

[1] In the isle of Mindanao. 　　[2] Islets.

[3] Sulu.　　　　　　　　　　　　　[4] Now named Basilan.

on shore. In these two districts of Cavit and Subanin, which are situated in the same island[1] as that in which are Butuan and Calagan, the best cinnamon of any grows. If we could have remained here only two days, we could have laden the ships with it; but we did not wish to lose time, but to profit by the favourable wind, for we had to double a cape and some islets which were around it. Wherefore, remaining under sail, we made a little barter, and obtained seventeen pounds of cinnamon for two big knives, which we had taken from the Governor of Pulaoan.

Having seen the cinnamon tree, I can give some description of it. It is a small tree, not more than three or four cubits high, and of the thickness of a man's finger, and it has not got more than three or four little branches. Its leaf is like that of the laurel. The cinnamon for use which comes to us, is its bark, which is gathered twice in the year. Its wood and leaves when they are green have the taste and force of the bark itself. Here it is called Cainmana, since *cain* means wood and *mana* sweet.[2]

Having set the head of the ship to north-east, we made for a large city called Maingdanao, situated in the same island in which are Butuan and Calagan, in order to get precise information of the position of Maluco. Following this course we took possession of a *bignaday*, a vessel similar to a prahu, and being obliged to have recourse to force and violence, we killed seven out of eighteen men who formed the crew. These men were better made and more robust than all those we had seen hitherto, and they were all chief men of Mindanao. There was among them a brother of the king who said that he well knew where Maluco was. Afterwards, following his indications, we left the north-east course which we held, and took a south-east course. We

---

[1] Mindanao.
[2] From this probably comes the word "Cinnamomum".

were then in 6° 7′ N. latitude and thirty leagues distant from
Cavit.

We were told that at a cape of this island near to a river
there are men who are rather hairy, great warriors, and
good archers, armed with swords a span broad. When
they make an enemy prisoner they eat his heart only, and
they eat it raw with the juice of oranges or lemons.[1] This
cape is called Benaian.[2]

Making for the south-east we found four islands, named
Ciboco, Birabam Batolac, Sarangani, and Candigar. Saturday, the 26th of October, about nightfall, whilst coasting the island of Birabam Batolac, we met with a very
great storm, before which we lowered all our sails, and
betook ourselves to prayer. Then our three saints appeared
upon the masts and dispersed the darkness. St. Elmo stood
for more than two hours at the mainmast head like a flame.
St. Nicholas at the head of the foremast, and St. Clara
on the mizenmast. In gratitude for their assistance we
promised a slave to each of the saints, and we gave to
each an offering.

Continuing our voyage we entered a port between the
two islands Sarangani and Candigar, and cast anchor to the
east, near a village of Sarangani, where pearls and gold are
found. This port is in 5° 9′ N. latitude, and fifty leagues
from Cavit. The inhabitants are Gentiles and go naked
like the others.

Having remained here a day we compelled by force two
pilots to come with us to show us the way to Maluco. We
were directed to take a south-south-west course, and passed
between eight islands partly inhabited, partly uninhabited,
which formed a kind of street. These were named Cheava,

---

[1] This receipt was recently attributed, in some newspaper paragraph,
to the Battas of Sumatra, 1874.

[2] Cape Benaian is the most northern cape of the island, and has still
the same name. Note, Milan edition.

Caviao, Cabiao Camanuca, Cabaluzao, Cheai, Lipan, and Nuza. At the end of these we reached an island which was very beautiful, named Sanghir.[1] But having a contrary wind, which did not allow us to double the cape, we tacked about backwards and forwards near it.

On this occasion, profiting by the darkness of the night, one of the pilots whom we had caught at Sarangani, and with him the brother of the king of Mindanao with his little son, escaped by swimming and reached that island; but we learned later that the son not being able to hold on well to his father's shoulders, was drowned.

Seeing that it was impossible to double the head of this island we passed below it, where we saw many small islands. This large island has four kings whose names are Raja Matandatu, Raja Laga, Raja Bapti, and Raja Parabu. These are Gentiles. It is in 3° 30′ N. latitude and twenty-seven leagues from Sarangani.

Continuing our course in the same direction we passed near five islands named Cheoma, Carachita, Para, Zangalura, and Cian.[2] This last is ten leagues distant from Sanghir. In this island there is a rather high mountain, but not one of great extent. Its king is named Raja Ponto. We came next to the island Paghinzara,[3] which has three high mountains, and in it the king is Raja Babintan. We saw at twelve leagues to the east of Paghinzara another island,

---

[1] The islands here mentioned belong to that group in which modern geographers reckon Kararotan, Linop, and Cabrocana; after which is found Sanghir, the beautiful island of the author: others name it Sanguil. This island has many islets to the S.W., which Pigafetta mentions later. Cabiu, Cabalussu, Limpang, and Nussa, are mentioned in the list of islands which in 1682 belonged to the King of Ternate. Note, Milan edition.

[2] In the list of islands belonging to the King of Ternate, are found Karkitang, Para, Sangaluhan, Siau.

[3] Pangazara, Talaut, and Mahono, are in the above quoted list.

Talant, and also two islands, not large but inhabited, called Zoar and Mean.

Wednesday, the 6th of November, having passed beyond these two islands, we discovered four other rather high islands at a distance of fourteen leagues towards the east. The pilot who had remained with us told us those were the Maluco islands, for which we gave thanks to God, and to comfort ourselves we discharged all our artillery. It need not cause wonder that we were so much rejoiced, since we had passed twenty-seven months less two days always in search of Maluco, wandering for that object among the immense number of islands. But I must say that near all these islands the least depth that we found was one hundred fathoms, for which reason attention is not to be given to all that the Portuguese have spread, according to whom the islands of Maluco are situated in seas which cannot be navigated on account of the shoals, and the dark and foggy atmosphere.

Friday, the 8th November of 1521, three hours before sunset, we entered a port of the island called Tadore,[1] and having gone near the shore, we cast anchor in twenty fathoms, and discharged all our artillery. Next day the king came to the ships in a prahu, and went round them. We went to meet him with a boat to show him honour, and he made us enter his prahu, and sit near him. He was sitting under a silk umbrella, which sheltered him. In front of him was his son with the royal sceptre, there were also two men with gold vases to give him water for his hands, and two others with gilt caskets full of betel.

The king gave us a welcome, and said that a long time back he had dreamed that some ships were coming to Maluco from distant countries, and that to assure himself with respect to this, he had examined the moon, and he had seen that they were really coming, and that indeed they

[1] Tidore.

were our ships. After that he came on board our ships, and we all kissed his hand : we then conducted him to the poop, but he, in order to avoid stooping, would not enter the cabin except by the upper opening. We made him sit down on a chair of red velvet, and placed on him a Turkish robe of yellow velvet. In order to do him more honour we sat down before him on the ground. When he had heard who we were, and what was the object of our voyage, he said that he and all his people were well content to be the most faithful friends and vassals of the King of Spain ;. that he received us in this island as his own sons ; that we might go on shore and remain there as in our own houses ; and that his island for the future should not be named Tadore, but Castile, in proof of the great love he bore to the king our master. Then we presented to him the chair on which he sat, and the robe which we had put on him, a piece of fine linen, four ells of scarlet cloth, a robe of brocade, a cloth of yellow damask, a piece of the whitest Cambay linen, two caps, six strings of glass beads, twelve knives, three large mirrors, six scissors, six combs, some gilt goblets, and other things. We gave to his son an Indian cloth of gold and silk, a large mirror, a cap and two knives. To each of the nine chief men of his suite we made a present of a piece of silk, a cap and two knives ; and to many others of his suite we made a present, to one of a cap, to another of a knife, until the king told us not to give any more presents. He then said that he had got nothing worthy to be sent as a present to our king, unless he sent himself, now that he considered him as his lord. He invited us to come closer to the city, and if any one attempted to come on board the ships at night, he told us to fire upon him with our guns. He came out of the stern cabin by the same way by which he had entered it, without ever bending his head. At his departure we fired all the cannon.

This king is a Moor, of about forty-five years of age,

rather well made, and of a handsome presence. He is a
very great astrologer. His dress consisted of a shirt of
very fine white stuff, with the ends of the sleeves embroidered with gold, and a wrapper which came down from
his waist almost to the ground. He was barefooted; round
his head he had a silk veil, and over that a garland of flowers.
He is named Raja Sultan Manzor.

On the 10th of November—a Sunday—we had another
conversation with the king, who wished to know how long
a time we had been absent from Spain, and what pay and
what rations the king gave to each of us; and we told him
all this. He asked us for a signature of the king and a
royal standard, since he desired that both his island of
Tadore, and also that of Tarenate (where he intended to
have his nephew named Calanogapi, crowned king) should
become subject to the King of Spain, for whose honour he
would fight to the death; and if it should happen that he
should be compelled to give way, he would take refuge in
Spain with all his family, in a new junk which he was having
constructed, and would take with him the royal signature
and standard.

He begged us to leave with him some of our men, who
would always keep alive his recollection of us and of our
king, as he would more esteem having some of us with him
than our merchandise, which would not last him a long time.
Seeing our eagerness to take cloves on board, he said that
for that purpose he would go to an island called Bachian,
where he hoped to find as much of them as were wanted,
since in his island there was not a quantity sufficient of dry
cloves to load the two ships. On that day there was no
traffic because it was Sunday. The holiday of these people
is on Friday.

It may please your illustrious lordship to have some
description of the islands where the cloves grow. They
are five—Tarenate, Tador, Mutir, Machian, and Bachian.

Tarenate is the principal island.   Its king, whilst he lived, had almost entire dominion over the other four.   Tadore, the island in which we were, has its own king.   Mutir and Machian have no king, but are governed by the people; and when the kings of Tarenate and Tidore are at war, they furnish them with combatants.   The last is Bachian, and it has a king.   All this province in which the cloves grow is called Maluco.

When we arrived here, eight months had not elapsed since a certain Portuguese, Francisco Serrano, had died in Tarenate.   He was captain-general of the King of Tarenate when he was making war on the King of Tadore; and he acted so strenuously that this king was compelled to give his daughter in marriage to the King of Tarenate, who also received as hostages almost all the sons of the chief men of Tadore.   Peace was then made, and from that daughter was born the nephew Calanopagi, of whom I have spoken.   But the King of Tadore never forgave Serrano in his heart; and he having come several years later to Tadore to traffic in cloves, the king had him poisoned with some betel leaves, so that he survived hardly four days. The King of Tarenate wished to have him buried according to their own usage, but three Christian servants that Serrano had with him did not consent to it.   In dying he left a little son and a little girl that he had of a lady he had taken in Java major, and two hundred bahars of cloves.

Francisco Serrano was a great friend and a relation of our unfortunate captain-general, and he it was who induced him to undertake that voyage, for when Magellan was at Malacca, he had several times learned by letters from Serrano that he was here.   Therefore, when D. Manuel, King of Portugal, refused to increase his pension by a single testoon[1] per month, an increase which he thought he had well deserved, he came to Spain and made the proposal to his Sacred Ma-

[1] A testoon was worth half a ducat.   Note, Milan edition.

jesty to come here by way of the west, and he obtained all
that he asked for.

Ten days after the death of Serrano, the King of Tarenate,
named Raja Abuleis,[1] drove out from his kingdom his son-
in-law the King of Bachian, whose wife, the daughter of the
King of Tarenate, came to Tarenate under the pretext of
concluding peace, and gave him (her father) such a poison
that he only survived two days, and dying left nine sons,
whose names were told to me as follows : Chechili[2]-Momuli,
Jadore Vunghi, Chechilideroix, Cilimanzur, Cilipagi, Chia-.
linchechilin, Cataravajecu, Serich, and Calanopagi.

Monday, the 11th of November, Chechilideroix, one of the
above-mentioned sons of the King of Tarenate, came with
two prahus to the ships sounding drums : he was dressed in
red velvet. We learned that he had near him the widow
and sons of Francisco Serrano. When we knew him, being
aware that he was an enemy of the King of Tadore, we sent
to ask him whether we might receive him in the ships,
which, as we were in his port, we would not do without his
consent. The king sent us word to do whatever we pleased.
But meantime Chechilideroix, seeing our hesitation, had
some suspicion, and moved further off from the ships. We
then went to him in a boat, and made him a present of an
Indian cloth of gold and silk, with some looking-glasses,
knives, scissors, etc. : these things he accepted but disdain-
fully, and soon after departed. He had with him an Indian
who had become a Christian, named Manuel, the servant of a
certain Pedro Alfonzo de Lorosa, a Portuguese, who, after
the death of Serrano, had come from Bandan to Tarenate.
Manuel being able to speak Portuguese, came on board the
ships, and told us that although the sons of the King of
Tarenate were enemies to the King of Tadore, yet they were

When the Portuguese, Brito, was sent to govern the Moluccas in
1511, this Raja Abuleis lived, and he names him Raja Beglif. Note,
Milan edition.   [2] " Chechil" or " Cachil", a title.

disposed towards the service of Spain. Then, by means of him, we wrote to De Lorosa to come to our ships without any suspicion or fear.

These kings have as many ladies as they please, but one only is the principal wife, and all the others are subject to her. The King of Tadore had a large house outside the city, where there were two hundred of the ladies he was most fond of, and as many more to serve them. The king eats alone, or with his principal wife, on a kind of raised dais, from which he can see all the others sitting round, and he decides upon the one who most pleases him to come to him. When the king's dinner is finished, the ladies all eat together if he permits it, or else each one goes to eat in her own room. No one without special permission from the king can see those ladies, and if anybody by day or by night were found near their house he would be killed immediately. Each family is bound to give one or two daughters to the king. Rajah Sultan Manzour had twenty-six children, of whom eight were boys and eighteen girls. In the island of Tadore there is a kind of bishop, and the one that was there in our time had forty ladies and very many children.

On Tuesday, the 12th of November, the king had a house built in the city for our merchandise, and it was built in one day. Thither we carried all that we had to barter, and placed it in the custody of three of our men, and the trade began at once. It was carried out in this manner. For ten ells of red cloth of pretty good quality they gave a bahar of cloves. A bahar is four quintals[1] and six pounds. For fifteen ells of middling quality a bahar, for fifteen hatchets a bahar, for thirty-five glass cups a bahar; and the king in this manner had from us almost all our goblets: for seventeen cathils of cinnabar a bahar; the same for as much quicksilver. For twenty-six ells of common linen a bahar, and the same for twenty-five ells of finer linen; for a hundred and fifty knives

---

[1] A hundredweight.

K

a bahar; for fifty scissors a bahar; for forty caps a bahar; for ten Guzerat cloths a bahar; for three of their cymbals two bahars: for a quintal of bronze a bahar. Almost all our mirrors were broken, and the few that remained entire the king wished to have. Many of the above-mentioned goods had been obtained by us by the capture of the junks, which I have related; and the haste we were in to return to Spain caused us to sell our goods at a lower price than we should have done had we not been in a hurry.

Every day there came to the ships many boats laden with goats, fowls, plantains, cocoanuts, and other victuals, that it was a wonder to see. We supplied the ships with good water taken from a spring whence it issued hot, but if it remains only one hour in the open air it becomes very cold. They say that it comes out like that because it issues from the mountain of the cloves. It may be seen from this how those lied who said that fresh water had to be brought to Maluco from distant countries.

The next day the king sent his son named Mossahap to the island of the Mutir for cloves with which to freight our ships. We had spoken to the king that day of some Indians whom we had captured, and he entreated us to make a present of them to him, as he had the intention of sending them back to their native country, accompanied by five men of Tadore, who, on restoring them to their country, would praise and commend the King of Spain and make a good name for the Spaniards. We gave him the three ladies whom we had destined for the queen, as has been said above, and all the men except those of Burné: he very much appreciated this gift.

The king then asked another favour—that was, that we should kill all the pigs we had on board, for which he would give an ample compensation in fowls and goats. We gave him satisfaction in this, cutting their throats and hanging them up under the deck, so that the Moors should not have occasion to see them, since if by accident they see any pig they covered their faces not to see it or perceive its smell.

In the evening of the same day Pedro Alfonso,[1] the Portuguese, came in a prahu, but before he came on board the ships the king sent to call him, and said to him, that although he belonged to Tarenate he should take good care not to answer falsely to the questions we were going to ask him. He indeed, after coming on board, told us that he had come to India sixteen years ago, and of these years he had passed ten in Maluco; and it was just ten years since those islands had been discovered by the Portuguese, who kept the discovery secret from us. He then related to us that a year, less fifteen days, had elapsed since a large ship had come hither proceeding from Malacca, and had gone away laden with cloves; but that, on account of the bad weather, she had been obliged to remain some months at Bandam. He added that her captain was Tristan de Meneses, a Portuguese, from whom, on asking what news there was in Europe, he had heard that a squadron of five ships had sailed from Seville to discover Maluco in the name of the King of Spain, and that the captain of this squadron was Ferdinand Magellan, a Portuguese, for which reason the King of Portugal, being angry that a subject of his should attempt to do a thing so opposed to him, had sent some ships to the cape of Good Hope, and others to the Cape Sta. Maria,[2] where the cannibals are, to impede their passage, but they had not fallen in with them. Having learned later that Magellan had passed by another sea, and was making for Maluco by way of the west, he had written to his Captain-Major of the Indies, named Diogo Lopez de Sequeira, to send six ships to Maluco against the Spanish squadron. But the captain-major, having at that time received information that the Grand Turk was planning an expedition against Malacca, was obliged to send against

---

[1] Pedro Alfonso de Lorosa.
[2] The northern cape at the mouth of the Rio de la Plata.

him sixty sail to the Straits of Mekkah, in the country of Jiddah, where, however, they only found a few galleys which had grounded near the beautiful and strong city of Aden, and they set fire to them.

This enterprise, added De Lorosa, had prevented the captain-major from immediately sending an expedition against Magellan; but a little later he had sent to Maluco a great galloon with two rows of cannon, commanded by Francisco Faria, a 'Portuguese: but neither did this one come, for on account of the shoals and currents which are near Malacca, and the contrary winds, it was unable to pass that promontory, and was compelled to turn back.

He also related that a few days before a caravel with two junks had come to these parts to get news of us. The junks had sailed to Bachian to load cloves, with seven Portuguese on board. These men, who did not respect the wives of the inhabitants, nor even those of the king, notwithstanding the warning they had received from the king himself, were all killed. The men of the caravel, on hearing of this, returned in haste to Malacca, abandoning the junks with four hundred bahars of cloves and as much merchandise as would have purchased another hundred bahars. He also related that every year many junks go from Malacca to Bandan to buy mace and nutmeg, and go thence to Maluco to purchase cloves. They make the voyage from Bandan to Maluco in three days, and employ fifteen in the voyage from Bandan to Malacca. He said, lastly, that since ten years back the King of Portugal had derived great profit from these islands, and he took especial care to keep these countries concealed from and unknown to the Spaniards. He related many other similar things, passing several hours in conversation with us: and we said and did so much, offering him a large salary, that we made him determine on coming with us to Spain.

Friday, the 15th of November, the king told us that he thought of going himself to Bachian to get the cloves which the Portuguese had left there, and asked us for presents to give to the two governors of Mutir in the name of the King of Spain. Meanwhile, having come close to our ships, he wished to see how we shot with the cross-bow, with guns, and with a swivel gun, which is a weapon larger than an arquebuse. He himself fired three times with a cross-bow, but he did not care to fire with a gun.

Opposite Tadore there is another very large island, called Giailolo[1], and it is so large that a prahu can with difficulty go round it in four months. It is inhabited by Moors and Gentiles. The Moors have two kings, one of whom, according to what the King of Tadore related to us, has had six hundred children, and the other has had five hundred and twenty-five. The Gentiles have not got so many women as the Moors, and are less superstitious. The first thing they meet in the morning when they go out of their houses is the object which they worship throughout that day. The king of these Gentiles is named Rajah Papua. He is very rich in gold, and inhabits the interior of the island. There grow here among the rocks bamboos as thick as a man's leg, full of water, which is very good to drink. We purchased many of them.

On Saturday the Moorish King of Giailolo came to the ships with many prahus, and we made him a present of a green damask robe, two ells of red cloth, some looking-glasses, scissors, knives, combs, and two gilt goblets, which things pleased him very much, and he said to us that, as we were friends of the King of Tadore, we were also his friends, since he loved that king like one of his own sons. He invited us to come to his country, promising to do us great honour. This king is powerful, and held in sufficient respect throughout all these islands. He is very old, and his name is Raja Jussu.

Sunday morning this same king came on board the ships

---

[1] Gilolo.

and wished to see how we fought, and how we discharged the bombards, at which he was greatly pleased, for in his youth he had been a great warrior.

The same day I went on shore to see how the cloves grow, and this is what I observed. The tree from which they are gathered is high, and its trunk is as thick as a man's body, more or less, according to the age of the plant. Its branches spread out somewhat in the middle of the tree, but near the top they form a pyramid. The bark is of an olive colour, and the leaves very like those of the laurel. The cloves grow at the end of little branches in bunches of ten or twenty. These trees always bear more fruit on one side than on the other, according to the seasons. The cloves are white when they first sprout, they get red as they ripen, and blacken when dry. They are gathered twice in the year, once about Christmas and the other time about St. John's day, when the air in these countries is milder, and it is still more so in December. When the year is rather hot, and there is little rain, they gather in each of these islands from three to four hundred bahars of cloves. The clove tree does not live except in the mountains, and if it is transferred to the plain it dies there.[1] The leaf, the bark, and the wood, as long as they are green, have the strength and fragrance of the fruit itself. If these are not gathered when just ripe they get so large and hard that nothing of them remains good except the rind. It is said that the mist renders them perfect, and indeed we saw almost every day a mist descend and surround one or other of the above-mentioned mountains. Among these people everyone possesses some of these trees, and each man watches over his own trees and gathers their fruit, but does not do any work round them to cultivate them. This tree does not grow except in the five mountains of the five Maluco islands. There are, however, a

---

[1] The Dutch observed later that this does not happen. Note, Milan edition.

few trees in Giailolo and in a small island between Tadore and Mutir named Mare, but they are not good.

There are in this island of Giailolo some trees of nutmegs. These are like our walnuts, and the leaves also are similar. The nutmeg, when gathered, is like the quince in form and colour, and the down which covers it, but it is smaller. The outside rind is as thick as the green rind of our walnuts, beneath which is a thin web, or rather cartilage, under which is the mace, of a very bright red, which covers and surrounds the rind of the nuts, inside which is the nutmeg properly so called.

There also grows in Tadore the ginger, which we used to eat green, instead of bread. Ginger is not a tree, but a shrub, which sends out of the earth shoots a span long like the shoots of canes, which they also resemble in the shape of the leaves, only those of the ginger are narrower. The shoots are good for nothing; that which makes ginger is the root. When green, it is not so strong as when it is dry, and to dry it they use lime, or else it would not keep.

The houses of these people are built like those already described, but are not so high above the ground, and are surrounded with canes after the fashion of a hedge. The women here are ugly, and go naked like the others, having only their middles covered with cloth made of bark. The men also are naked, and notwithstanding that their women are ugly, they are exceedingly jealous; and amongst other things which displeased them, was that we came ashore without cloaks,[1] because they imagined that might cause temptation to their wives. Both men and women always go barefoot.

Since I have spoken of cloth, I will relate how they make it. They take a piece of bark and leave it in water until it has grown soft; they then beat it with wooden clubs to extend it in length and breadth, as much as they please;

[1] This refers to the dress of men at arms of the period, which was not decent.

thus it becomes like a veil of raw silk with filaments enlaced within it, so that it appears as if it was woven.

Their bread is made with the wood of a tree like a palm tree, and they make it in this way. They take a piece of this wood, and extract from it certain long black thorns[1] which are situated there; then they pound it, and make bread of it which they call sagu. They make provisions of this bread for their sea voyages.

Every day there came from Tarenate many boats laden with cloves, but we, because we were waiting for the king, would not traffic for those goods, but only for victuals: and the men of Tarenate complained much of this.

On Sunday night, the 24th of November, the king arrived, and on entering the port had his drums sounded, and passed between our ships. We fired many bombards to do him honour. He told us that for four days we should be continually supplied with cloves.

In effect, on Monday he sent seven hundred and ninety one catils, without taking tare. To take tare means to take spice for less than what it weighs, and the reason of this is because when they are fresh, every day they diminish in weight. As these were the first cloves which we took on board, and the principal object of our voyage, we fired our bombards for joy. Cloves are called *Gomode* in this place; in Sarangani where we took the two pilots they are called *Bonglavan*, and in Malacca *Chianche*.[2]

Tuesday the 26th November the King came to tell us that for us he had done what a King never does here, that was to leave his own island; but he had gone to show the affection he had for the King of Castile, and because when we had got our cargo, we could sooner return to Spain, and afterwards return with greater forces to avenge the death

[1] Perhaps these are what the Malays use for pens.
[2] Chingké, Chinese for "odorous nails".

of his father, who had been killed in an island called Buru, and his body had been thrown into the sea.

He afterwards added that it was the custom in Tadore, when the first cloves were embarked in a vessel, or in junks, that the king gave a feast to their crews and merchants, and they made prayers to God to bring them in safety to their port.   He wished to do the same for us, and at the same time the feast would serve for the King of Bachian, who was coming with a brother of his to pay him a visit, and on that account he had the streets cleaned. Hearing this, some of us began to suspect some treachery; all the more because we learned that, not long before, three Portuguese of the companions of Francisco Serrano had been assassinated at the place where we got water, by some of the islanders concealed in the thickets; also we often saw them whispering with the Indians whom we had made prisoners.   Therefore, although some of us were inclined to accept the invitation, we concluded not to betake ourselves thither, recollecting the unfortunate feast given to our men in the island of Zubu, and we decided on a speedy departure.

Meantime a message was sent to the king to thank him, and to ask him to come soon to the ships, where we would deliver to him the four men we had promised him, with the goods which we had destined for him.   The King came soon, and on entering the ship, as though he had observed that we had doubts, said that he entered with as much confidence and security as into his own house.   He made us feel how much he was displeased by our unexpected haste to depart, since ships used to employ thirty days in taking in their cargo; and that if he had made a journey out of the island, he certainly had not done it to injure us but to assist us, so that we might more speedily obtain the cloves which we required, and a part of which we were still expecting.   He added that it was not then

a fit season for navigating in those seas, on account of the
many shoals near Bandan, and besides it would be a
likely thing that we should fall in with some Portuguese
ships. When, in spite of what he had said, he saw we
were still determined on going away, he said that we must
take back all that we had given him, since the Kings,
his neighbours, would consider him as a man without
reputation for receiving so many presents in the name of
so great a king as the King of Spain, and he had given
nothing in return, and perhaps they would suspect that
the Spaniards had gone away in such haste for fear of
some treachery, so that they would fix upon him the name
of traitor. Then, in order that no suspicion might remain
in our minds of his honesty and good faith, he ordered
his Koran to be brought, and kissing it devoutly he placed
it four or five times on his head whilst whispering certain
words to himself, with a rite which they call Zambehan,[1]
and he said in the presence of us all, that he swore by
Allah and by the Koran, which he held in his hand, that
he would ever be faithful and a friend to the King of
Spain. He said all this almost weeping and with so great
an appearance of sincerity and cordiality, that we promised
to prolong our sojourn at Tadore for another fortnight.
We then gave him the Royal signature and standard.
We learned later, by a sure and certain channel, that
some of the chiefs of those islands had indeed counselled
him to kill all of us, by which thing he would have acquired
for himself great merit with the Portuguese, who would
have given him good assistance to avenge himself on the
King of Bachian, but he, loyal and constant to the King
of Spain, with whom he had sworn a peace, had answered
that he would never do such an act on any account whatever.

Wednesday, the 27th November, the king issued a pro-

---

[1] "Subhan", or giving praise.

clamation that whoever had cloves might freely sell them to us. For which reason all that and the following day, we bought cloves like mad.[1]

Friday, in the afternoon, the governor of Machian came with many prahus, but he would not come on shore, because his father and his brother, who had been banished from Machian, had taken refuge here.

The following day the King of Tadore, with his nephew, the governor, named Huma[1], a man of twenty-five years of age, came on board the ships, and the king, on hearing that we had no more cloth, sent to fetch from his house six ells of red cloth, and gave them to us in order that we might, by adding other objects, make a fitting present to the governor. We made him the present, and he thanked us much, and said that soon he would send us plenty of cloves. At his departure from the ship we fired several bombards.

Sunday the 1st day of December, the above-mentioned governor departed from Tadore; and we were told that the king had made him a present of some silk cloths and drums, for him to send us the cloves sooner. On Monday, the king himself went again out of the island for the same object. Wednesday morning, as it was the day of St. Barbara,[1] and on account of the King's arrival all the artillery was discharged. The king came to the beach to see how we fired rockets and fire balls, and took great pleasure in them.

Thurday and Friday we purchased a good many cloves both in the city and at the ships at a much lower price, as the time of our departure grew nearer. For four ells of riband[3] they gave a bahar of cloves, for two little chains of

---

[1] " A furia."

[2] S. Barbara is the patroness of powder magazines, which on board French ships are called Sainte Barbe.

[3] "Frixeto," " nastro," or " settuccia," "ribbon," is so called now in Genoese. Note, Milan edition.

brass which were worth a marcello,[1] they gave us a
hundred pounds ; and at last each man being desirous of
having his portion of the cargo, and as there were no more
goods to give in exchange for cloves, one gave his cloak,
another his coat, and another a shirt or other clothes to
obtain them.

On Saturday three sons of the King of Tarenate, with
their wives, who were daughters of our King of Tadore,
and afterwards Pedro Alfonso, the Portuguese, came to
the ships. We gave a gilt glass goblet to each of the
brothers, and to the three wives scissors and other
things ; and when they went away we fired several bombards in their honour. We afterwards sent on shore a
present of several things to the widow of the King of
Tarenate, daughter of the King Tadore, who had not ven-
tured to come on board the ships.

Sunday the 8th December, we fired many bombards,
rockets, and fireballs to celebrate the Conception of our
Lady. Monday in the afternoon, the King came to the
ships with three women who carried his betel. It is to be
observed that no one can take women about with him
except the king. Afterwards the King of Giailolo came
to see again our gun exercise.

Some days later, as the day of our departure grew near,
the king showed us a sincere affection, and among other
obliging things, said to us that it seemed to him that he
was a sucking child whom its mother was about to leave,
and that he remained disconsolate all the more now that he
had become acquainted with us and liked several things
of Spain, for which reason he entreated us not to delay our
return thence to Tadore. Meantime, he begged us to leave

---

[1] Marcello, a coin struck at Venice by the Doge Nicolò Marcello in
1473, of silver, weighing as much as a sequin, and worth about sixpence.
Note, Milan edition.

him some of our swivel guns[1] for his own defence. He warned us at the same time not to navigate except by daylight, on account of the shoals and reefs which exist in these seas; but we answered him that because of our need to arrive in Spain as soon as possible, we were obliged to navigate night and day: he then added that, being unable to do anything else, he would pray God every day to bring us home in safety.

During this time Pedro Alfonso de Lorosa had come to the ships with his wife and property to return with us. Two days after, Kechilideroix, son of the King of Tarenate, came with a prahu well filled with men, and approaching the ships requested Lorosa to come into his prahu; but Lorosa, who suspected him, refused to do so, and told him he had determined on going away with those ships to Spain. For the same suspicion he advised us not to receive him in the ships; and we did not choose that he should come on board when he asked to do so. It was known later that Kechili was a great friend of the Portuguese captain of Malacca, and had the intention of seizing Lorosa and of conducting him thither; and on that account he severely reprimanded those persons with whom this Portuguese lived, for having let him depart without his permission.

The king had informed us that the King of Bachian would soon arrive, with a brother of his who was going to marry one of his daughters, and had asked us to do him honour by firing bombards on his arrival. He arrived on Sunday the 15th of December, in the afternoon, and we did him honour as the king had desired; we did not, however, discharge the heavier cannon, as we were heavily laden. The king and his brother came in a prahu with three banks of rowers on each side, a hundred and twenty in number. The prahu was adorned with many streamers made of white, yellow and red parrot's feathers. They were

[1] "Verzi."

sounding many cymbals, and that sound served to give the measure to the rowers to keep time. In two other prahus were the damsels who were to be presented to the bride. They returned us the salute by going round the ships and round the port.

As it is the custom that no king disembarks on the land of another king, the King of Tadore came to visit him of Bachian in his own prahu: this one, seeing the other coming, rose from the carpet on which he was sitting, and placed himself on one side to make way for the king of the country: but he, out of ceremony, would not sit on the carpet, but sat on the other side of it, leaving the carpet between them. Then the King of Bachian gave to him of Tadore five hundred *patol*, as if in payment of the daughter he was giving as a wife to his brother. *Patols* are cloths of gold and silk worked in China, and are very much prized in these islands. Each of these cloths is paid for with three bahars of cloves more or less, according as they are more or less rich in gold and embroidery. Whenever one of the chief men die, his relations put on these cloths to do him honour.

Monday, the King of Tadore sent a dinner to the king of Bachian, carried by fifty women clothed with silk from their waists to their knees. They went two and two with a man between in the midst of them. Each one carried a large dish upon which were small dishes with various viands; ten of the oldest of these women were the mace-bearers. They proceeded in this way to the prahu, and presented everything to the king who was sitting on a carpet under a red and yellow canopy. As they were returning, they caught some of our men who had come out of curiosity and who were obliged to make them presents of some trifle to get free. After that the king sent also to us a present of goats, cocoanuts, wine, and other things.

This day we bent on the ships new sails, upon which was

the cross of St. James, of Gallicia, with letters which said : "This is the figure of our good fortune."

Tuesday, we presented to the king some pieces of artillery ; that is some arquebuses which we had taken as prizes in the Indies, and some of our swivel-guns with four barrels of powder. We took on board each ship eighty barrels of water. Wood we were to find at the island of Mare, where the king had already five days ago sent a hundred men to prepare it, and near which we were to pass.

This day, the King of Bachian, with the consent of the King of Tadore, came on shore, preceded by four men holding up daggers in their hands, to make alliance with us : he said, in the presence of the King of Tadore and of all his suite, that he would always be ready for the service of the King of Spain, that he would keep in his name the cloves left in his island by the Portuguese, until another Spanish squadron arrived there, and he would not give them up without his consent. He sent through us to the King of Spain a present of a slave and two bahars of cloves. He would have wished to have sent ten bahars, but our ships were so heavily laden, that we could not receive any more.

He also gave us for the King of Spain two most beautiful dead birds. These birds are as large as thrushes ; they have small heads, long beaks, legs slender like a writing pen, and a span in length ; they have no wings, but instead of them long feathers of different colours, like plumes : their tail is like that of the thrush. All the feathers, except those of the wings, are of a dark colour; they never fly, except when the wind blows. They told us that these birds come from the terrestrial Paradise, and they call them " bolon dinata" that is divine birds.

The King of Bachian was a man of about seventy years of age. Not only did the King of Bachian recognise the King of Spain as his Sovereign ; but every king of

Maluco wrote to him that he desired always to be his faithful subject.

One day the King of Tadore sent to tell our men, who dwelt in the magazine for the merchandise, that they should take care not to go out of the house by night, since there were certain men, natives of the country, who by anointing themselves, walk by night in the shape of men without heads : and if they meet anyone to whom they wish ill, they touch his hand and anoint his palm, and that ointment causes him soon to grow ill, and die at the end of three or four days. But if they meet three or four persons together they do not touch them, but make them giddy. He added that he had a watch kept to discover them, and he had already had several executed.

When they build a new house, before going to inhabit it, they make a fire round it, and give many feasts there. Then they fasten to the roof of the house a pattern or sample of everything that is to be found in the island, persuaded that by that means none of those things will be ever wanting to whoever inhabits the house.

Wednesday morning everything was prepared for our departure from Maluco. The Kings of Tadore, of Giailolo, and of Bachian, and a son of the King of Tarenate had come to accompany us as far as the island of Mare. The ship "Victoria" made sail and stood out a little, waiting for the ship "Trinity"; but she had much difficulty in getting up the anchor, and meanwhile the sailors perceived that she was leaking very much in the hold. Then the "Victoria" returned to anchor in her former position. They began to discharge the cargo of the "Trinity" to see if the leak could be stopped, for it was perceived that the water came in with force as through a pipe, but we were never able to find out at what part it came in. All that day and the next we did nothing else but work at the pumps, but without any advantage.

Hearing this, the King of Tadore came at once to the ships, and occupied himself with us in searching for the leak. For this purpose he sent into the sea five of his men, who were accustomed to remain a long time under the water, and although they remained more than half-an-hour they could not find the fissure. As the water inside the ship continually increased, the king, who was as much affected by it as we were, and lamenting this misfortune, sent to the end of the island for three other men, more skilful than the first at remaining under water.

He came with them early the next morning. These men dived under water with their hair loose, thinking that their hair, attracted by the water which penetrated into the ship, would indicate to them the leak, but though they remained more than an hour in the water, they did not find it. The king, seeing that there was no remedy for it, said with lamentation, "Who will go to Spain to take news of me to the king our lord?" We answered him that the "Victoria" would go there, and would sail at once to take advantage of the east winds, which had already commenced. The "Trinity," meanwhile, would be refitted and would wait for the west winds and go to Darien, which is on the other side of the sea, in the country of Diucatan.[1] The king approved our thoughts, and said that he had in his service two hundred and twenty-five carpenters who would do all the work under the direction of our men, and that those who should remain there would be treated as his own children, and he said this with so much emotion that he moved us all to tears.

We, who were on board the "Victoria," fearing that she might open, on account of the heavy cargo and the long voyage, lightened her by discharging sixty hundred weight of cloves, which we had carried to the house where the crew of the "Trinity" were lodged. Some of our own

[1] Yucatan.

crew preferred to remain at Maluco rather than go with us to Spain, because they feared that the ship could not endure so long a voyage, and because, mindful of how much they had suffered, they feared to die of hunger in mid-ocean.

Saturday, the 21st December, day of St. Thomas the Apostle, the King of Tadore came to the ships and brought us the two pilots, whom we had already paid, to conduct us out of these islands. They said that the weather was then good for sailing at once, but, having to wait for the letters of our companions who remained behind, and who wished to write to Spain, we could not sail till midday. Then the ships took leave of one another by a mutual discharge of bombards. Our men accompanied us for some distance with their boat, and then with tears and embraces we separated. Juan Carvalho remained at Tadore with fifty-three of our men: we were forty-seven Europeans and thirteen Indians.

The king's governor[1] came with us as far as the island of Mare: we had hardly arrived there when four prahus laden with wood came up, which in less than an hour we got on board. We then took the south-west course.

In all the above-mentioned islands of Maluco are to be found cloves, ginger, sagu, which is their bread made of wood, rice, cocoa-nuts, plantains, almonds larger than ours, sweet and bitter pomegranates, sugar-canes, oil of cocoa and of sesame, melons, cucumbers, pumpkins, comilicai,[2] which is a refreshing fruit the size of a water-melon, another fruit like a peach called guave, and other eatable vegetables. They also have goats and fowls, honey produced by bees not larger than ants, which make their hives in trunks of trees. There are also parrots of many kinds, and amongst them there are white ones called Catara, and red ones called

---

[1] Or minister.
[2] A kind of Ananas. Note, Milan edition.

Nori, which are the most sought after, not so much for the beauty of their plumage, as because they talk more clearly. One of these is sold for a bahar of cloves.

It is hardly fifty years since the Moors conquered Maluco and dwelt there. Before that, these islands were inhabited only by Gentiles, who did not care for the cloves. There are still some families of them who have taken refuge in the mountains, where the cloves grow.

The island of Tadore is in 0 deg. 27 min. North latitude, and 161 deg. west of the line of demarcation ;[1] it is 9 deg. 30 min. distant from the first island of this archipelago, named Zamal, to the south-east and a quarter south. The island of Tarenate is in 0 deg. 40 min. of N. latitude. Mutir is exactly under the equinoctial line. Machian is in 0 deg. 15 min. S. latitude, and Bachian in 1 deg. of the same latitude. Tarenate, Tadore, Mutir, and Machian, are like four high and pointed mountains,[2] upon which the clove trees grow. Bachian is not visible from these four islands, but it is a larger island than any of those. Its clove mountain is not so high nor so pointed as those of the other islands, but it has a larger base.

(Book IV of the Milan Edition.)

RETURN FROM THE MOLUCCAS TO SPAIN.

Pursuing our voyage, after having taken in wood at the islet of Mare, we passed between the following islands :— Caioan, Laigoma, Sico, Giogi, Cafi, Laboan,[3] Toliman,

---

[1] The longitude is wrong, as usual. Note, Milan edition.

[2] The volcanoes of Ternate and Machian, which caused such havoc in the last century by their explosions, did not then emit flames or smoke, since Pigafetta would not have omitted to mention them.

[3] Laboan, an islet considered now as part of Bachian. Note, Milan edition.

Titameti, Bachian, Latalata, Jabobi, Mata, and Batutiga. They told us that in the island of Cafi the people were small and dwarfed like the Pigmies; they have been subjected by force by the King of Tadore. We passed outside of Batutiga to the west, and we steered between west and south-west, and we discovered some islets to the south, on which account the pilots of Maluco said it would be better to cast anchor so as not to drift at night among many islets and shoals. We, therefore, altered our course to south-east, and went to an island situated in 2 deg. S. latitude, and fifty-three leagues from Maluco.

This island is named Sulach;[1] its inhabitants are Gentiles, and have not got a king. They eat human flesh; both men and women go naked, except a piece of the bark of a tree of two fingers' breath before their natural parts. There are many other islands around here inhabited by anthropophagi. These are the names of some of them :—Silan, Noselao, Biga, Atulabaon, Leitimor, Tenetum, Gonda, Kailaruru, Mandan and Benaia.[2] We left to the east the islands named Lamatola and Tenetum.

Having run ten leagues from Sulach in the same direction, we went to a rather large island named Buru, in which we found plenty of victuals, such as pigs, goats, fowls, sugar-canes, cocoa-nuts, sagu, a certain food of theirs made of bananas called kanali, and chiacare, which here they call Nanga.[3] The chiacare are fruit like water-melons, but knotty on

---

[1] "Xulla" of Robert's Atlas, and "Xoula" of the Dutch. Note, Milan edition.

[2] Comparing this with what the author writes a little further on, there is another proof that he took down the names of the islands, and laid down their positions, as he thought he understood the pilots who spoke a language which he little understood. He here notes ten islands, and he has drawn six without names to the North of Sulach, where other geographers also lay down a few islets; but of these ten, Tenetum Kalairuru, Mandan, and Benaia, are again named and drawn further on; and Leytimor is a peninsula attached to Amboina. Note, Milan edition.

[3] The jack fruit, called Nangka throughout the Malay seas.

the outside; inside they have some small red fruit like plums, they have not got a stone in the middle, but instead of that have a certain pith like a white bean, but larger, they are tender to eat like chestnuts. We found here another fruit which externally is like a pine cone, and it is yellow, but white inside; on cutting, it is something like a pear, but much softer and better tasted. Here it is called comilicai. The inhabitants of this island are Gentiles, and have no king: they go naked like those of Sulach. The island of Buru is in 3 deg. 30 min. S. latitude, and seventy-five leagues from Maluco.

To the east of this island, at a distance of ten leagues, there is another one larger, and which borders on Giailolo, and it is named Ambon.[1] It is inhabited by Moors and Gentiles, but the former are on the sea shore, and the others in the interior; these are also anthropophagi. The products of this island are the same as those of Buru. Between Buru and Ambon, there are three islands surrounded by reefs named Vudia, Kailaruru and Benaia. To the south of Buru, at a distance of four leagues, is another small island named Ambalao.

At thirty-five leagues from Buru, south and a quarter south-west, is Bandon, with thirteen other islands. In six of them grow mace and nutmeg. Zoroboa is the largest of them, Chelicel, Saniananpi, Pulai, Puluru, and Rasoghin, the other six are Unuveru, Pulanbaracan, Lailaca, Mamica, Man, and Meut. In these islands nutmegs are not found, but only sagu, rice, cocoanuts, bananas, and other fruits, and they are near one another. The inhabitants of these are Moors, and have no king. Bandan is in 6 deg. of S. latitude, and 163 deg. 30 min. longitude from the line of demarcation. As this island was a little out of our course, we did not go to it.

[1] Amboina. Pigafetta appears to refer to the large island of Ceram. Note, Milan edition.

Leaving the island of Buru in the direction south-west and a quarter west, about eight degrees of latitude,[1] we arrived at three other islands near each other named Zolot,[2] Nocemamor, and Galian. Whilst we sailed amidst these islands, a great storm fell upon us, for which we made a vow of a pilgrimage to our Lady della Guida. We put the ship before the storm and made for a rather high island, which afterwards we learned was named Mallua, but before we could reach it, we had to struggle much with the squalls of wind which descended from the mountains and with the currents. The inhabitants of this island are savages, and more beasts than men; they eat human flesh; they go naked, except the usual piece of bark to cover their natural parts. But when they go to fight they wear on the back, the breast, and the flanks, pieces of buffalo hide, orna-mented with shells,[3] and boars' tusks, and tails of goat skins, hanging before and behind. They wear the hair raised high up by means of cane combs with long teeth, which go through it. They wrap up their beards with leaves, and enclose them in cases or tubes of reed, a thing which seemed to us very ridiculous. In one word these were the ugliest men we had seen in these Indies. Both their bows and arrows are made of reeds, and they carry their food in bags made of leaves. When their women saw us they came towards us with their bows drawn, but when we had given them some presents we soon became friends.

We passed fifteen days in this island in caulking the ship whose sides had suffered. We found here goats, fowls, wax, cocoanuts, and pepper. For a pound of old iron they gave fifteen pounds of wax or of pepper.

There are two kinds of pepper here, the long and the round. The long pepper is like the flower of the hazel tree

---

[1] The Milan MS. says "longitude", which must be an error of the scribe. Note, Milan edition.　　　　[2] Solor.　　　　[3] "Cornioli."

in winter; its plant is like ivy, and like it clings to trees; its leaves are like those of the mulberry tree; it is called luli. The round pepper grows like the other, but its fruit is in ears like Indian corn, and the grains are pulled off in the same manner; it is called lada. The fields here are full of pepper plants.

Here we took a man to conduct us to some island where we could find plenty of victuals.

The island of Mallua is in 8 deg. 30 min. S. latitude, and 169 deg. 40 min. longitude from the line of demarcation.

The old pilot from Maluco related to us, whilst sailing, that in this neighbourhood there was an island named Aruchete, the inhabitants of which, men and women, are not more than one cubit high, and they have ears as large and as long as themselves, so that when they lie down one serves them for a mattress, and with the other they cover themselves.[1] They are shorn and naked, their voices are shrill, and they run very swiftly. They dwell under ground, live on fish and a certain substance which grows between the bark and the wood of a tree, which is white and round like coriander comfits, and which is named ambulon. We would have gone there willingly, but the shoals and currents did not allow of it.

Saturday the 25th of January, (1522), at 22 o'clock,[2] we left the island of Mallua; and the following day, having run five leagues to the south-south-east, we arrived at a large island called Timor. I went ashore alone to speak to the head man of a village named Amaban, about his providing us with victuals. He offered me buffaloes, pigs, and goats, but when it was a question of the goods which he wanted in exchange, we could not come to an agreement, because he asked a great deal, and we had got very little to give. Then as we were constrained by hunger, we took the

---

[1] Strabo (Geogr., lib. xv).
[2] The Italian method of reckoning time.

measure of detaining on board the ship the chief of another village named Balibo, who had come there in good faith with a son of his; and we imposed upon him as a ransom for recovering his liberty, to give six buffaloes, ten pigs, and ten goats. He, being much afraid that we should kill him, quickly gave orders to have all this brought to us; and as there were only five goats and two pigs, they gave us instead an additional buffalo. We then sent him ashore with his son, and he was well pleased when we not only left him free, but also gave him some linen, some Indian cloths of silk and cotton, some hatchets, some Indian knives, scissors, looking-glasses, and some of our knives.

The chief man, whom I went to speak to first, has only women in his service; all were naked like those of the neighbouring islands, and wear in their ears small gold rings with tufts of silk hanging from them; on their arms they wear many rings of gold and copper, which often cover them up to the elbow. The men are naked like the women, and wear attached to their necks round plates of gold, and on their heads reed combs ornamented with gold rings. Some of them, instead of gold rings, wore in their ears dried necks of gourds.

In this island there are buffaloes, pigs, and goats, as has been said; there are also fowls and parrots of various colours. There is also rice, bananas, ginger, sugar canes, oranges, lemons, beans and almonds.

We had approached that part of the island where there were some villages with their chiefs or head men. On the other side of the island are the dwellings of four kings, and their districts are named Oibich, Lichsana, Suai, and Cabanaza. Oibich is the largest place. We were told that in a mountain near Cabanaza, very much gold is found, and its inhabitants buy whatever they want with small pieces of gold. All the trade in sandal wood and wax, carried on by the people of Malacca and Java, is done here; and indeed, we found here a junk which had come from Lozon[1] to trade in sandal wood; for white sandal wood only grows in this country.

These people are Gentiles; we were told that when they go to cut sandal wood, the devil appears to them in various forms, and tells them that if they want anything they should ask him for it; but this apparition frightens them so much, that they are ill of it for some days.[2] The sandal wood is cut at a certain phase of the moon, and it is asserted that if cut at another time it would not be good. The merchandise most fitting for bartering here for sandal wood is red cloth, linen, hatchets, iron, and nails.

This island is entirely inhabited. It extends a long way from east to west, and little from north to south. Its south latitude is in 10 deg., and the longitude 174 deg. 30 min. from the line of demarcation.

In all these islands that we visited in this archipelago, the evil of Saint Job prevailed, and more here than in any other place, where they call it "for franki", that is to say, Portuguese illness.[3]

We were told that at a day's voyage, west-north-west from Timor, there was an island in which much cinnamon grows, called Ende;[4] its inhabitants are Gentiles, and have no king. Near this are many others forming a series of islands as far as Java Major, and the Cape of Malacca. The names of these islands are Ende, Tanabuton, Crenochile, Bimacore, Azanaran, Main, Zubava, Lombok, Chorum, and Java Major, which by the inhabitants is not called Java but Jaoa.

---

[1] Luzon.

[2] Bomare says that those who cut sandal wood fall ill from the miasma exhaled by the wood. Note, Milan edition.

[3] A note to the Milan edition suggests that it was too early in the century for this to be the Frank disease, and that it must have been leprosy. This is more probable.

[4] Ende, or Flores.

In this island of Java are the largest towns; the principal of them is Magepaher,[1] the king of which, when he lived, was the greatest of all the kings of the neighbouring islands, and he was named Raja Patiunus Sunda. Much pepper grows there. The other towns are—Dahadama, Gagiamada, Minutarangam, Ciparafidain, Tuban, Cressi,[2] and Cirubaya.[3] At half a league from Java Major are the islands of Bali, called Java Minor, and Madura, these are of equal size.

They told us that in Java Major, it was the custom when one of the chief men died, to burn his body; and then his principal wife, adorned with garlands of flowers, has herself carried in a chair by four men throughout the town, with a tranquil and smiling countenance, whilst comforting her relations, who are afflicted because she is going to burn herself with the corpse of her husband, and encouraging them not to lament, saying to them, "I am going this evening to sup with my dear husband, and to sleep with him this night." Afterwards, when close to the place of the pyre, she again turns towards the relations, and after again consoling them, casts herself into the fire and is burned. If she did not do this she would not be looked upon as an honourable woman, nor as a faithful wife.

Our old pilot related to us other extravagant things. He told us that the young men of Java . . . . and that in an island called Ocoloro, below Java Major, there are only women who become pregnant with the wind, and when they bring it forth, if the child is a male, they kill it, and if a female, they bring it up; and if any man visits their island, whenever they are able to kill him, they do so.

They also related to us that beyond Java Major, towards the north in the Gulf of China, which the ancients named Sinus Magnus, there is an enormous tree named Campang-

---

[1] Majapahit.   [2] Gresik.   [3] Surabaya.

anghi,[1] in which dwell certain birds named Garuda,[2] so large that they take with their claws, and carry away flying, a buffalo, and even an elephant, to the place of the tree, which place is named Puzathaer. The fruit of this tree is called Buapanganghi, and is larger than a water melon. The Moors of Burné, whom we had with us in the ships, told us they had seen two of these birds, which had been sent to their king from the kingdom of Siam. No junk, or other vessel, can approach this tree within three or four leagues, on account of the great whirlpools which the water makes there. They related to us, moreover, how in a wonderful manner what is related of this tree became known, for a junk, having been carried there by the whirlpools, was broken up, and all the seamen perished, except a child who attached himself to a plank and was miraculously borne near the tree, upon which he mounted. There he placed himself under the wing of one of these birds, which was asleep, without its perceiving him, and next day the bird having taken flight carried him with it, and having seen a buffalo on the land, descended to take it; the child took advantage of the opportunity to come out from under its wing, and remained on the ground. In this manner the story of these birds and of the tree became known, and it was understood that those fruits which are frequently found in the sea came from that place.

We were told that there were in that kingdom, on the banks of the rivers, certain birds which feed on carrion, but which will not touch it unless another bird has first eaten its heart.

The Cape of Malacca is in 1 deg. 30 min. of S. latitude. To the east of that Cape are many cities and towns, of a few of which I will note the names—Singapola, which is at the Cape, Pahan, Kalantan, Patani, Bradlini, Benan,

---

[1] "Campong anghin," the place of wind.
[2] Sanscrit and Malay, a griffin.

Lagon, Cheregigharan, Trombon, Joran, Ciu, Brabri, Banga, Iudia, Jandibum, Laun, Langonpifa. All these cities are constructed like ours, and are subject to the King of Siam who is named Siri Zacabedera, and who inhabits Iudia.

Beyond Siam is situated Camogia; its king is named Saret Zacabedera; next Chiempa, the king of which is named Raja Brahami Martu. There grows the rhubarb, and it is found in this manner: men go together in companies of twenty or twenty-five, to the woods, and at night ascend the trees, both to get out of the way of the lions, the elephants, and other wild beasts, and also to be able better to smell the odour of the rhubarb borne to them by the wind. In the morning they go to that quarter whence they have perceived that the odour comes, and seek for the rhubarb till they find it. This is the rotten wood of a large tree, which acquires its odour by putrefaction.[1] The best part of the tree is the root, but the trunk is also good, which is called Calama.

The kingdom of Cocchi[2] lies next, its sovereign is named Raja Seri Bummipala. After that follows Great China, the king of which is the greatest sovereign of the world, and is called Santoa raja. He has seventy crowned kings under his dependence; and some of these kings have ten or fifteen lesser kings dependent on them. The port of this kingdom is named Guantan,[3] and among the many cities of this empire, two are the most important, namely Nankin and Comlaha, where the king usually resides.

He has four of his principal ministers close to his palace, at the four sides looking to the four cardinal winds, that is, one to the west, one to the east, to the south, and

---

[1] Pigafetta has confounded rhubarb with the decayed wood of a tree found in Siam, which, when burnt, gives a very sweet perfume, and which sells at a high price.

[2] Cochin.   [3] Kwantung or Canton.

to the north. Each of these gives audience to those that come from his quarter. All the kings and lords of India major and superior obey this king, and in token of their vassalage, each is obliged to have in the middle of the principal place of his city the marble figure of a certain animal named Chinga, an animal more valiant than the lion; the figure of this animal is also engraved on the king's seal, and all who wish to enter his port must carry the same emblem in wax or ivory.

If any lord is disobedient to him, he is flayed, and his skin, dried in the sun, salted, and stuffed, is placed in an eminent part of the public place, with the head inclined and the hands on the head in the attitude of doing zongu, that is obeisance to the king.

He is never visible to anybody; and if he wishes to see his people, he is carried about the palace on a peacock most skilfully manufactured, and very richly adorned, with six ladies dressed exactly like himself, so that he cannot be distinguished from them. He afterwards passes into a richly-adorned figure of a serpent called Naga, which has a large glass in the breast, through which he and the ladies are seen, but it is not possible to distinguish which is the king. He marries his sisters in order that his blood should not mix with that of others.

His palace has seven walls round it, and in each circle there are daily ten thousand men on guard, who are changed every twelve hours at the sound of a bell. Each wall has its gate, with a guard at each gate. At the first stands a man with a great scourge in his hand, named Satuhoran[1] with Satubagan; at the second a dog called Satuhain;[2] at the third, a man with an iron mace, called Satuhoran with pocumbecin;[3] at the fourth, a man with a bow in his hand, called Satuhoran with anatpanan;[4] at the fifth, a man with

[1] "Satu orang," one man.
[2] "Anjing," a dog.
[3] "Pokoh bisi," club of iron.
[4] "Panah," a bow.

a lance, called Satuhoran, with tumach ;[1] at the sixth, a lion called Satuhorimau ;[2] at the seventh, two white elephants called Gagiapute.

The palace contains seventy-nine halls, in which dwell only the ladies destined to serve the king ; there are always torches burning there. It is not possible to go round the palace in less than a day. In the upper part of it are four halls where the ministers go to speak to the king : one is ornamented with metal, both the pavement and the walls ; another is all of silver, another all of gold, and the other is set with pearls and precious stones. The gold and other valuable things which are brought as tribute to the king are placed in these rooms ; and when they are there deposited, they say, Let this be for the honour and glory of our Santoa Raja. All these things and many others relating to this king, were narrated to us by a Moor, who said that he had seen them.

The Chinese are white, and are clothed ; they eat on tables like us. They have crosses, but it is not known why they have them.

It is from China that musk comes ; the animal which produces it is a kind of cat, like the civet cat; it eats nothing but a certain soft wood, slender as a finger, named chamaru. To extract the musk from this animal they attach a leech to it, and leave it till it is full of blood, and when they see that it is well filled, they crush it, and collect the blood in a plate, and put it in the sun for four or five days, moistening it every day with urine. In this way it becomes perfect musk. Whoever keeps one of these cats pays a tribute to the king. The grains of musk which come to Europe as musk, are only small pieces of kid's flesh soaked in real

[1] "Tombak," a lance.
[2] "Harimau," a tiger; not a lion. All these words are Malay, the language in which the whole of this information must have been conveyed to Pigafetta.

musk, and not the blood, since though it can be made into grains, it easily evaporates. The cat which produces musk is called castor, and the leech is called Linta.

Continuing along the coast of China, many nations are met with, and they are these: the Chienchi, who inhabit the islands in which they fish for pearls, and where the cinnamon grows. The Lecchii inhabit the mainland: the entrance to their port is traversed by a large rock, for which reason all the junks and vessels which wish to enter must take down their masts. The king of this country is called Moni. He has on the mainland twenty kings under him, and he is subject to the King of China: his capital is Baranaci, and here is situated Oriental Cathay. Han is a high and cold island, where there is copper, silver, pearls, and silk; its king is named Raja Zotra. There is also Miliaula, the king of which is named Raja Quetischeniga, and Guio, the king of which is Raja Sudacali. These places are cold and on the mainland. Friagonba and Trianga are two islands which also produce copper, silver, pearls, and silk; their king is Raja Ruzon. Bassi is a low land on the continent. There come afterwards Sumbdit and Pradit, two islands very rich in gold, where the men wear a large ring of gold round the ancle. In the neighbouring mountains dwell people who kill their parents when they are old, so that they may cease from travail. All the people of these countries are Gentiles.

Tuesday night (between it and Wednesday,) on the 11th of February of 1522, we left the island of Timor, and entered upon the great sea named Laut Chidol,[1] and taking a west-south-west course, we left to the right and to the North, from fear of the Portuguese, the island of Zumatra, anciently named Taprobana; also Pegu, Bengala, Urizza, Chelim, where are the Malabars, subjects of the King of Narsinga: Calicut which is under the same king; Cambaya

---

[1] "Laut Kidol," Javanese, the Southern Ocean.

in which are the Guzeratis; Cananor, Goa, Armus, and all the other coast of India major.

In this kingdom dwell six classes of persons, that is to say : Nairs, Panicals, Franas, Pangelins, Macuas, and Poleas. The Nairs are the chiefs; the Panicals are the townspeople; these two classes live and converse together. The Franas collect the wine from the palm trees and the bananas. The Macuas are fishermen; and the Poleas sow and harvest the rice; these last always dwell in the fields, and never enter the city, and when it is desired to give them anything, it is placed on the ground and they take it. When they go along the roads they always cry out, po, po, po, that is take care of yourself; and we were told that a Nair who had been accidentally touched by a Polea, not to survive such a disgrace, had himself killed.

In order to double the Cape of Good Hope, we went as far as 42° South latitude, and we remained off that cape for nine weeks, with the sails struck on account of the Western and North-western gales which beat against our bows with fierce squalls. The Cape of Good Hope is in 34° 30′ South latitude, 1600 leagues distant from the Cape of Malacca, and it is the largest and most dangerous cape in the world.

Some of our men, and among them the sick, would have liked to land at a place belonging to the Portuguese called Mozambique, both because the ship made much water, and because of the great cold which we suffered; and much more because we had nothing but rice and water for food and drink, all the meat of which we had made provision having putrified, for the want of salt had not permitted us to salt it. But the greater number of us, prizing honour more than life itself, decided on attempting at any risk to return to Spain.

At length, by the aid of God, on the 6th of May, we passed that terrible cape, but we were obliged to approach it within only five leagues distance, or else we should never have passed it. We then sailed towards the north-west for two whole months without ever taking rest; and in this short time we lost twenty-one men between Christians and Indians. We made then a curious observation on throwing them into the sea, that was that the Christians remained with the face turned to the sky, and the Indians with the face turned to the sea. If God had not granted us favourable weather, we should all have perished of hunger.

Constrained by extreme necessity, we decided on touching at the Cape Verde Islands, and on Wednesday the 9th of July, we touched at one of those islands named St. James's. Knowing that we were in an enemy's country, and amongst suspicious persons, on sending the boat ashore to get provision of victuals, we charged the seamen to say to the Portuguese that we had sprung our foremast under the equinoctial line (although this misfortune had happened at the Cape of Good Hope), and that our ship was alone, because whilst we tried to repair it, our captain-general had gone with the other two ships to Spain. With these good words, and giving some of our merchandise in exchange, we obtained two boat-loads of rice.

In order to see whether we had kept an exact account of the days, we charged those who went ashore to ask what day of the week it was, and they were told by the Portuguese inhabitants of the island that it was Thursday, which was a great cause of wondering to us, since with us it was only Wednesday. We could not persuade ourselves that we were mistaken; and I was more surprised than the others, since having always been in good health, I had every day, without intermission, written down the day that was current. But we were afterwards advised that there was no error on our part, since as we had always sailed towards the west, following the course of the sun, and had returned to the same place, we must have gained twenty-four hours, as is clear to any one who reflects upon it.

M

The boat, having returned for rice a second time to the shore, was detained, with thirteen men[1] who were in it. As we saw that, and, from the movement in certain caravels, suspected that they might wish to capture us and our ship, we at once set sail. We afterwards learned, some time after our return, that our boat and men had been arrested, because one of our men had discovered the deception, and said that the captain-general was dead, and that our ship was the only one remaining of Magellan's fleet.

At last, when it pleased Heaven, on Saturday the 6th of September of the year 1522, we entered the bay of San Lucar; and of sixty men who composed our crew when we left Maluco, we were reduced to only eighteen,[1] and these for the most part sick. Of the others, some died of hunger, some had run away at the island of Timor, and some had been condemned to death for their crimes.

From the day when we left this bay of San Lucar until our return thither, we reckoned that we had run more than fourteen thousand four hundred and sixty leagues, and we had completed going round the earth from East to West.

Monday the 8th of September, we cast anchor near the mole of Seville, and discharged all the artillery.

Tuesday, we all went in shirts and barefoot, with a taper in our hands to visit the shrine of St. Maria of Victory, and of St. Maria de Antigua.

Then, leaving Seville, I went to Valladolid, where I presented to his Sacred Majesty Don Carlos, neither gold nor silver, but things much more precious in the eyes of so great a Sovereign. I presented to him among other things, a book written by my hand of all the things that had occurred day by day in our voyage. I departed thence as I was best able, and went to Portugal, and related to King John the things which I had seen. Returning through Spain, I came to France, where I presented a few things

[1] See statement of Herrera, p. 175.

from the other hemisphere to Madam the Regent, mother
of the most Christian King Don Francis.[1]   Afterwards, I
turned towards Italy, where I established for ever my abode,
and devoted my leisure and vigils to the very illustrious
and noble lord, Philip de Villiers Lisleadam, the very worthy
grand master of Rhodes.

The Chevalier,

ANTHOYNE PIGAPHETE.

[1] Francis I.

TREATISE OF NAVIGATION

OF THE

CHEVALIER ANTONY PIGAFETTA.

THE armillary sphere, of which the author gives a drawing, serves to explain the system of the world according to
Ptolemy, and could also serve as an astrolabe, for one sees
at the top of it a kind of handle or ring, by which to hold
it suspended, as is seen in the above-mentioned drawing.
He begins his treatise by giving us an idea of that system,
as have done all those after him, who have written of the
elements of the nautical art and of pilotage.

"The earth is round," he says, "and remains suspended and
immovable in the midst of all the celestial bodies. The
first index fixed on two poles, the arctic and antarctic, which
are supposed to correspond with the poles of the earth. It
runs from East to West, and transports with itself all the
planets and stars. Besides this there is the eighth sphere,
the poles of which are at 23 deg. 33 min.,[1] it runs from
West to East.

"It is supposed that all the circumference of the earth is
divided into 360 degrees; and each degree is of 17 leagues
and a half, consequently the circumference of the earth is
6,300 leagues. Land leagues are of three miles and sea
leagues of four miles.[2]

---

[1] Now the declination of the ecliptic, which answers to the poles of
the eighth sphere of Pigafetta, is 23 deg. 28 min. 30 sec. Note, Milan
edition.

[2] Supposing that the surface of the globe under the equator were

"The ten circles of the armillary sphere, of which the six major pass through the center of the earth, serve to determine the situation of countries and climates. The Ecliptic determines the movement of the sun and the planets : the two Tropics indicate the point to which the sun declines from the equator towards the North in summer, and towards the South in winter. The Meridian, always variable, because it passes through all points of the equator, cutting it perpendicularly, designates the longitude, and it is on it that the latitudes are marked."

OF LATITUDE.

After having well explained the armillary sphere with all its parts, and their use according to the system of Ptolemy, the author goes on to teach the method of taking the altitude of the pole, on which the latitude is calculated ; fixing the pole at 0° and the equator at 90°.

"The Polar star," he says, "is not precisely on the point corresponding to the axis of the earth; but it turns round it, as do all the other stars. In order to know its true position with regard to the pole, it must be observed where the Guard stars[1] stand. If these are on the western arm,[2] the polar star stands one degree above the pole : if they

---

half land and half sea, and then giving to each league three and a half miles, we should have 22,050 miles for the circumference of the earth : a measure very little differing from that which results from giving to each degree at the equator sixty Italian miles, by which the circumference is 21,600 miles. Note, Milan edition.

[1] The guard stars are β and γ of Ursa Minor, which form a triangle with the pole and pole star ; now γ of the belt of Cassiopeia is used. Note, Milan edition.

[2] This means the arm of the instrument used; it might be the meteoroscope of Regiomontano, which had a cross in the middle: or an astrolabe like it; or the common astrolabe with a dioptron, or mediclino, as Pigafetta calls it, placed on the equator. Note, Milan edition.

are on the line[1] the pole star stands 3 deg. 30 min.[2] below the pole : if they are on the eastern arm the pole star is one degree below the pole. When one wishes to take the altitude of the pole star, in whichever of the above-mentioned four places the Guard stars may be, the degrees which the pole star has above the pole will be subtracted from its altitude, or those which it has below the pole will be added to it. I have spoken in the account of the voyage of the stars of the Antarctic Pole.

"The latitude of the place may also be ascertained by the sun's altitude. 1. If you find yourself between the equinoctial and the arctic pole and the shadow falls towards that pole, look how many degrees and minutes meridianal declination the sun has that day; and this you will subtract from the altitude of the sun which you have taken : afterwards, deducting the remaining degrees from 90 deg., you will have in the residue the number of degrees of North latitude, that is your distance from the equator. 2. If the sun has a boreal declination, in such a manner that the shadow falls towards the south, take the sun's declination on that day, and add it to the sun's altitude which you have taken, from that sum subtract 90 degs., and the remaining degrees will indicate your boreal latitude. 3. If the sun is between the equinoctial and the antarctic, and the shadow falls towards the antarctic, observe the sun's declination for that day, subtract it from the altitude taken, according to the first rule, and you will have the degrees of south latitude. 4. If, when you and the sun are between the equinoctial and the antarctic pole, the shadow falls to-

[1] That is the meridian line from the pole to the equator. Note, Milan edition.

[2] Though the radius of the circle which the pole star goes round is now little more than a degree and a half, in the time of Pigafetta it was 3 deg. 17 min. 37 sec., so that if he reckoned it at 3 deg. 30 min. it is wonderful that he should have made so small an error, notwithstanding the imperfection of his instruments. Note, Milan edition.

wards the north, you will add the altitude you have taken to the sun's declination that day, and act according to the second rule. 5. When you have an altitude of 90 deg., you will be so many degrees distant from the equator as there are degrees of the sun's declination, and if the sun has no declination you will be under the equator. 6. If you are to the north of the equator, and the sun is in the southern signs you will look what is its declination, you will add these degrees of declination to those of the altitude observed, and as many degrees as are wanting from 90 deg., so many will you be distant from the equinoctial. 7. You will do the same when you find yourself to the south of the equinoctial, whilst the sun is in the northern signs.

" Of Longitude.

"Longitude indicates the degrees from east to west: I have considered many methods or means for ascertaining it, and I have found three methods[1] fitting for that object. The last is the most convenient for those who do not know astrology. At the present time the pilots content themselves with knowing the latitude; and are so proud that they will not hear speak of longitude.

"1. From the latitude of the moon the longitude is calculated of the place in which the observation is made. The distance of the moon from the ecliptic is called its latitude: the ecliptic is the path of the sun. The moon, in its movement, always increases its distance until it reaches the furthest point of its distance: and thence it returns back, to diminish, so to say, its latitude, until it is with the head or tail of the dragon :[2] there it cuts the ecliptic. And since

---

[1] These three methods are probably those which, according to Castañeda, Faleiro taught to Magellan. Note, Milan edition.

[2] That is to say, the knot where the orbit of the moon cuts the ecliptic. Note, Milan edition.

the moon, whilst it lengthens its distance from the ecliptic, has more degrees towards the west than towards the east, it must necessarily have more latitude on one side (*of the globe*) than on the other: and when the latitude is known, by measuring the degrees and minutes with the astrolabe, it will be known whether it is found, and how far it is found towards the east or the west. But in order to ascertain the longitude, you must know in what latitude the moon ought to be at that same moment in the place from which you sailed, for instance, in Seville. By knowing the latitude and longitude of the moon at Seville in degrees and minutes, and seeing also the latitude and longitude which it has in the place where you are, you will know how many hours and minutes you are distant from Seville; and afterwards you will calculate the distance in east or west longitude.

" II. The moon furnishes another method for ascertaining the longitude, but that is when I knew the precise hour in which the moon observed at Seville ought to be in conjunction with a given star or planet, or ought to be in a certain opposition to the sun, of which the degrees are determined: and this I can know by means of an almanack. And since that happens in the east before it happens in the west, as many as may be the hours and minutes that may elapse from the time when the conjunction took place at Seville, till the time in which I observe it to take place, so much will be my longitude west of Seville. But if I should see the conjunction take place before the hour in which it ought to happen with respect to Seville, then my distance in longitude will be east. For each hour, fifteen degrees of longitude are calculated.

" To understand this does not require any great genius. It should be borne in mind that the moon has a motion opposed to the general motion of the heavens; that is, it goes from west to east, and in every two hours it progresses a degree and a few minutes ; and since it is in the first heaven, and the stars are in the eighth, it certainly never enters in conjunction with them ; but sometimes it interposes itself before the rays which come from them to our eye : but this does not happen at the same time to those who are at Seville, and to those who are at Valencia. The annexed figure will give an idea of this, from which it is seen that the ray of the star D is intercepted by the moon C for those who are at A, and not for those who are at B, for whom it was intercepted when the moon was at E.

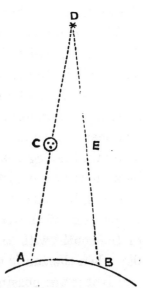

" III. The compass can also supply a method, still easier, for finding the longitude of the place in which you are. It is known that the compass, or the magnetised needle which is in it, directs itself to a given point, because of the tendency which the loadstone has towards the pole. The reason of this tendency is because the loadstone does not find in the heavens any other spot in repose except the pole, and on that account directs itself towards it. This is an explanation of the phenomenon which I propose; and I believe it to be true, so long as experience does not inform us of some better explanation.

" In order to know, by means of the needle, the degrees of longitude, form a large circle, in which place the compass, and divide it into 360 deg.: and having placed the needle, at 360 deg., where it indicates the arctic pole; when the needle is in repose, draw a thread, which should pass from the arctic pole, pointed out by the needle to the antarctic pole, and let this thread be longer than the diameter. After that take the south, which you will know by the greatest

altitude of the sun. Turn the compass, until the thread
which traverses it coincides with the direction of the meridian shade; then, from the antarctic pole of the needle, with
the thread which remained over, draw another thread to
the arctic pole, that is, to the flower;[1] and you will thus
find how many degrees the needle of the compass is distant
from the meridian line, that is, from the true pole. So
many will be the degrees of longitude, which you will have
from the place where the compass begins to set itself in
motion.[2] Therefore, with the more accuracy you take the
true meridian so much the more exactly will you be able to
ascertain the degrees of longitude. And from this it may
be seen that the meridian should never be taken with the
compass, because it north-easts or north-wests,[3] as soon as
it goes out of the true meridian; but take an observation
of the south[4] with the astrolabe, and judge that it is midday when the sun is at its greatest height.

" If it is not possible to take the sun's altitude at midday,
that can be determined with an hour-glass of sand, taking
the hours of the night from sunset till the moment of its
rising. Having learned the hours of the night, you will
know how many are wanting of the twenty-four, and these
you will divide into two equal parts. When half of this has
elapsed, be sure that it is midday, and that the shadow indicates to you the true meridian. But since the sand clock
may often be inexact, it will be better to take the sun's altitude with the astrolabe by means of its mediclino.[5]

---

[1] The fleur-de-lys placed at the north.

[2] That is, where it coincides with the meridian and begins to deviate
or vary. Note, Milan edition.

[3] That is, varies east or west.   [4] Or of midday.

[5] I do not find any mention of the *mediclino* in any writer of the times
near that of Pigafetta who have treated of the astrolabe, such as Regio-
montanus, Appianus, Gimma Frisius, Danti, Clavius, etc.; but from
what our author says here and elsewhere, it appears that the mediclino
is that movable rule, fixed on the centre of the astrolabe, which turns

" The true meridian may also be ascertained, or rather the equinoctial line, which cuts the meridian at right angles, by observing the points where the sun rises and sets, and by observing how much they are distant from the equinoctial either to the north or to the south. For this purpose an astrolabe is formed with the globe; that is, a circle is made representing the earth's circumference, divided into 360 deg. At sunrise fix two pins in the circumference, in such a manner that a line drawn from one to the other should pass through the centre, and place the pins so that both should be in a line opposite the sun's center. Place two other pins in the same way in the circumference when the sun sets. You will thus see how much the sun declines from the equinoctial line, either to the north or to the south. And as many degrees as the pins are distant from the equinoctial, so many degrees are the sun's declination. Having found the sun's rising and setting, you will also find the medium distance; that is, the meridian line, and afterwards you will see how much the compass or magnetic needle north-easts or north-wests. You will infer from this how far you are from the Fortunate islands; that is, from Tenerife towards the east or the west. This method has been tried by experience.[1]

round it, and is named sometimes alhidade, or dioptron, or traguardo, or linea di fiducia. Note, Milan edition.

[1] Amoretti, in his introduction to this Treatise of Navigation, in the Milan edition, observes that Pigafetta was misled by a false theory when he supposes that there is in the heavens a point in repose to which the magnetic needle tends, but that the exact direction of the magnetic needle coincided, or at least approximated, to the meridian of the isle of Ferro, which is not now the case; and that in some other places the variations of the compass had been observed to correspond with that of the longitude. By the table of variations of the compass published by Lambert in the Ephemerides of Berlin (*Astronomische Jahrbuch*) for the year 1779, it is seen by an easy calculation that at the beginning of the sixteenth century the magnetic equator or zero of deviation was very near the isle of Tenerife. Now it is further off, and the distance

"DIRECTION OF THE SHIP.

"If you wish to navigate to any place, you must first know its position ; that is, its latitude and longitude. Then, by means of the compass you will point directly to that place. And since the compass varies to east and west, you must, by the methods above described, ascertain its variation, and subtract or add that which is necessary, so that the ship's head, regulated by the compass, may have the required direction.

"Should the compass be lost, or if its variation east or west is not known, you may regulate yourself by the sun at mid-day. When you have fixed the meridian in such a manner that it cuts the ship in its width, it will be easy to direct the prow wherever you wish. Here is an example: suppose you wish to go from north-east to south-west, place the chart in such manner that the ship should have her head to west and the poop to the east; then on the circle of the winds, divided into 360, or in four times 90, fix two pins, one at 45 degrees between east and north, the other at 45 degrees between west and south; bring the two pins on the line of the meridian by turning the ship's head for that purpose, and the prow will be directed to the place to which you are going. If the pins do not come in a line with the meridian, it is a sign that you are navigating in a false direction, and you must rectify the course. When you reach land, you will see that what I have said is true.

"With an astrolabe made with plates,[1] observations may be taken of the meridian line, the poles, and the equinoctial

increases. M. de Bougainville found there the deviation to the west to be 14 deg. 41 min.; and Staunton, the companion of Lord Macartney, found it to be 17 deg. 35 min.

[1] We have two astrolabes in our museum constructed with several plates: one is of brass, and another of card, for more easy manipulation. Note, Milan edition.

line, at any hour of the day or night, looking at the moon or any star; and for these, place in the middle of the astrolabe instead of the *verghezita* or sight,[1] two straight bars between which you will observe the star."

Thus the method being known by which the required direction is given to the ship, the author teaches the method for determining the point or degree on the chart of the winds,[2] to which the ship on leaving a place to go to a given country should be directed. For clearness, he gives some examples of this. "Do you wish," he says, "to go from south to north, or *vice versâ*, on the same longitude? always proceed on the same meridian. Do you wish to go from east to west, or *vice versâ*, in the same latitude? always proceed on the same parallel. Do you wish to go from one place to another as many degrees distant in longitude as it is different in latitude? Then take the course of 45 degrees either to the south-west or south-east, or north-west or north-east. If the latitude is greater than the longitude, then add to the 45 degrees as many degrees towards the nearest pole, as the number of degrees by which the latitude exceeds the longitude. For instance, if I wish to go from Cape St. Vincent to Cape Bojador, I reckon the degrees of longitude and those of latitude to know the difference between these two capes. I find that the degrees of longitude are five and a half, and those of latitude are eleven, from which I subtract the degrees of longitude and there remain 5 deg. 30 min. Then, instead of going in the direction of from north-east to south-west (as I should do if the longitude were equal to the latitude), I go from 5 deg. 30 min. above north-east towards north, to 5 deg. 30 min. below south-west towards south. If the longitude is greater than the latitude, the lesser number is still subtracted from the greater; and the direction will be 45 deg. after deducting the residue.

[1] " Traguardo," level or traverser.
[2] " Rosa dei venti."

For instance, do you want to go from the island of Ferro to Guadeloupe; you know that the first is in 27 deg. latitude and the second in 15 deg.; then take their difference, which is 12 deg.: look at the map for their longitude, and you see that Ferro is in 1 deg. and Guadeloupe in 45 deg., whence their difference is 44 deg.: subtract from these the 12 deg. residue of latitude, and there remain 32 deg. Then you must subtract these 32 deg. from 45 deg., and there will remain 13 deg. Therefore your course will be from north-east 13 deg. north to south-west 13 deg. south.

" DIRECTION OF THE WINDS.

" The rose of the winds, divided into 360 deg., will give a clearer idea of what has been here said; it being well understood that the pilot must place the center of the winds on the point from which he starts, or from which he takes the course, and he must fix the pole to the true pole observed from the sun, and not trusting to the compass, which north-easts or north-wests.

" Then, to ascertain whence comes the wind, place a little stick with a little sail[1] in the centre of your rose or circle of winds, divided into 360 deg., and placed in such a manner that north and south stand on the true Solar meridian. The direction of the vane moved by the wind will indicate exactly which wind blows: on the equinoctial is east and west; at 45 deg. there is north-east, south-west, north-west, and south-east; at 22½ deg. towards north you have north-north-east, and so on with the others."

---

[1] Or flag, as appears from the drawing.

NAMES OF THE FIRST CIRCUMNAVIGATORS.

HERRERA (Dècade III, lib. iv, cap. 4) mentions the arrival of the *Victoria*, and says that an accountant and thirteen Castilians had remained behind, arrested at Cape Verde, and that the King of Portugal's factor sent them on to Lisbon in a ship which came at that time from Calicut.

Herrera then gives the names of those who came in the *Victoria*, and who went to Court. They were—

1. Miguel de Rodas, master.
2. Martin de Insaurraga, pilot.
3. Miguel de Rodas, seaman.
4. Nicolas Griego.
5. Juan Rodriguez.
6. Vasco Gallego (Portuguese).
7. Martin de Judicibus.
8. Juan de Santander.
9. Hernando de Bustamante.
10. Antonio Lombardo (*Pigafetta*).
11. Francisco Rodriguez.
12. Antonio Fernandez.
13. Diego Gallego.
14. Juan de Arratia.
15. Juan de Apega.
16. Juan de Acurio.
17. Juan de Zubieta.
18. Lorenzo de Iruña.
19. Juan de Ortega.
20. Pedro de Indarchi.
21. Ruger Carpintete.
22. Pedro Gasco.
23. Alfonso Domingo, seaman.
24. Diego Garcia.
25. Pedro de Valpuesta.
26. Ximeno de Bargos.
27. Juan Martin.
28. Martin de Magallanes.
29. Francisco Alvaro (probably Albo, the pilot).
30. Roldan de Argote (from whom must be named the mountain, which in the Strait of Magellan, is now called the Campaña de Roldan).
31. Juan Sebastian del Cano.

This number, 31, will agree with Pigafetta's 13, who remained at Cape Verde, and 18 who landed from the *Victoria*.

Sebastian del Cano was very well received by the emperor, and Herrera mentions the safe arrival of some of the Molucca Indians: "One of whom," he says, "was so sharp, that the first thing he did was to inquire how many reals a ducat was worth, and a real how many maravedises, and how much pepper was given for a maravedi; and he went from shop to shop to get information of the value of spices, and with this he gave cause that he did not return to his country, although the others returned." This probably means that he was not allowed to return, lest he should raise the price of spices in the Molucca Islands.

ORDER OF THE DAY OF MAGELLAN,

Given in the Straits, which 'fell into the hands of the Portuguese, along with the Papers of the Astrologer ANDRES DE SAN MARTIN, *at the Moluccas:* taken 'from BARROS, Decade III, Liv. v, Cap. 19.

───────────

"I FERNAN DE MAGALHAES, Knight of the Order of St. James, and captain-general of this fleet, which his majesty sent for the discovery of the spices, etc. I make known to you, Duarte Barbosa, captain of the ship *Victoria,* and to the pilots, masters, and quarter-masters of that ship, as I have understood that it seems to you all a serious matter, that I am determined to go forward, because it seems to you that the weather is little fitted for this voyage on which we are going; and inasmuch as I am a man who never rejected the opinion or counsel of any one, but rather all my affairs are discussed and communicated generally to all, without any person being affronted by me; and since, because of that which happened in the port of S. Julian with respect to the death of Luis de Mendoça, Gaspar de Quexada, and the banishment of Juan de Cartagena and Pero Sanches de Reina, the priest, you, from fear, desist from telling me, and counselling all that may appear to you to be for the service of his majesty, and the safe conduct of this fleet, and you have not told it me nor counselled it: you err in the service of the emperor and king our sovereign, and go against the oath and plighted homage which you have made to me; for which I command you on the part of the said

N

sovereign, and on my part beseech you and charge you, that with respect to all that you think is fitting for our voyage, both as to going forward, and as to turning back, that you give me your opinions in writing each one for himself: declaring the circumstances and reasons why we ought to go forward or turn back, not having respect to anything for which you should omit to tell the truth. With which reasons and opinions, I will say mine, and my decision for coming to a conclusion as to what we have to do. Done in the Channel of All Saints, opposite the river of the islet, on Wednesday, twenty-first of November, in fifty-three degrees, of the year one thousand five hundred and twenty."

Andres de San Martin replied, giving his opinion that, though he doubted there being any opening in the channel by which to go to the Moluccas, yet he thought they should go forward till the middle of January, as long as the summer and long days lasted.

Magellan, having received this and the other opinions, which he had asked for only to please and content his people, gave a full answer, with long reasons for going forward; and he swore by the habit of St. James, which he wore, that so it seemed to him to be for the good of the fleet. This opinion was notified to the fleet, and next day he set sail.

A LETTER

FROM

MAXIMILIANUS TRANSYLVANUS

TO THE

MOST REVEREND CARDINAL OF SALZBURG,

VERY DELIGHTFUL TO READ,

CONCERNING THE MOLUCCA ISLANDS, AND ALSO MANY
OTHER WONDERS, WHICH THE LATEST VOYAGE OF
THE SPANIARDS HAS JUST DISCOVERED.

(THE TITLE IN RAMUSIO'S COLLECTION RUNS THUS)—

A Letter of Maximilianus Transylvanus, Secretary to His Majesty the
Emperor, written to the Most Illustrious and Reverend Lord
the Cardinal of Salzburg, concerning the wonderful and
astonishing Voyage made by the Spaniards in the
Year 1519, round the World.

M. GIOVANNI BATTISTA RAMUSIO

VOYAGE MADE BY THE SPANIARDS ROUND THE WORLD.

THE voyage made by the Spaniards round the world in the space of three years is one of the greatest and most marvellous things which have been heard of in our times; and, although in many things we surpass the ancients, yet this expedition far excels every other that has been made up till now. The voyage was described very minutely by Peter Martyr, who belonged to the Council of the Indies of His Majesty the Emperor, and to whom was entrusted the duty of writing this history; and by him were examined all those who remained alive of that expedition, and who reached Seville in the year 1522. But, as it was sent to be printed in Rome, it was lost in the miserable sacking of that city; and nothing is known even now as to where it is. And he who saw it, and read it, bears testimony to the same; and, amongst other things worthy of recollection that the aforesaid Peter noted concerning the voyage, was this, that the Spaniards, having sailed about three years and one month, and the greater part of them, as is usual amongst seafaring men, having noted down the days of the months one by one, found, when they arrived in Spain, that they had lost a day, for the day on which they arrived at Seville, which was the 7th of September, was, by their reckoning, the 6th. And the aforesaid Peter having mentioned this peculiarity to a certain excellent and extraordinary man, who was at that time ambassador for his Republic to His Majesty; and, having asked him how it could be, he, who was a great philosopher and learned in Greek and Latin literature, so that for his singular learning and rare excellence, he was afterwards promoted to much higher rank, gave this explanation: That it could not have fallen out otherwise, as they had travelled for three years continuously and always accompanied the sun, which was going westward. And he told him besides, that those who sailed due westwards towards the sun, lengthen their day very much, as the ancients also had noticed. Now, the book of the aforesaid Peter having disappeared, Fortune has not allowed the memory of so marvellous an enterprise to be entirely lost, inasmuch as a certain noble gentleman of Vicenza called Messer Antonio Pigafetta (who, having gone on the voyage and returned in the ship *Vittoria*, was made a Knight of Rhodes), wrote a very exact and full account of it in a book, one copy of which he presented to His Majesty the Emperor, and another he sent to the most Serene Mother of the most Christian King, the Lady Regent. She entrusted to an excellent Parisian philosopher called Jacomo Fabre, who had studied in Italy, the work of translating it into French.[1] This worthy person, I suppose to save himself trouble, made only a summary of it, leaving out what seemed fit to him; and this was printed, very incorrectly, in France, and has now come into our hands; and along with it a letter from one called Maximilianus of Transylvania, a secretary of His Majesty the Emperor, to the most Reverend Cardinal of Salzburg. And this we have wished to add to this volume of travels, as one of the greatest and most remarkable that there has ever been, and one at which those great philosophers of old, hearing of it, would have been stupified and beside themselves. And the city of Vicenza may well boast, among the other cities of Italy, that in addition to its nobility

[1] It was written in French. See Introduction.

and high qualities; in addition to its many rare and excellent geniuses, both in letters and arms, there has been a
gentleman of such courage as the aforesaid Messer Antonio
Pigafetta, who has circumnavigated the whole globe, and
has described it so exactly. There is no doubt that the
ancients would have erected a statue of marble to him, and
would have placed it in an honourable position, as a memorial and example to posterity of his great worth, and in
acknowledgment of so stupendous an enterprise. But if, in
this letter or in the summary, there be seen any discrepancy
of names or things, let no one be astonished; for the bent
of men's minds is various, and one notices one thing and
one another, just as the things appear most deserving of
attention. Let it suffice if, in the principal things they
agree, and many parts which are left out in one can be read
at length in the other. Fabulous stories, too, are noted for
what they are. This may be safely affirmed by anyone, that
the ancients never had such a knowledge of the world,
which the sun goes round and examines every twenty-four
hours, as we have at present, through the industry of the
men of these our times.

Most Reverend and Illustrious Lord, my only Lord, to you
I most humbly commend myself.

One of those five ships has lately returned which Cæsar
sent in former years, when he was living at Saragossa, to a
strange, and for so many ages, an unknown world, in order
to search for the islands where spices grow. For though
the Portuguese bring a great quantity of them from the
Golden Chersonesus, which we now suppose to be Malacca,
yet their own Indies produce nothing but pepper. Other
spices, such as cinnamon, cloves, and the nutmeg, which

we call muscat, and its covering (mace), which we call muscat flower, are brought to their own Indies from distant
islands till now only known by name, and in ships which
are fastened together not by iron but by palm leaves. The
sails of these ships are round and woven, too, of the palm-
fibre. This sort of ships they call junks, and they only use
them with a wind directly fore and aft.

It is no wonder that these islands should be unknown
to any human beings almost up to our time. For whatever we read concerning the native soil of the spices has
been told us by ancient authors, and is partly, certainly,
fabulous; and, partly, so far from the truth, that even the
very countries in which they said that they grew naturally,
are but little less distant from those where it is now
known that they grow, than we are. For to omit others,
Herodotus, in other respects a most famed author, has said
that cinnamon is found in birds' nests, to which the birds
have brought it from most distant regions, and specially
the Phœnix, and I know not who has seen his nest. But
Pliny, who thought himself able to give more certain information, because, before his time, many things had been
made clear by the voyages of the fleets of Alexander the
Great and of others, relates that cinnamon grows in Æthiopia on the borders of the land of the Troglodytæ, whilst
now it is known that cinnamon is produced very far from
any part of Æthiopia, and specially from the Troglodytæ
(that is, the dwellers in subterranean caverns). But our
men, who have now returned, and who were perfectly acquainted with Æthiopia, have been obliged to make a complete circuit of the world, and that a very wide one, before
they could find the islands and return. As this voyage may
be considered marvellous, and not only unaccomplished, but
even unattempted either in our age or in any previous one,
I have resolved to write as truly as possible to your Reverence the course (of the expedition) and the sequence of the

whole matter. I have taken care to have everything related
to me most exactly by the captain and by the individual
sailors who have returned with him. They have also related
each separate event to Cæsar and to others with such good
faith and sincerity, that they seemed not only to tell nothing
fabulous themselves, but by their relation to disprove and
refute all the fabulous stories which had been told by old
authors. For who can believe that these were Monosceli,
Scyopodæ, Syritæ, Spitamei, Pygmies, and many others,
rather monsters than men. And as so many places beyond
the Tropic of Capricorn have been sought, found, and carefully examined, both by the Spaniards in the south-west
and by the Portuguese sailing eastwards, and as the remainder of the whole world has now been sailed over by our
countrymen, and yet nothing trustworthy has been heard
concerning these man-monsters, it must be believed that the
accounts of them are fabulous, lying, and old women's tales,
handed down to us in some way by no credible author.
But lest I, who have to travel over the whole world, should
seem too diffuse in my introduction, I return to my story.
When, nearly thirty years ago, the Spaniards in the west,
and the Portuguese in the east, began to search for new
and unknown lands, their two kings, lest one should be a
hindrance to the other, divided the whole globe between
them by the authority, most likely, of Pope Alexander the
Sixth, in this manner: that a straight line should be drawn
360 miles, which they call leucæ, west of the islands of the
Hesperides, which are now called the islands of Cape Verd;
towards the north, and another towards the south Pole, till
they should meet again, and so divide the world into two
equal parts. And whatever strange land should be discovered eastwards (of this line) should be ceded to the Portuguese, and whatever west of it to the Spaniards. In this
manner it happened that the Spaniards always sailed south-
west, and there they discovered a very large continent and

very great and innumerable islands, rich in gold and pearls
and in other wealth, and now, quite lately, have they discovered the vast Mediterranean city, Tenostica,[1] situated in
a lake, like Venice.   About this city Peter Martyr, an
author more careful about his facts than the elegance of his
style, has written many wonderful, and yet true, things.
But the Portuguese, passing southwards by the shores of
the Hesperides, and of the ichthyophagous Æthiopians, and
crossing the equinoctial line and the Tropic of Capricorn,
sailed eastward, and discovered many great and unknown
islands, and afterwards the sources of the Nile and the land
of the Troglodytæ.   Thence they sailed past the Arabian
and Persian Gulfs to the shores of India, within the Ganges,
where there is now the mighty emporium and kingdom of
Calicut.   Thence they sailed to Taprobanes, which they now
call Zamatara.   For there is now no island which either
can be, or can be supposed to be, Taprobanes, in the position
in which Ptolemy, Pliny, and the other cosmographers
placed it.   Going thence, they arrived at the Golden Chersonesus, where now is situated that most famous city of Malacca, the greatest emporium of the East.   After this they
entered the Great Gulf,[2] which reaches as far as the country
of the Sinæ, which they now call Schinæ, where they found
a white and tolerably civilised people, like our Germans.
They believe that the Seres and the Asiatic Scythians extend as far as there.   And though there was a certain
rumour afloat that the Portuguese had progressed so far to
the east as to cross their own limits and enter the territory
of the Spaniards, and that Malacca and the Great Bay were
within our limits, still all these things were said rather than
believed, until four years ago Ferdinand Magellan, a distinguished Portuguese, who, for many years had explored the
coasts of the whole of the East as Admiral, took a great
hatred to his king, whom he complained of as being most

---

[1] " Tenistitan," Ramusio.   [2] Gulf of Siam.

ungrateful to him, and came to Cæsar.   Christopher Haro, too, my own father-in-law's brother, who had traded for many years in the East by means of his agents, he himself staying in Ulyssipone, commonly called Lisbon, and who had lastly traded with the Chinese, so that he has great practice in such things, having also been unjustly treated by the King of Portugal, came also home to Spain.   And they both showed Cæsar that though it was not yet quite sure whether Malacca was within the confines of the Spaniards or the Portuguese, because, as yet, nothing of the longitude had been clearly proved, yet that it was quite plain that the Great Gulf and the people of Sinæ lay within the Spanish boundary.   This, too, was held to be most certain, that the islands which they call the Moluccas, in which all the spices are produced, and are thence exported to Malacca, lay within the Spanish western division, and that it was possible to sail there ; and that spices could be brought thence to Spain more easily, and at less expense and cheaper, as they came direct from their native place.

Their course would be this, to sail westward, coasting the southern hemisphere (till they came) to the East.   The thing seemed almost impossible and useless, not because it was thought a difficult thing to go from the west right to the east under the hemisphere, but because it was uncertain whether ingenious nature, which has done nothing without the greatest foresight, had not so dissevered the east from the west, partly by sea and partly by land, as to make it impossible to arrive there by either land or sea travelling. For it had not then been discovered whether that great region which is called Terra Firma did separate the western sea from the eastern ; it was clear enough that that continent, in its southern part, trended southwards and afterwards westwards.   It was clear, also, that two regions had been discovered in the North, one of which they called Regio Bacalearum (Cod-fish Land), from a new kind of fish ;

and the other Terra Florida. And if these two were united
to that Terra Firma, it was impossible to get to the east by
going from the west, as nothing had ever been discovered of
any channel through this land, though it had been sought
for most diligently and with great labour. And they considered it a very doubtful and most dangerous enterprise to
go through the limits of the Portuguese, and so to the east.
For which reason it seemed to Cæsar and to his counsellors
that these men were promising a thing from which much
was to be hoped, but still of great difficulty. When they
were both brought to an audience on a certain day, Magellan offered to go himself, but Christopher offered to fit out
a fleet at his own expense and that of his friends, but only
if it were allowed to sail under the authority and protection
of Cæsar. Whilst they both persisted rather obstinately in
their offers, Cæsar himself equipped a fleet of five ships, and
appointed Magellan its admiral. Their orders were, to sail
southwards along the coast of Terra Firma till they found
either its termination or some channel through which they
might reach the spice-bearing Moluccas. So Magellan set
sail on the 10th of August, 1519, with five ships from
Seville. A few days after he reached the Fortunate Islands,
which are now sometimes called the Canaries. Thence
they arrived at the Islands of the Hesperides,[1] from which
they took a south-western course towards that continent
which we mentioned before; and after some days' fair sailing they sighted a promontory, to which the name of Santa
Maria has been given. Here Juan Ruy Diaz Solis had
been eaten, with some of his companions, by the anthropophagi, whom the Indians call cannibals, whilst, by order of
Ferdinand the Catholic, he was exploring the coast of this
continent with a fleet. Sailing thence, our men coasted in
an unbroken course along the coasts of this continent, which
extend a very long way south, and tend a little west, so that

[1] Cape Verde Islands.

they crossed the Tropic of Capricorn by many degrees. I think that this continent should be called that of the Southern Pole. But it was not so easy as I have said; for not till the last day of March of the following year did they reach a bay, to which they gave the name of Saint Julian. Here they found the Antarctic Pole star $49\frac{1}{2}$ degrees above their horizon, both by the altitude and declination of the sun from the Equinoctial, and also by the altitude of the Antarctic (Pole star) itself. This star our sailors generally make use of more than of any other. They state also that the longitude was 56 deg. west of the Fortunate Isles. For, as the ancient cosmographers, and specially Ptolemy, reckoned the longitude from the Fortunate Islands eastward to Catigara at 180 deg., so our men, sailing as far as they could westward also, began to reckon another 180 deg. westward to Catigara, as was right. Yet our sailors seem to me rather to be mistaken in the calculation of the longitudes (of distances?) than to have fixed them with any certainty, because in so long a voyage, and being so distant from the land, they cannot fix and determine any marks or signs for the longitude. Still I think that these accounts, whatever they be, should not be cast aside, but rather accepted till more certain information be discovered.

This Gulf of Saint Julian seemed very great, and had the appearance of a channel. Wherefore Admiral Magellan ordered two ships to explore the Gulf and anchored the rest outside. After two days, information was brought to him that the Gulf was full of shoals, and did not extend far inland. Our men, on their way back, saw some Indians picking up shell-fish on the shore; for they call the natives of all unknown lands Indians. They were of extraordinary height, that is to say, about ten spans, were clothed in the skins of wild beasts, and seemed darker than would be expected from the situation of the country. When some of our men went on shore to them and showed them bells and pictures painted on paper, they began a hoarse chant and an unintelligible song, dancing round our men, and, in order to astonish them, they passed arrows a cubit and a half long down their throats to the bottom of their stomachs, and without being sick. And forthwith drawing them out again, they seemed to rejoice greatly, as having shown their bravery by this exploit.

At last three came as ambassadors, and prayed our men, by certain signs, to go further inland with them, as if they would receive them with all hospitality. Magellan sent seven men, well armed, with them, to investigate as carefully as possible both country and people. When they had gone with them about seven miles inland, they came to a thick and pathless wood.

Here was a rather low hut, covered with skins of wild beasts. There were two apartments in it; in one lived the women with their children, in the other the men. There were thirteen women and children, and five men. These received their guests with a (ferali apparatu[1]) barbarous pomp, which seemed to them a royal one. An animal was slaughtered, which seemed to differ little from the onager, and they served it up half roasted to our men, without any other food or drink. Our men were obliged, contrary to their custom, to sleep under skins, on account of the severity of the snow and wind. Wherefore, before they slept, they set watch. The Indians did the same, and lay down near our men, snoring horribly.

When the day had broken, our men asked them to return with them to the ships, with the whole family. When the Indians had refused for a considerable time, and our

---

[1] Literally, with funereal or lugubrious state; but Maximilian and his translators appear to have thought that *feralis* is derived from *fera*. Ramusion translates: "Dando loro a mangiar carne di fiere;" and the Spanish version in Navarrete has: "Con su aparato y cerimonias bestiales." Ducange has an adverb, *feraliter*, with the sense of beastly.

men had insisted upon it rather imperiously, the men entered the den-like[1] women's apartment. The Spaniards thought that they were consulting with their wives concerning this expedition; but they returned covered, from the sole of their feet to the crown of their heads, with different horrible skins, and with their faces painted in different colours, and equipped in this terrible and horrible garb with bows and arrows for battle, and (seemingly ?) of much greater stature than before. The Spaniards, who thought that it would come to a fight, ordered (a shot) to be fired. Though this shot was harmless, still the giants, who looked just before fit to contend with Jove, were so frightened by this sound, that they began forthwith to speak of peace. The upshot was, that three men returned with our fellows to the ships, having sent away the rest of the family. So they started for the ships. But, as our men could not only not keep up with these almost giants when the latter were running, but could not, even by running, keep up with them walking, two of them escaped upon the march, on the pretext of pursuing an onager, which they saw feeding at a distance upon a mountain. The third was brought to the ship, but died, within a few days, of fasting, which he had imposed upon himself, according to the habit of the Indians, through homesickness. And though the admiral sent again to that hut, in order to catch some one of these giants to take to Cæsar on account of their novelty, yet no one was found there, but all had gone elsewhere with the hut. Whence it seems clear that that race is a wandering one, nor did our men ever see another Indian on that coast, though they remained in that bay for many days, as we shall mention farther on. They did not think that there was anything in that region of sufficient importance to justify their exploring it and the interior any farther. Though Magellan perceived that any longer stay there was useless, yet, as the sea for several

[1] " Feralis," again.

days was stormy and the sky threatening, and the land
stretched continuously southwards, so that the farther they
went the colder they would find that region, his departure
was necessarily put off from day to day, till the month of
May was close upon them, from which time the winter there
begins to be most severe, so that it became necessary to
winter at the very time when we have our summer. Magellan foreseeing that the voyage would be a long one, ordered
provisions to be served out more sparingly among his crews,
so that the stock might last longer. When the Spaniards
had borne this patiently for some days, fearing the severity
of the winter and the barrenness of the country, they at last
petitioned their admiral, Magellan, that, as he saw that the
land stretched uninterruptedly to the south, and that no
hope remained of its terminating or of the discovery of a
strait through it, and that a severe winter was imminent,
and that many of them were dead of starvation and hardships; and declared that they could no longer bear the rule
which he had made about the allowance of provisions (lex
sumptuaria), and begged that he would increase the allowance of provisions, and think about going home; that
Cæsar never intended that they should too obstinately
attempt what nature itself and other obstacles opposed;
that their exertions were already sufficiently known and
approved of,—for they had gone farther than either the
boldness or rashness of mortals had ever dared to go as yet;
and that they could easily reach some milder shore, if they
were to sail south (north?) for a few days, a south wind being then blowing. But in reply, Magellan, who had already
made up his mind either to die or to complete his enterprise, said that his course had been laid down for him by
Cæsar himself, and that he neither could nor would depart
from it in any degree, and that he would in consequence
sail till he found either the end of the land or some strait
(through it).

That though they could not at present succeed whilst winter was against them, yet that it would be easy in the summer of that region. But that, if they would continue towards the Antarctic portion of this country, the whole of its summer would be one perpetual day. That there were means if they would only try them, by which they might avoid famine and the rigour of the winter, inasmuch as there was abundance of wood, and the sea provided shell-fish and many sorts of the very best fish. The springs there were wholesome, and birdfowling and hunting would supply many wants; and neither bread nor wine had as yet been lacking, nor would they lack in future if they would only bear that they should be served out when needed, or for health's sake, and not for pleasure or for luxury. They had done nothing as yet worthy of admiration, or which could serve as an excuse for their return, inasmuch as the Portuguese crossed the tropic of Capricorn by as much as 12 deg. not only every year, but almost every day, when they were sailing eastwards. They would be thought worthy of very little praise who had gone only 4 deg. southwards. He had certainly made up his mind to endure the worst rather than return ignominiously to Spain, and he trusted that all his comrades, or at least those in whom the noble Spanish spirit was not yet dead, would be of the same mind.

He advised them to bear at least the remainder of the winter patiently, and said that their rewards would be the more abundant the more difficulties and dangers they had endured in opening to Cæsar a new unknown world, rich in spices and gold. Magellan thought that the minds of his crews were soothed and cheered by this harangue, but within a few days was harassed by a shameful and foul conspiracy. For talking began amongst the crews about the old eternal hatred between the Portuguese and the Spaniards, and about Magellan's being a Portuguese. He,

o

they said, could do nothing more glorious for his own country than to cast away this fleet, with so many men. Nor was it credible that he should wish to discover the Moluccas, even if he were able; but he would think it sufficient if he could lure Cæsar on for some years with a vain hope, and meanwhile something new would turn up, by which the Spaniards would for the future be diverted from the search for spices. Nor even had their course begun to turn towards those happy Moluccas, but rather to distant snows and ice, and to perpetual storms.

Magellan, very much enraged by these sayings, punished the men, but rather more harshly than was proper for a foreigner, especially when commanding in a distant country. So, having planned a conspiracy, they seize upon a ship, and make ready to return to Spain. But he, with the rest whom he had still obedient to his commands, attacked that ship, and put to death the head man and the other ringleaders, those even who could not lawfully be so treated sharing the same fate. For these were certain servants of the king, upon whom no one but Cæsar and his Council could lawfully pronounce a sentence of death. Nevertheless, no one from that time dared to disparage the power of the commander. Still, there were not wanting some who whispered that Magellan would, in the same manner, murder all the Spaniards to the last man, until he, having got rid of them all, might return with the few Portuguese with the fleet to his own country. And so this hatred settled more deeply in the hearts of the Spaniards.

As soon as ever Magellan saw the storminess of the sea and the rigour of the winter mitigated, he set sail from the gulf of St. Julian on the 24th of August. And, as before, he followed the course of the coast southwards for many days. A promontory was at last sighted, which they called Santa Cruz, when a severe storm, springing from the east, suddenly caught them, and one of the five ships was cast on shore, the men being all saved, with the merchandise and equipment, except one Ethiopian slave, who was caught and drowned by the waves. After this the land seemed to bear a little east and south, and this they began to coast along as usual, and on the 26th of November certain inlets of the sea were discovered, which had the appearance of a strait. Magellan entered them forthwith with the whole fleet, and when he saw other and again other bays, he gave orders that they should be all carefully examined from the ships, to see if anywhere a passage might be discovered; and said that he would himself wait at the mouth of the strait till the fifth day, to hear what might happen.

One of the ships, which Alvarus Meschito, his nephew, commanded, was carried back by the tide to the sea, to the very place where they entered the gulf. But when the Spaniards perceived that they were far away from the other ships, they made a plot to return home, put Alvarus, their captain, in irons, bent their course northwards, and were at last carried to the coast of Æthiopia (Guinea), and, having victualled there, they reached Spain eight months after they had deserted the rest. There they compel Alvarus to stand his trial in chains (causam ex vinculis dicere faciunt quasi), for having, by his counsel and advice, induced his uncle Magellan to practise such harshness on the Spaniards.

But when Magellan had waited for this ship some days longer than the time fixed, another returned, which had discovered nothing but a bay full of shoals and shingle, and very lofty cliffs. The third ship, however, reported that the largest bay had the appearance of a strait, as in three days' sail they had found no way out; but the farther they had gone the narrower the sea was, and they had not been able to sound the depth of it in many places by any length of line, and that they had also noticed that the tide was rather stronger than the ebb, and that so they were per-suaded that a passage was open in that direction to some other sea. He made up his mind to sail through it. This channel, which they did not then know to be a channel, was at one place three Italian miles wide, at another two, some-times ten, and sometimes five, and pointed a little west-ward. The altitude of the southern pole was found to be 52 deg., and the longitude to be the same, as at St. Julian's Bay. The month of November was upon them (Aderat jam mensis Novembris), the night was rather more than five hours long, and they had never seen any human beings on the shore.

But one night a great number of fires were seen, mostly on their left hand, from which they guessed that they had been seen by the natives of the region. But Magellan, see-ing that the country was rocky, and also stark with eternal cold, thought it useless to waste many days in examining it; and so, with only three ships, he continued on his course along the channel, until, on the twenty-second day after he had entered it, he sailed out upon another wide and vast sea. The length of the channel they attest to be nearly a hundred Spanish miles.

There is no doubt that the land which they had upon their right was the continent of which we have spoken, but they think that the land on the left was not a main-land, but islands, because sometimes on that side they heard on a still farther coast the beating and roaring of the sea.

Magellan saw that the continent stretched northwards again in a straight line; wherefore, leaving that huge con-tinent on the right hand, he ordered them to sail through that vast and mighty sea (which I do not think had ever seen either our or any one else's ships) in the direction whence the wind called Corus[1] generally blows—that is, 'twixt north and west—so that he might, by going through

[1] Or, Caurus.

west to east, again arrive at the torrid zone ; for he thought
that it was proved sufficiently clearly that the Moluccas
were in the most remote east, and could not be far from
the equator. They kept this course uninterruptedly, nor
did they ever depart from it, except when rough weather
or violent winds compelled them to diverge ; and when
they had in this manner been carried for forty days by a
strong and generally favourable wind, and had seen nothing but sea, and everywhere sea—when they had almost
reached the tropic of Capricorn once more, two islands
were sighted, but small and barren. These they found
uninhabited when they tried to land ; still, they stopped
there two days for their health's sake, and general recruit-
ing of their bodies, for there was very fair fishing there.
They named these the Unfortunate Islands by common
consent. Then they again set sail thence, following their
original course and direction of sailing. And when, for
three months and twenty days, they had been sailing over
this ocean with great good fortune, and had traversed an
immense part of the sea—more vast than mind of man can
conceive, for they had been driven almost continuously by
a very strong wind—they were now at last arrived on this
side of the equinoctial line, and at last they saw an island,
called, as they learnt afterwards, Inuagana by the natives.
When they had approached nearer, they discovered the
altitude of the Arctic pole to be 11 deg. The longitude
they thought to be 158 deg. west of Gades. Then they
saw other and still more islands, so that they knew they
had arrived at some vast archipelago. When they reached
Inuagana, the island was discovered to be uninhabited.
They then approached a rather small island, where they
saw two Indian canoes—for that is the name by which this
strange kind of boat is called by the Indians. The canoes
are cut and hollowed out of a single trunk of a tree, and
hold one, or, at most, two men ; and they usually speak by

gestures and signs, as if the dumb were talking with the dumb.

They asked the Indians the names of the islands, and where they could get provisions, of which they were in great want. They understood that the island in which they had been was called Inuagana, and that the one where they now were was Acaca, but both of them uninhabited. They said that there was an island not far off, which was called Selani, and which they almost showed with their finger, and that it was inhabited, and that an abundance of everything necessary for life was to be found there.

Our men, having taken in water in Acaca, sailed towards Selani; here a storm took them, so that they could not bring the ships to that island, but were driven to another island called Massaua, where lives a king of (the?) three islands, after that they arrived at Subuth. This is an excellent and large island, and, having made a treaty with its chieftain, they landed immediately to perform divine service, according to the manner of Christians, for it was the feast of the resurrection of Him who was our salvation. Wherefore they built a small chapel of the sails of the ships, and of boughs, and in that they built an altar according to the Christian rites, and performed service after their home fashion. The chieftain came up with a great number of Indians, who seemed in every way delighted by this wor-ship of the gods. They led the admiral and some of the officers to the chief's hut, and put before them whatever food they had. Their bread, which they call sago, was made of the trunk or wood of a tree, rather like a palm. This, when cut in pieces, and fried in oil in a pan, supplies them with bread, a small piece of which I send to your reverence. Their drink was a liquor which flows and trickles from the boughs of the palm-trees when cut. Fowling, too, supplied the feast, and the rest was the fruit of that region.

Magellan beheld, in the chief's hut, one sick, and almost

at the last gasp. He asked who he was, and what illness he was suffering from. He learnt that he was the chief's grandson, and had now suffered for two years from a raging fever. But he told him to be of good cheer, and that he would immediately recover his health and former strength, if he would only become a Christian. The Indian accepted the condition, and, having adored the Cross, he received baptism, and the next day declared that he was well, rose from his bed, walked, and took food like the rest. He told I know not what visions to the Indians. What need I say more? The chief himself, with two thousand two hundred Indians, was baptized, and professed the name and religion of Christ. But Magellan, judging this island to abound in gold and ginger, and, besides, to be convenient from its position with respect to the neighbouring islands, for exploring with ease their wealth and produce of the earth, goes to the Chief of Subuth, and persuades him that as he had abandoned that vain and impious worship of the gods, and had turned to the religion of Christ, it was only fair that the kings of the neighbouring isles should be subject to his rule and command; and he said that he had resolved to send ambassadors concerning this, and compel by arms those who did not listen to his command.

This proposition pleased the savage, and the ambassadors were sent. The chiefs came in one by one, and did homage. The nearest island was called Mauthan, the king of which excelled the others in number of soldiers and in arms, and he refused to do homage to one whom he had been accustomed for so long to command.

Magellan, who desired to finish what he had once begun, gave orders that forty of his men, whose bravery and prowess he had proved, should arm, and he crossed over to Mauthan in boats, for the island was very near. The Chief of Subuth added some of his own men to show him the situation of the island, and to fight, if matters came to that.

The King of Mauthan, seeing our men coming, draws up about three thousand of his subjects in the field, and Magellan draws up his on the shore, with their guns and warlike engines, though only a few ; and though he saw that he was far inferior to the enemy in number, yet he thought it better to fight this warlike race, which made use of lances and other long weapons, than either to return or to use the soldiers from Subuth. So he orders his men to be of good cheer and brave hearts, and not to be alarmed at the number of the enemy, for they had often seen, as formerly, so in quite recent times, two hundred Spaniards in the island of Yucatan put sometimes two or three hundred thousand men to flight. But he pointed out to the Subuth islanders that he had brought them, not to fight, but to watch their bravery and fighting power (robur in acie). So, having charged the enemy, both sides fought valiantly : but, as the enemy were more numerous, and used longer weapons, with which they did our men much damage, Magellan himself was at last thrust through and slain. But the rest of our men, though they did not seem quite conquered, yet retreated, having lost their leader. And the enemy dared not follow them, as they were retreating in good order.

So the Spaniards, having lost their admiral, Magellan, and seven of their comrades, returned to Subuth, where they chose another commander, John Serrano, a man not to be despised. He immediately renewed with fresh gifts the alliance that had been made with the King of Subuth, and promised to subdue the King of Mauthan.

Magellan had a slave, born in the Moluccas, whom he had bought in Malacca some time back; this man was a perfect master of the Spanish language, and, with the assistance of one of the islanders of Subuth as interpreter, who knew the language of the Moluccas, our men managed all their communications. This slave had been present at the battle of Mauthan, and had received some slight wounds in it. For which reason he lay all day long nursing himself. Serrano, who could manage nothing without him, spoke to him very harshly, and told him that he had not ceased to be a slave and bondsman because Magellan was dead, but that the yoke of slavery would be heavier, and that he would be severely flogged unless he did the services required of him more zealously.

This slave conceived an intense hatred of us from these words ; but, concealing his anger, he went a few days after to the Chief of Subuth, and told him that the greed of the Spaniards was insatiable, that they had resolved and determined, after they had conquered the King of Mauthan, to make a quarrel with him and take him away prisoner, and there was no other remedy possible than to anticipate their treachery by treachery. The savage believed it all. He made peace secretly with the King of Mauthan and the others, and they plotted our destruction. Serrano, the commander, with all the rest of his officers, who were about twenty-seven in number, were invited to a solemn banquet. They, suspecting no evil—for the savages had cunningly dissimulated in everything—land, careless and unsuspecting, as men who were going to dine with the chief would do. Whilst they were feasting they were set upon by those who had been placed in ambush. Shouts were raised on all sides, and news flew to the ships that our men were murdered, and that everything on the island was hostile to us. Our men see from the ships that the beautiful cross which they had hoisted on a tree was hurled to the ground, and kicked to pieces by the savages with great fury. But the remaining Spaniards, who had stopped on board, when they knew of their comrades' murder, feared some still greater treachery. Wherefore, when they had weighed anchor, they begin to set sail quickly. Shortly after, Serrano was brought down to the shore bound most cruelly, and he begged them to redeem him from so harsh a captivity. He said he had prevailed upon them to permit his being ransomed, if our men would only do it.

Though our men thought it shameful to leave their commander in this way, yet, fearing fraud and treachery, they put out to sea, leaving Serrano on the shore, weeping bitterly, and imploring the help and assistance of his fellow-countrymen with great and grievous lamentation. The Spaniards sailed along, sad and anxious, having lost their commander and their shipmates, not only alarmed by their loss and by the slaughter of their mates, but because their number was reduced so low that it was quite insufficient for the management of three ships. Wherefore they hold a council, and, having taken the votes, they agree that there was nothing better to do than to burn some one of the three ships, and keep only two.

So they go to an island near, Cohol[1] by name, and transfer the equipment to the other two ships, and burn the third. Then they sailed to the island called Gibeth. Though they found that it was rich in gold and ginger and many other things, yet they thought it better not to stay there long, because they could not, by any kindness, attract the Indians to them. And their scantiness of number prevented their fighting. Thence they went to the island Porne (Borneo). There are two great and rich islands in this archipelago, one of which was called Siloli, the king of which had six hundred children; and the other Porne.

Siloli was greater than the one called Porne. For it takes nearly six months to sail round it, but Porne only three. But just so much as the former is larger, so much is the latter better situated as regards fertility of soil, and more famed also for the size of a city of the same name as itself. And, as Porne must be considered of more importance than any of the other islands which they had examined, and

[1] Bohol.

seemed to be the source whence the others received their good customs and civilization (cultum vitæ), I have resolved to touch, in a few words, upon the customs and laws of these peoples. All these islanders are Caphræ, that is, heathen, and worship the sun and moon. They ascribe the rule of the day to the sun, but that of the night to the moon; the former they call male, and the latter female; and them, too, they call the parents of the stars, which they deem to be all gods, though small ones. They salute the rising sun with certain hymns before they worship it. This they do also to the moon, when it shines at night, to whom they pray for children, and fruitful increase of cattle, and abundant fruits of the earth, and other things of that sort.

But they practise justice and piety, and specially do they love peace and quiet, but war they greatly detest, and they honour their king as a god whilst he is bent upon peace. But if he be too desirous of war, they rest not till he has fallen by the hand of the enemy in battle. Whenever he has determined to wage war, which is rarely done, he is placed by his subjects in the vanguard, where he is compelled to bear the whole onslaught of the enemy. Nor do they fight against the enemy with any spirit until they know that their king is dead; then, first do they begin to fight for their liberty and for their future king, nor has there ever been seen among them a king who began a war who has not died in battle. Wherefore they rarely wage war, and think it unjust to extend their territories; but the special care of all is not wantonly to attack either the neighbouring or the distant peoples. But if at any time they are attacked, they meet force by force (par pari referunt). But lest the mischief should spread farther they look immediately to making peace. There can be nothing more honourable among them than to be the first to ask for peace, nor more disgraceful than to be anticipated in asking for it, and they think it shameful and hateful to refuse it to anyone, even if he had attacked them without provocation. And all the neighbouring people unite against the one (who refuses peace) for his destruction, as against a cruel and impious man. Whence it happens that they almost always enjoy quiet and repose. There is no robbery among them, and no murder. No one but his wives and children may speak to the king, except by means of canes, which they place to his ear from a distance, and whisper what they wish through them. They say that man, after his death, has no feeling, as he had none before his birth. They have small houses, built of logs and of earth, partly roofed with rubble, and partly with palm leaves. [Ædes habent exiles ex lignis & terra constructas, partim rudere, partim palmatis frondibus coopertas.] It is, though, quite certain that in Porne there are twenty thousand houses. They marry as many wives as they can afford, and live on food, which bird-fowling or fishing supplies them with. They make bread of rice, and a drink which drops from the severed branches of the palm, as we said before.

Some carry on traffic in the neighbouring islands, to which they go in junks; some devote themselves to hunting; some to fishing; and others to agriculture. They have dresses of cotton, and almost all the animals that we have, except the sheep, the ox, and the ass; but their horses are very small and feeble. The produce of camphor, of ginger, and of cinnamon, is great among them. Thence our men, having saluted this king, and heaped him with presents, directed their course to the Moluccas, which had been pointed out to them by the same king. They came to the shores of the island of Solo, where they heard that there were pearls as big as dove's eggs, and sometimes as hen's eggs, but which can only be fished up from the very deepest sea. Our men brought no large pearl, because the season of the year did not allow of the fishery. But they testify that they had taken an oyster in that region, the flesh of which weighed forty-seven pounds. For which reason I could easily believe that pearls of that great size are found there; for it is clearly proved that pearls are the product of shell-fish. And to omit nothing, our men constantly affirm that the islanders of Porne told them that the king wore in his crown two pearls of the size of a goose's egg. Hence they went to the island of Gilo, where they saw men with ears so long and pendulous, that they reached to their shoulders. When our men were mightily astonished at this, they learnt from the natives that there was another island not far off where the men had ears not only pendulous, but so long and broad, that one of them would cover the whole head, if they wanted it (cum ex usu esset). But our men, who sought not monsters but spices, neglecting this non-sense, went straight to the Moluccas, and they discovered them eight months after their admiral, Magellan, had fallen in Mauthan. The islands are five in number, and are called Tarante, Muthil, Thidore, Mare, and Matthien: some on this side, some on the other, and some upon the equinoctial line.

One produces cloves, another nutmegs, and another cinnamon. All are near to each other, but small and rather narrow.

The kings (of?) Marmin began to believe that souls were immortal a few years ago, induced by no other argument than that they saw that a certain most beautiful small bird never rested upon the ground nor upon anything that grew upon it; but they sometimes saw it fall dead upon the ground from the sky. And as the Mahometans, who travelled to those parts for commercial purposes, told them that this bird was born in Paradise, and that Paradise was the abode of the souls of those who had died, these kings (reguli) embraced the sect of Mahomet, because it promised wonderful things concerning this abode of souls. But they call the bird Mamuco Diata, and they hold it in such reverence and religious esteem, that they believe that by it their kings are safe in war, even though they, according to custom, are placed in the fore front of battle. The common folk are Caphræ, and of almost the same manners and laws as the islanders of Porne; they are rather poor, as would be likely with people in whose land nothing grows except spices. These they willingly barter for poisons, namely, arsenic and what is commonly called sublimate of mercury, and for linens, in which they generally are dressed; but for what purpose they use these poisons, we have not yet found out. They live on sago bread and fish, and sometimes on parrots, and they shelter in low huts. What need of many words. Everything there is humble, and of no value, but peace, quiet, and spices. The best and noblest of which, and the greatest good possible, namely, peace, seems to have been driven by men's wickedness from our world to theirs. But avarice and the insatiable greed of the belly, have driven us to seek for spices in their unknown world. (Adeo hominum protervia salubria quaeque haud longius satis nequet protudere neque quæ luxus et libidinis appetere.) But, our men having carefully inspected the position of the Moluccas and of each separate island, and also having inquired about the habits of the kings, went to Thedori, because they learnt that in that island the supply of cloves was far above that of the others, and that its king also surpassed the other kings in wisdom and humanity. So, having prepared their gifts, they land, and salute the king, and they offer the presents as if they had been sent by Cæsar. He, having received the presents kindly, looks up to heaven, and says: "I have known now for two years from the course of the stars, that you were coming to seek these lands, sent by the most mighty King of Kings. Wherefore your coming is the more pleasant and grateful to me, as I had been forewarned of it by the signification of the stars."

   And, as I know that nothing ever happens to any man

which has not been fixed long before by the decree of fate and the stars, I will not be the one to attempt to withstand either the fates or the signification of the stars, but willingly and of good cheer, will henceforth lay aside the royal pomp and will consider myself as managing the administration of this island only in the name of your king. Wherefore draw your ships into port, and order the rest of your comrades to land; so that now at last, after such a long tossing upon the seas, and so many dangers, you may enjoy the pleasures of the land and refresh your bodies. And think not but that you have arrived at your king's kingdom. Having said this, the king, laying aside his crown, embraced them one by one, and ordered whatever food that land afforded to be brought. Our men being overjoyed at this, returned to their comrades, and told them what had happened. They, pleased above measure with the friendly behaviour and kindness of the king, take possession of the island. And when their health was completely restored, in a few days, by the king's munificence, they send envoys to the other kings, to examine the wealth of the islands, and to conciliate the other kings. Tarante was the nearest, and also the smallest, of the islands; for it has a circumference of a little more than six Italian miles. Mathien is next to it, and it, too, is small. These three produce a great quantity of cloves, but more every fourth year than the other three. These trees only grow on steep rocks, and that so thickly as frequently to form a grove. This tree is very like a laurel (or bay tree) in leaf, closeness of growth, and height; and the gariophile which they call clove from its likeness (to a nail, clavus) grows on the tip of each separate twig. First a bud, and then a flower, just like the orange flower is produced.

The pointed part of the clove is fixed at the extreme end of the branch, and then growing slightly longer, it forms a spike. It is at first red, but soon gets black by the heat of the sun. The natives keep the plantations of these trees separate, as we do our vines.   They bury the cloves in pits till they are taken away by the traders.

Muthil, the fourth island, is not larger than the rest, and it produces cinnamon.   The tree is full of shoots, and in other respects barren; it delights in dryness, and is very like the tree which bears pomegranates.   The bark of this splits under the influence of the sun's heat, and is stripped off the wood; and, after drying a little in the sun, it is cinnamon.   Near to this is another island, called Bada,[1] larger and more ample than the Moluccas.   In this grows the nutmeg, the tree of which is tall and spreading, and is rather like the walnut tree, and its nut, too, grows like the walnut; for it is protected by a double husk, at first like a furry calix, and under this a thin membrane, which embraces the nut like network.   This is called the Muscat flower with us, but by the Spaniards mace, and is a noble and wholesome spice.   The other covering is a woody shell, like that of hazel-nut, and in that, as we have already said, is the nutmeg.   Ginger grows here and there in each of the islands of the archipelago.   It sometimes grows by sowing, and sometimes spontaneously; but that which is sown is the more valuable.   Its grass is like that of the saffron, and its root is almost the same too, and that is ginger.   Our men were kindly treated by the chiefs in turn, and they, too, submitted freely to the rule of Cæsar, like the King of Thidori.   But the Spaniards, who had but two ships, resolved to bring some of each (spice) home, but to load the ships with cloves, because the crop of that was most abundant that year, and our ships could contain a greater quantity of this kind of spice.   Having, therefore, loaded the ships with cloves, and having received letters and presents for Cæsar from the kings, they make ready for their departure. The letters were full of submission and respect.   The gifts were Indian swords, and things of that sort.   But, best of all,

---

[1] Bandan.

the Mamuco Diata ; that is, the Bird of God, by which they believe themselves to be safe and invincible in battle. Of which five were sent, and one I obtained from the captain (con gran prieghi), which I send to your reverence, not that your reverence may think yourself safe from treachery and the sword by means of it, as they profess to do, but that you may be pleased by its rareness and beauty. I send also some cinnamon and nutmeg and cloves, to show that our spices are not only not worse, but more valuable than those which the Venetians and Portuguese bring, because they are fresher. When our men had set sail from Thedori, one of the ships, and that the larger one, having sprung a leak, began to make water, so that it became necessary to put back to Thedori. When the Spaniards saw that this mischief could not be remedied without great labour and much time, they agreed that the other ship should sail to the Cape of Cattigara, and afterwards through the deep as far as possible from the coast of India, lest it should be seen by the Portuguese, and until they saw the Promontory of Africa, which projects beyond the Tropic of Capricorn, and to which the Portuguese have given the name of Good Hope ; and from that point the passage to Spain would be easy. But as soon as the other ship was refitted, it should direct its course through the archipelago, and that vast ocean towards the shores of the continent which we mentioned before, till it found that coast which was in the neighbourhood of Darien, and where the southern sea was separated from the western, in which are the Spanish Islands, by a very narrow space of land. So the ship sailed again from Thedori, and, having gone twelve degrees on the other side of the equinoctial line, they did not find the Cape of Cattigara, which Ptolemy supposed to extend even beyond the equinoctial line ; but when they had traversed an immense space of sea, they came to the Cape of Good Hope and afterwards to the Islands of the Hesperides.

And, as this ship let in water, being much knocked about by this long voyage, the sailors, many of whom had died by hardships by land and by sea, could not clear the ship of the water. Wherefore they landed upon one of the islands, which is named after Saint James, to buy slaves. But as our men had no money, they offered, sailor fashion, cloves for the slaves. This matter having come to the ears of the Portuguese who were in command of the island, thirteen of our men were thrown into prison. The rest were eighteen in number. Frightened by the strangeness of this behaviour, they started straight for Spain, leaving their shipmates behind them. And so, in the sixteenth month after leaving Thedori, they arrived safe and sound on the sixth of September, at the port near Hispalis (Seville). Worthier, indeed, are our sailors of eternal fame than the Argonauts who sailed with Jason to Colchis. And much more worthy was their ship of being placed among the stars than that old Argo; for that only sailed from Greece through Pontus, but ours from Hispalis to the south; and after that, through the whole west and the southern hemisphere, penetrating into the east, and again returned to the west.

I commend myself most humbly to your Reverence. Given at Vallisoleti, on the 23rd of October, 1522.

Your most Reverend and Illustrious Lordship's

Most humble and constant servant,

MAXIMILIANUS TRANSYLVANUS.

(Printed at) Cologne, in the house of Eucharius Cervicornus, in the year of the Virgin's Child, 1523, in the month of January.

A DERROTERO OR LOG-BOOK

OF THE VOYAGE OF FERNANDO DE MAGALLANES IN SEARCH OF THE STRAIT, FROM THE CAPE OF ST. AUGUSTIN.   FRANCISCO ALBO, 1519,

Copied from the Original in "Simancas en un legajo suelto".
Additional MS., British Museum, 17, 621.
(Published by Navarrete.)

———

TUESDAY, 29th day of November, I began to take the altitude of the sun whilst following the said voyage; and whilst in the vicinity of Cape St. Augustine, and in 7° altitude on the S. side, and at a distance from the said cape a matter of 27 leagues to S.W. Wednesday, 30th of said month, I took the sun in 76°, and its declination was 22° 59', and its polar altitude was 8° 59', and the course was S.S.W.

On the 1st December, Thursday, the sun had 78° meridian altitude, and 23° 4' declination, and our distance (from the equator) 11° 4', and the course was S.S.W.

Friday, the 2nd of the said month, I took the sun in barely 80°, and its declination was 23° 3', the altitude was just 13°, and the course S.S.W.

Saturday, the 3rd of the said month, I took the sun in 82° 15', which had 23° 13' declination, and our distance was 14° 58', and the course was S.S.W.

Sunday, the 4th of the said month, the sun had 83° altitude, and 23° 17' declination; and our distance came to be 16° 17', and the course was S.S.W.

Monday, 5th of the said month, I took the sun in barely 84°, and it had 23° 21' declination; and our distance to the South came to be 17° 13', and the course was S.S.W. ¼ W.

Tuesday, 6th of the said month, the sun had 85° meridian altitude, and 23° 25' declination; and the height to the S. Pole came to be 18° 25'; the course was S.W. ¼ S.

Wednesday, 7th of the said month, I took the sun in 86° 30', and it had 23° 29' declination; our distance from the line came 18° 57', and the course was to W.S.W.

Thursday, 8th of the said month, I took the sun in 86° 30', and it had 23° 29' declination; and so our altitude came to be 19° 59', and the course was S.W., and we sounded here, and found bottom at 10 fathoms; and this day we saw land, flat beaches, and it was the day of the Conception of our Lady.

Friday, 9th of the said month (December), I took the sun in 88°, and its declination was 23° 31'; and our distance from the equinoctial line towards the South part came to be 21° 31', and the course was S.S.W., and we arose in the morning to the right of St. Thomas, on a great mountain, and south slopes along the coast in the S.S.W. direction; and on this coast, at 4 leagues to sea, we found bottom at 25 fathoms, free from shoals; and the mountains are separated one from another, and have many reefs round them; and in Brazil and St. Thomas there are many rivers and ports; and going along the coast 6 leagues there are many shoals 2 leagues out to sea, and there is a depth of 12 fathoms on them, and 10, and 8; but the coast runs N.E. and S.W. to Cape Frio, and there are many islands and rivers.

At Cape Frio there is a very large river, and to the N.E., at three leagues distance, there is the peak of a high mountain and three islands; and the cape is in 23°, and at the said cape there are three islands, and you leave them out-

side. Passing the said cape there is a large bay, and
at its entrance there is a low island, and the bay within
is very large, with many ports; it extends two leagues
from the mouth, and it is called Bay of St. Lucy; and
if you wish to pass the island, you leave it on the left
hand, and (the entrance) is narrow; but there is a depth
of 7 fathoms, and a foul bottom; but outside there is
a depth of 20 to 25 fathoms, and within, where there is
anchorage, there are 18 fathoms. In this bay there are
good people, and plenty of them, and they go naked, and
barter with fish-hooks, and looking-glasses, and little bells,
for victuals. There is a good deal of brazil wood, and this
bay is in 23°, and we entered here the day of St. Lucy, and
remained till the day of St. John, which is the 27th of the
month of December; and we set sail the same day, and
went to W.S.W., and found seven islets, and to the right
of them there is a bay, and it is called the Bay of Kings;
it has a good entrance, and in this neighbourhood, on the
31st of the month, I took the sun in 86° 45', and its declination was 22° 8', and our latitude came to be 25° 23'.

Sunday, 1st of January of the year 1520, I took the sun
in 84°, and it had 21° 23' declination; and the altitude
from the pole came to be 27° 29'; and on the days after the
first day we went to S.W., and the other to W., and the
fourth day to S.W.¼S. Thursday, the 5th, the sun was in
85° 30' of altitude, and 23° 19' of declination; so that our
distance from the line came to be 29° 49', and the course
was S.W.¼S.

On the 6th, the day of the Kings, the sun was in barely
80°, and had 21° 8' of declination; and the altitude from
the pole came to be 31°, and the course was S.W.¼W.

Saturday, the 7th, I took the sun in 78°; it had 20° 56'
of declination, and our parallel was 32° 56'; the course was
to S.W.¼S., and we went along the coast.

On the 8th I did not take the sun, but we went to

S.W.$\frac{1}{4}$S., and at night we sounded and found 50 fathoms ; and we altered the course, and went on the 9th of the said month to W.S.W.; and in the morning we sounded, and found 15 fathoms, and we went till midday, and saw land, and there I took the sun in 76°, and it had 20° 31' of declination ; and at night we anchored in a bottom of 12 fathoms—34° 31'.

Tuesday, 10th January (1520), I took the sun in 75°; it had a declination of 20°, and our latitude came to 35°. We were to the right of the Cape of Sta. Maria. Thence forward the coast runs East and West, and the land is sandy ; we gave it the name of Montevidi (now they call it correctly Santovidio), and between it and the Cape Sta Maria there is a river which is called (de los Patos) Duck River. From thence we went on forward through fresh water, and the coast runs E.S.E. and W.N.W. for ten leagues distance ; after that it trends N.E. and S.W. as far as 34$\frac{1}{2}$°, with a depth of 5, 4 and 3 fathoms; there we anchored, and sent the ship *Santiago* along the coast to see if there was a roadstead, and the river is in 33$\frac{1}{2}$°. To the N.E. we found some islets, and the mouth of a very large river (it was the river of Solis), and it went to the N. Here they turned back to the ships, and the said ship was away from us a matter of 25 leagues, and they were 15 days in coming ; and during this time two other of our ships went in a southerly direction to see if there was a roadstead for staying at ; and those went in the space of two days, and the Captain-General went thither, and they found land to the S.S.W., 20 leagues distance from us, and they were four days in coming ; and on returning we took in water and wood, and we went away from there, tacking from one tack to the other with contrary winds, until we came in sight of Montevidi ; and this was on the 2nd day of the month of February, the day of our Lady of the Candlemas ; and at night we anchored at 5 leagues from the mountain, and it lay to

the S.E. and a quarter S. of us. Afterwards, on the morning of the 3rd, we set sail for the South, and we sounded,
and found 4, 5, 6, and 7 fathoms, always increasing in
depth; and this day we took the sun in 68° 30'; it had
13° 35' declination, and our latitude came to 35°.

Saturday, 4th February, we anchored in a depth of seven
fathoms, the ship San Antonio having got leaky, and we
were there till the 5th, and afterwards we weighed on the
6th, and stood on the south course, and at night we anchored
in eight fathoms, and remained there till next day.

The 7th we set sail to reconnoitre better the coast, and
we saw that it trended S.E. $\frac{1}{4}$ S.; after that we took another
tack and anchored in 8 fathoms, and there we took the sun
in 66° 30', and it had 12° 15' declination, with which our
distance from the equinoctial line to the south came to be
$35\frac{3}{4}$°; after that we sailed the same day, and at night we
anchored in 9 fathoms, and stood for Cape Santanton [Cabo
Blanco] it was to the south in 36°, and this was Tuesday,
the 7th.

On the 8th we set sail from the said point, and it is north
and south with Montevidi, and 27 leagues distant from it;
this coast runs N. and S. [the width of the Rio de la Plata
is 27 leagues]; from that place forward we went along the
coast round the cape of St. Polonia; after that the coast
trends from N.E. to S.W. The said cape is in 37°, and the
land sandy and very low, it has sea of shallow depth for
a distance of two leagues from land, of 8, 9, and 10 fathoms;
so we ran all this day to the S.W., and the night and day.

Thursday, 9th of February, I took the sun in $63\frac{1}{4}$°; it
had $11\frac{1}{2}$° declination, and the altitude came to be 38° 30';
the coast can be sounded, and not very high nor moun-
tainous, and we made out many smokes along the coast;
this coast runs E.W. $\frac{1}{4}$ N.W. S.E., and the point is called
Punta de las Arenas.

On the 10th I took the sun in 62° $\frac{1}{3}$, and it had 11° 8'

declination, our distance from the equinoctial came to be
38° 48', and the coast runs E. W., and it is a very pretty
coast for running in one or other direction.

On the 11th of the said month, I took the sun in 62°, it
had 10° 47' declination, and the altitude came to be 38° 47',
and the course was W. ¼ N.W., and the coast ran east and
west from the Point de las Arenas; to this place there is a
very good coast, with soundings, with many little green
hills and low land.

Sunday the 12th, we did not take the sun, but from the
day before till midday we began to run to S.W. and to
S.W. and a quarter W., and to W.S.W., and W. and a
quarter S.W., but I calculate that the whole course was
W.S.W., and this run was from midday of the 11th, till
nightfall of the 12th, and at that hour we anchored in 9
fathoms, and further on in 13 fathoms, and after that we
had anchored we saw land, and we set sail to the N., and
this was on the 13th, and in the morning we were alongside
of some shoals, where the Victoria bumped several times.

Item, the same day we were at anchor, and we did not
take the sun's altitude, and we were in soundings of 7
fathoms, and we remained there till the 14th, and the said
day I took the sun in 60½°, and it had 9° 41' declination,
and our altitude came to 39° 11'.

On the 15th of the said month I took the sun in 60°, and
it had 9° 13' declination, and our distance came to be
39° 19', and we sailed a south course.

Thursday the 16th, we could not take the sun until the
18th, and on that day we were in 39¼°; and the next day,
the 19th, we were in 39⅓°, and this day we went to S.W.,
and we went by this course, and could not take the sun
until the 20th of the month.

On the 20th I took the sun in 57°, it had 7° 27' declination, and our distance to the south came to 40° 17'.

. On the 21st, I took the sun in 55°, it had 7° 4' declination, our altitude came to 42° 4', the course was S.W. ¼ W., and we sounded and found bottom at 55 fathoms.

Wednesday the 22nd, I took the sun in 53°, it had 6° 41' declination, and our distance came to 43° 26', the course was S.W. ¼ W.; at night we sounded and found bottom at 55 fathoms.

On the 23rd I took the sun in 53¼°, it had 6° 18' declination, our distance from the line came to be 43° 3', the course was W.N.W.

On the 24th I took the sun in 53°, it had 5° 54' declination, our altitude from the pole came to 42° 54', and our course was W.N.W., and we were to the right of a very large bay, to which we gave the name of Bay of St. Matthew, because we found it on his day; we entered well in, and could not find bottom until we were entirely inside, and we found 80 fathoms, and it has a circuit of 50 leagues, and the mouth is to the N.W., and it is in the altitude of 42½°.

On the 25th I did not take the sun, but I took it on the 26th, in 51⅔°, and it had 5° 7' declination, by which we found ourselves in 43° 27' to the south of the line, and the coast runs N.W. S.E. ¼ N.S.

On the 27th I took the sun in 50¼°, and it had 4¾° declination, and so our altitude came to be 44°; and here to the right hand we found a bay, and three leagues before it there are two rocks, and they lie East and West with the said bay, and further on we found another (bay), and there were in it many sea wolves, of which we caught eight, and on this land there are no people, but it is very good land, with pretty plains without trees, and very flat country.

Tuesday, 28th, I took the sun in 48½°, and it had 4° 21' declination, and so we found ourselves in 44° 21', and the course was to the south, and at night we saw land to W.N.W.

On the 29th I took the sun in 48½°, and this day it had

4° declination, by which we found ourselves in 45½°, and the
course was to S.S.W. and to W.S.W. and to W.N.W., and
I give the whole of the run as to W.S.W. until I took the
sun, and afterwards we were two days that we could not
take it.

On Friday, 2nd of March, I took the sun in 43° 50′, it
had 3° 10′ declination, with which our distance came to be
47°; and after that we did not take the sun again until we
entered a port called St. Julian, and we entered there on
the last day of March, and remained there till the day of
St. Bartholomew, which is the 24th of August, and the
said port is in 49⅔°, and there we caulked the ships, and
many Indians came there, who go covered with skins of
antas, which are like camels without humps, and they carry
some bows of canes very small like the Turkish, and the
arrows are like theirs, and at the point they have a flint tip
for iron, and they are very swift runners, and well made
men, and well fashioned. We sailed thence on the 24th of
the said month of August, and went along the coast to
S.W. ¼ W., a matter of 30 leagues, and found a river called
Santa Cruz, and we entered there on the 26th of August,
and remained till the day of S. Lucas, which is the 18th of
the month of October, and there we caught much fish, and
we took in water and wood, and this coast is well defined
and with good marks.

Thursday, the 18th of October, we sailed from the said
river of Santa Cruz, with contrary winds, we went for two
days tacking about, and then we had a fair wind, and went
to the S.S.W. for two days, and in that time we took the
sun in 50⅔°, and it was on the 20th.

On the 21st of the said month, I took the sun in exactly
52°, at five leagues from the land, and there we saw an opening like a bay, and it has at the entrance, on the right
hand a very long spit of sand, and the cape which we discovered before this spit, is called the Cape of the Virgins,

and the spit of sand is in 52° latitude, and 52½° longitude, and from the spit of sand to the other part, there may be a matter of 5 leagues, and within this bay we found a strait which may be a league in width, and from this mouth to the spit you look East and West, and on the left hand side of the bay there is a great elbow, within which are many shoals, but when you enter the strait, keep to the North side, and when you are in the strait go to the S.W., in the middle of the channel, and when you are in the strait, take care of some shallows less than three leagues from the entrance of the straits, and after them you will find two islets of sand, and then you will find the channel open, proceed in it at your pleasure without hesitation; and passing this strait we found another small bay, and then we found another strait of the same kind as the first, and from one mouth to the other runs East and West, and the narrow part runs N.E. and S.W., and after we had come out of the two straits or narrows, we found a very large bay, and we found some islands, and we anchored at one of them; and took the sun, and found ourselves in 52⅓°, and thence we came in S.S.E. direction, and found a spit on the left hand, and from thence to the first mouth there will be a matter of 30 leagues; after that we went to S.W. a matter of 20 leagues, and there we took the sun, and we were in 53⅔°, and from there we returned to N.W., a matter of 15 leagues, and there anchored in 53° latitude. In this strait there are a great many elbows, and the chains of mountains are very high and covered with snow, with much forest. After that we went to N.W. and a quarter W., and in this course there are many islets; and issuing from this strait the coast turns to the north, and on the left hand we saw a cape with an island, and we gave them the name of Cape Fermoso and Cape Deseado, and it is in the same latitude as the Cape of the Virgins, which is at the beginning of the straits, and from the said Cape Fermoso we afterwards went to N.W. and to N., and to N.N.E., and we went in this course two days and three nights, and in the morning we saw land of pointed hills, and it runs North and South (thus runs the coast of the South sea) and from this land to Cape Fermoso there is a matter of 20 leagues, and we saw this land the 1st December.

Now I will commence the course and latitude of this voyage after this land, and the 1st day of December, when we were opposite to it; it is in latitude 48°.

December—

On the 2nd of December we did not take the sun, but we went to the N.N.E., and were in 47¼°, and this day we found ourselves that much ahead,[1] as all this country is in the same altitude.

On the 3rd, we went N.W., and found ourselves in 46° 30′.

,,	4th, to N.W.,	45½
,,	5th, to N. ¼ N.W.	44¼
,,	6th, to N.E. ¼ E.	44
,,	7th, to N.E. ¼ E.	43⅔
,,	8th, to N.E. ¼ N.	43¼
,,	9th, to N.N.E.	42⅔
,,	10th, to N.E. ¼ E.	42 12′.
,,	11th, to N.E. ¼ E.	41⅔
,,	12th, to N.E. ¼ E.	41¼ .
,,	13th, to N.E. ¼ N.	40
,,	14th, to N.	38¾
,,	15th, to N. ¼ N.E.	38
,,	16th, to N. ¼ N.W.	36½
,,	17th, to N.W. ¼ N.	34½
,,	18th, to N. ¼ N.W.	33½
,,	19th, to N.W.	32¾
,,	20th, to N.W.	31¾
,,	21st, to N.W.	30⅔

---

[1] "Tanto abante." These words are doubtful.

On the 22nd, to W. $\frac{1}{4}$ S.W., and found ourselves in 30$\frac{2}{3}$°

   ,,   23rd, to W.N.W.   ..   30

   ,,   24th, to W.N.W.   29$\frac{3}{4}$

   ,,   25th, to W.N.W.   29$\frac{1}{2}$

   ,,   26th, to N.W. $\frac{1}{4}$ W.   28$\frac{3}{4}$

   ,,   27th, to N.W. $\frac{1}{4}$ W.   27$\frac{2}{3}$

   ,,   28th, to N.W. $\frac{1}{4}$ W.   26$\frac{2}{3}$

   ,,   29th, to W.N.W.   26$\frac{1}{3}$

   ,,   30th, to W., 12 leagues.

   ,,   31st, to N.W.   25$\frac{1}{2}$

Year 1521—January—

On the 1st, to W. $\frac{1}{4}$ N.W.   25

   ,,   2nd, to W.N.W.   24

   ,,   3rd, to N.W. $\frac{1}{4}$ W.   23$\frac{1}{2}$

   ,,   4th, to W.N.W.   22

   ,,   5th, to W. $\frac{1}{4}$ S.W.   23

   ,,   6th, to W. $\frac{1}{4}$ NW.   22

   ,,   7th, to W., 25 leagues.

   ,,   8th, to W., 23 leagues.

   ,,   9th, to W. $\frac{1}{4}$ N.W.   ,,   22$\frac{1}{4}$

   ,,   10th, to W. $\frac{1}{4}$ N.W.   22

   ,,   11th, to W. $\frac{1}{4}$ N.W.   21$\frac{3}{4}$

   ,,   12th, to W. $\frac{1}{4}$ N.W.   21$\frac{1}{3}$

   ,,   13th, to W. $\frac{1}{4}$ N.W,   21

   ,,   14th, to N.W. $\frac{1}{4}$ W.   20$\frac{1}{2}$

   ,,   15th, to W.N.W.   19$\frac{1}{2}$

   ,,   16th, to W.N.W.   ,, -   19

   ,,   17th, to W.N.W.   18$\frac{1}{4}$

   ,,   18th, to W.N.W.   17$\frac{1}{2}$

   ,,   19th, to N.W. $\frac{1}{4}$ W.   16$\frac{1}{4}$

   ,,   20th, to N.W. $\frac{1}{4}$ W.   ,,   .   15

   ,,   21st, to S.W.   15$\frac{2}{3}$

   ,,   22nd, to S.W.   16$\frac{3}{4}$

   ,,   23rd, to W. $\frac{1}{4}$ N.W.   16$\frac{1}{2}$

   ,,   24th, to W. $\frac{1}{4}$ N.W.   16$\frac{1}{4}$

And in this neighbourhood we found an islet with trees on it. It is uninhabited; and we took soundings at it, and found no bottom, and so we went on our course. We called this islet San Pablo, having discovered it on the day of his conversion, and it is......[1] leagues from that of Tiburones.

On the 25th of the said month, to N.W. $\frac{1}{4}$ W., in 15$\frac{3}{4}$°

,,	26th	,,	to N.W. $\frac{1}{4}$ W., in 15$\frac{1}{3}$
,,	27th	..	to N.W. $\frac{1}{4}$ W., in 15
,,	28th	..	to W.N.W., in 14$\frac{1}{2}$
,,	29th	,,	to W.N.W., in 13$\frac{3}{4}$
,,	30th		to W. $\frac{1}{4}$ N.W., in 13$\frac{1}{2}$
,,	31st	,,	to W. $\frac{1}{4}$ N.W., in 13$\frac{1}{3}$

February—

On the	1st		to N.W., in 13
,,	2nd		to N.W., in 12$\frac{1}{2}$
,,	3rd	,,	to N.W., in 11$\frac{3}{4}$
,,	4th	,,	to N.W., in 11$\frac{3}{4}$

In this latitude we found an uninhabited island, where we caught many sharks, and therefore we gave it the name of Isle of Tiburones, and it is with the Strait N.W. and S.E. $\frac{1}{4}$ E. and W., and it is in 10$\frac{2}{3}$° S. latitude, and is distant . . . leagues from the Ladrone Islands.

On the 5th Feb.,		to N.W.,	in 10°
,,	6th ,,	to N.W.,	in 9$\frac{1}{4}$
,,	7th ,,	to N.W.,	in 8$\frac{2}{3}$
..	8th ,,	to N.W.,	in 7$\frac{2}{3}$
,,	9th ,,	to N.W. $\frac{1}{4}$ W.,	in 6$\frac{1}{2}$
,,	10th ,,	to N.W.,	in 5
..	11th ,,	to N.W.,	in 2$\frac{1}{2}$
,,	12th ,,	to N.W.,	in 1
..	13th ,,	to N.W.,	in – 30' N. of the line.
,,	14th ,,	to N.W.,	in 1 N. latitude.
,,	15th ,,	to N.W.,	in 1$\frac{3}{4}$

---

[1] The MS. of the British Museum has "9", which must be an error.

On the 16th Feb., to W.N.W.,   in $2\frac{1}{2}°$

  ,,   17th   ,,   to W.N.W.,   in $3\frac{1}{2}$

  ,,   18th   ,,   to W.N.W.,   in   5

  ,,   19th   ,,   to W.N.W.,   in $5\frac{3}{4}$

  ,,   20th   ,,   to W.N.W.,   in $6\frac{1}{2}$

  ,,   21st   ,,   to W.N.W.,   in   8

  ,,   22nd   ,,   to W.N.W.,   in $9\frac{1}{2}$

  ,,   23rd   ,,   to W.N.W.,   in $11\frac{1}{2}$

  ,,   24th   ,,   to W. $\frac{1}{4}$ N.W., in 12

  ,,   25th   ,,   to W. $\frac{1}{4}$ N.W., in $12\frac{1}{3}$

  ,,   26th   ,,   to W.,   in 12

  ,,   27th   ,,   to W.,   in 12

  ,,   28th   ,,   to W. $\frac{1}{4}$ N.W., in 13

March, 1521—

On the 1st March, to W.,   in 13

  ,,   2nd   ,,   to W.,   in 13

  ,,   3rd   ,,   to W.,   in 13

  ,,   4th   ,,   to W.,   in 13

  ,,   5th   ,,   to W.,   in 13

On the 6th (March), to W., in 13°. This day we saw land, and went to it, and there were two islands, which were not very large; and when we came between them, we turned to the S.W., and left one to the N.W., and then we saw a quantity of small sails coming to us, and they ran so, that they seemed to fly, and they had mat sails of a triangular shape, and they went both ways, for they made of the poop the prow, and of the prow the poop, as they wished, and they came many times to us and sought us to steal whatever they could; and so they stole the skiff of the flag-ship, and next day we recovered it; and there I took the sun, and one of these islands is in $12\frac{2}{3}°$, and the other in 13° and more (N. latitude); and this island of 12° is with that of Tiburones W.N.W. and E.S.E. (and it appears to be 20 leagues broad at the N. end), from the island of 12° we

sailed on the 9th of March, in the morning, and went W. $\frac{1}{4}$
S.W.

The islands of Ladrones are 300 leagues from Gilolo.

On the 9th of March, to W. $\frac{1}{4}$ S.W., in 12°

   ,,   10th   ,,   to W. $\frac{1}{4}$ S.W., in 12$\frac{1}{3}$

   ,,   11th   ,,   to W. $\frac{1}{4}$ S.W., in 11$\frac{1}{2}$

   ,,   12th   ,,   to W. $\frac{1}{4}$ S.W., in 11

   ,,   14th   ,,   to W. $\frac{1}{4}$ S.W., in 10$\frac{2}{3}$

   ,,   15th   ,,   to W. $\frac{1}{4}$ S.W., in 10

On the 16th (March) we saw land, and went towards it
to the N.W., and we saw that the land trended north, and
that there were many shoals near it, and we took another
tack to the south, and we fell in with another small island,
and there we anchored: and this was the same day, and
this island is called Suluano, and the first one is named
Yunuguan; and here we saw some canoes, and we went to
them, and they fled; and this island is in 9$\frac{2}{3}$° N. latitude and
in 189° longitude from the meridian. To these first islands,
from the archipelago of St. Lazarus. . . .

Ytem. From the Strait of All Saints and Cape Fermoso
to these two islands, there will be 106° 30' longitude, which
strait is with these islands in a straight course W.N.W.
and E.S.E., which brings you straight to them. From here
we went on our course.

Leaving these islands, we sailed W., and fell in with the
island of Gada, which is uninhabited, and there we provided
ourselves with water and wood. This island is very free
from shoals.

From here we departed and sailed W., and fell in with a
large island called Seilani, which is inhabited, and contains
gold; we coasted it, and went to W.S.W., to a small inhabited island called Mazaba. The people are very good,
and there we placed a cross upon a mountain; and from
thence they showed us three islands in the W.S.W. direction,
and they say there is much gold there, and they showed us

how they gather it, and they found small pieces like beans and like lentils ; and this island is in $9\frac{1}{3}$° N. latitude.

We departed from Mazaba and went N., making for the island of Seilani, and afterwards coasted the said island to the N.W. as far as 10°, and there we saw three islets; and we went to the W., a matter of 10 leagues, and then we fell in with two islets, and at night we stopped ; and on the morrow we went S.W. and $\frac{1}{4}$ S., a matter of 12 leagues, as far as $10\frac{1}{3}$°, and there we entered a channel between two islands, one called Matan, and the other Subo ; and Subo, with the isle of Mazaba and Suluan, are E.W. $\frac{1}{4}$ N.W.S.E. ; and between Subo and Seilani we saw a very high land to the north, which is called Baibai, and they say that there is in it much gold and provisions, and much extent of land, that the end of it is not known.

From Mazaba and Seilani and Subo, by the course which we came, towards the south part, take care ; for there are many shoals, and they are very bad ; for this a canoe would not stop which met us in this course.

From the mouth of the channel of Subo and Matan we went west in mid-channel, and met with the town of Subu, at which we anchored, and made peace, and there they gave us rice and millet and flesh ; and we remained there many days ; and the king and the queen, with many people, became Christians of their free will.

We sailed from Subu, and went S.W. till $9\frac{3}{4}$° between the head of Subu and an island called Bohol; and on the W. side of the head of Subu there is another, which is named Panilongo, and it belongs to black men ; and this island and Subu contain much gold and much ginger, and it is in $9\frac{1}{3}$°, and Subu in $10\frac{1}{3}$°; and so we came out of the channel, and came ten leagues to the S., and anchored off the island of Bohol, and there of the three ships we made two, and burned the other, not having crews enough ; and this island is in $9\frac{1}{2}$°.

Q

We sailed from Bohol to Quipit.to the S.W., and came to anchor at the same anchorage to the right of a river; and in the offing to the N.W. part there are two islets, which are in 8½°, and there we could not get provisions, for there were none, but we made peace with them; and this island of Quipit has much gold, ginger, and cinnamon, and so we decided on going to seek provisions; and from this head of Quipit to the first islands there will be a course of 112 leagues; it lies with them E.W.¼N.E. S.W., and this island lies due East and West.

From thence we sailed and went to W.S.W., and to S.W. and W., until we fell in with an island in which there were very few people, and it was named Cuagayan; and here we anchored on the N. side of it, and we asked where the island of Poluan was, to get provisions of rice, for there is much of it in that island, and they load many ships for other parts; and so they showed us where it was, and so we went to the W.N.W., and fell in with the head of the island of Poluan. Then we went to N.¼N.E., coasting along it until the town Saocao, and there we made peace, and they were Moors; and we went to another town, which is of Cafres; and there we bought much rice, and so we provisioned ourselves very well; and this coast runs N.E. S.W., and the cape of the N.E. part is in 9⅓°, and the part of S.W. is in 8⅓°; and so we returned to S.W. as far as the head of this island, and there we found an island, and near it there is a shoal, and in this course, and along Poluan, there are many shoals, and this head lies E.W. with Quipit, and N.W. S.E.¼E.W. with Cuagayan.

From Poluan we sailed for Borney, and we coasted the above-named island, and went to its S.W. head, and near there found an island which has a shoal on the E.; and in 7½° we had to change the course to W., until running 15 leagues; after that we ran S.W., coasting the island of Bornei until the city itself; and you must know that it is

necessary to go close to land, because outside there are
many shoals, and it is necessary to go with the sounding
lead in your hand, because it is a very vile coast, and
Bornei is a large city, and has a very large bay, and inside
it and without it there are many shoals; it is, therefore,
necessary to have a pilot of the country. So we remained
here several days, and began to trade, and we made good
agreements of peace; and after that they armed many
canoes to take us, which were 260 in number, and they
were coming to us, and as we saw them we sailed in great
haste, and we went outside and we saw some junks coming,
and we went to them, and we captured one, in which was
a son of the King of Luzon, which is a very large island,
and also the captain let him go without the counsel of anyone.

Borney is a large island, and there is also in it cinnamon,
mirabolams, and camphor, which is worth much in these
countries; and they say that when they die they embalm
themselves with it. Borney is in 5° 25′ latitude—that is,
the port itself—and 201° 5′ of longitude from the line of
demarcation, and from here we sailed and returned by the
same road; and this port of Borney lies E.N.E. W.S.W.
with the isle of Mazaba, and in this course there are many
islands; and from the cape at the N.E. of Bornei to Quipit
is E.W.¼N.E. S.W.

We sailed from Borney, and returned by the same course
which we had come, and so we passed between the head of
the isle of Bornei and Poluan; and we went to the W.,[1] to
fall in with the isle of Cuagayan; and so we went by the
same course to make for the island of Quipit on the S. side,
and in this course, between Quipit and Cuagayan, we saw
to the S. an island which they call Solo, in which there are
many pearls, very large—they say that the king of this
island has a pearl like an egg. This island is in 6° latitude;

[1] Query, east.

and so, going on this course, we fell in with three small
islands; and further on we met with an island named
Tagima, and they say there are many pearls there; and
this island lies with Solo N.E. S.W.¼E.W., and Tagima is
in 6⅚°. It is opposite the Cape of Quipit, and the said
cape is in 7¼°, and lies with Paluan E.S.E. W.N.W.

From here we coasted the island of Quipit on the south
side, and we went to E.¼S.E. as far as some islets; and
along the coast there are many villages, and there is much
good cinnamon in this island, and we bought some of it;
and there is much ginger on this coast; and so we went to
E.N.E., until we saw a gulf; then we went to S.E. until we
saw a large island, and thence to the cape at the east of the
island of Quipit, and at the cape of this island there is a
very large village, which collects much gold from a very
large river, and this cape is 191½° of the meridian.

We sailed from Quipit to go to Maluco, and went to S.E.,
sighting an island called Sibuco; after that we went to
S.S.E., and saw another island, called Virano Batolague;
and we went by the same course as far as the cape of this
island, and after that we saw another, which they call Candicar; and we went to the E. between the two, until we
went ahead of it; and there we entered a channel between
Candicar and another, which they call Sarangani; and at
this island we anchored and took a pilot for Maluco; and
these two islands are in 4⅔°, and the cape of Quipit in 7¼°,
and the Cape of Sibuco, on the south side, is in 6°, and the
Cape of Viranu Batologue in 5°, and from the Cape of
Quipit and Candicar the run is from N.N.W. to S.S.E.,
without touching any cape.

We sailed from Sarangani, and went S.¼S.E., until we
came opposite an island called Sanguin, and between the
two are many islets, and they are on the West side, and
this island is in 3⅔°. From Sangui we went S.¼S.E. to an
island called Sian; between them there are many islets,

and this island is in just 3°.   From Sian we went to
S¼S.W., as far as an island called Paginsara, it is in 1⅙°;
and from this island to Sarangani the run is N.S¼N.E. S.W.
in sight of all these islands.

From Paginsara we went to S.¼S.E., until we came between two islets, which lie together, N.E. and S.W., and
that one to the N.E. is named Suar, and the other is named
Atean, and one is in 1° 45′, and the other in 1½°.

From Atean we went S.S.E. until we sighted the Molucos,
and then we went to East, and entered between Mare and
Tedori, at which we anchored, and there we were very well
received, and made very good arrangements for peace, and
made a house on shore for trading with the people, and so
we remained many days, until we had taken in cargo.

The islands of the Malucos are these : Terrenate, Tidori,
Mare, Motil, Maquian, Bachian, and Gilolo, these are all
those which contain cloves and nutmeg ; and there are also
several others among them, the names of which I will mention, and in what altitude they are, and the first is Terrenate, which is on the side of the equinoctial line.

Terrenate is in altitude of	-	-	1°	0′
Tidori	„	„	- - 0	30
Mare	„	„	- - 0	15
Motil is on the line			- 0	
Maquian is to the south		-	- 0	15
Cayoan	„	„	- - 0	20
Bachian	„		- 1	
La Talata	„	„	- - ˙1	¼

La Talata (Lata-lata) lies north of Terrenate N.N.E. and
S.S.W., and that which is on the equinoctial line is 190° 30′
of longitude from the line itself, and the island of Motil
itself with Cagayan lies N.W. and S.E., and with Tagima,
which is opposite the island of Quipit, it lies N.E. and
S.W. ¼ N.S., but in these courses one cannot venture to
pass, for they say there are many shoals, and so we came

by another course, coasting the said islands. From the
islands of Maluco we sailed Saturday, 21st December, of
the said year 1521, and we went to the island of Mare, and
there took in wood to burn, and the same day we sailed
and went to S.S.W., making for Motil, and thence we went
by the same course, making for Maquian, and thence we
went to S.W., running by all these islands, and others,
which are these :—Cuayoan, Laboan, Agchian, Latalata,
and other small islands, which remain in the N.W. quarter,
and now I will say in what latitude and longitude are each
one separately, and which are those which contain cloves
and other spices. The first to the North is Terrenate,
which is in 1° North, and Tidore 40′ and Mare 15′, and
Motil on the equinoctial line, and these lie North and
South. The others to the South are these : Maqui is
in 20′, Cuayoan in 40′, and Laboan in 1°, and Latalata
in 1° 15′, ·and Bachian lies with Terrenate E.N.E. and
W.S.W. ; and to the S.E. of all these islands there is a very
large island called Gilolo, and there are cloves in it, but
very few ; therefore there are seven islands which contain
cloves, and those which have a large quantity are these :
Terrenate, Tidore, Motil, Maqui, and Bachian, which are
the five principal ones, and some of them contain nutmeg
and mace. Motil is on the line, and is in longitude of the
meridian of 191° 45′.

From Latalata we went to S.W. ¼ W., and fell in with
an island which is called Lumutola, it is in 1¾°, and on the
W. side there is another island called Sulan, and at these
islands there are many shoals, and from hence we took the
course to the South, towards an island named Buro, and
between these three, there is another island which is named
Fenado, it is in 2½°, and Buro is in 3½°, and it lies with
Bachian N.E. and S.W. ¼ N.S. in longitude 194°; and to the
East of Buro there is a very large island called Ambon, in
which they make much cotton cloths, and between it and

Buro there are some islets; take care of them, for this it is
necessary to coast the island of Buro to the East, and to
the South of it. I took the sun in 70° 24', it had 22° 36'
declination, and so the latitude came to be 3°. I was in
the Southern part of the island, and this was on the 27th
of December, on Friday. On the 28th of the said month,
I did not take the sun, but we were in the neighbourhood
of the said isle of Buro, and Bidia, which lies to the eastward.

Sunday, 29th, I took the sun in 71½°, it had 22° 21' declination, and our distance came to be 3° 51', and we were
opposite the isle of Ambon.

On the 30th I took the sun in the altitude of the day
before, in calm, it was Monday.

On the 31st I did not take the sun, we were a matter of
12 leagues from the Isle of Ambon E.N.E. and W.S.W.,
the day was Tuesday.

1522—

The 1st day of January, 1522, I took the sun in barely
73°, it had 21° 54' declination, the altitude came to be
4° 45'.

On the 2nd of the month, I took the sun in 73¾°, it had
21¾° declination, our distance came to be 5½°, the course
was to S.W., and it was Thursday.

Friday, 3rd, I did not take the sun, but the ship made
the course of S.S.W., in latitude of 6⅓°, after that we took
the course to N.W.

On the 4th of the month I did not take the sun, but
we were in 5¾°, the course was to N.W., and the day
Saturday.

Sunday, the 5th, I took the sun in 75°, it had 21° 14'
declination, the latitude came to 6° 14'.

On the 6th, Monday, I took the sun in 76°, it had 21° 2'
declination, the latitude came to be 7° 2'.

On the 7th, I took the sun in 76⅔°, it had 20° 50' decli-

nation, the latitude came to be $7\frac{1}{2}°$, and the course was to
S.W. Tuesday.

On the 8th of the month, I took the sun in $77\frac{1}{2}°$, it had
20° 37' declination, and the latitude came to be 8° 7', the
course was to S.W., and the day Wednesday, and this day
we saw some islands, which lie East and West, and this
day we entered between two of them, which are these,
Lamaluco and Aliguom; between them are two little ones
which you will leave on the right hand after entering the
channel, they are inhabited; this channel lies N.E. S.W. $\frac{1}{4}$
E.W., with Buro, and all these islands are ten in number,
and they lie E.W. $\frac{1}{4}$ N.E. S.W., and they have of longitude
a matter of 50 leagues; we ran along them, with very bad
weather from the South; we coasted them and anchored
off the last, which is called Malua, which is in $8\frac{1}{3}°$, the
others are named Liaman, Maumana, Cui, Aliguim, Bona,
Lamaluco, Ponon, Vera. We sailed from Malua and went
to the South, and found the island of Timor, and we coasted
the coast from east to west, on the north side of this
island, which is in the latitude of 9°, and the nearest land
on the north side, and this land will have 10 leagues
journey, and this coast lies with Buro N.E. S.W. $\frac{1}{4}$ N.S.,
in longitude of 197° 45', and of this island of Timor we
coasted all the coast from east to west, as far as the village
of Manvai; and first we came near the village of Queru,
and from Queru to Manvai, the coast runs N.E. S.W. $\frac{1}{4}$
N.S., and here I took the sun on the 5th day of February,
in $86\frac{2}{3}°$, and it had 12° 44' declination, so that the latitude
came to be 9° 24', and this island is very large and popu-
lous, and all the island has much sandal wood, and there
are many towns in it.

On the 8th of February I took the sun in $87\frac{1}{2}°$, and it
had 11° 42' of declination, with which our distance came to
be $9\frac{1}{6}°$, and we were at the head of the island of Timor, at

the West end, and from here to the Eastern cape the coast
runs E.N.E. to W.S.W., and it was Saturday.

Sunday, 9th of the said month, I took the sun in $88\frac{1}{6}°$,
and it had $11\frac{1}{3}°$ declination. Our latitude came to be 9° 35′,
and we were at the most salient cape of all the island, and
from there it goes falling off to the S.W. and S.

On the 10th of the same month I took the sun in $88\frac{1}{4}°$,
it had 10° 58′ declination ; our latitude came to be 9° 28′,
and the head of the island lay to the south, and the day
was Monday.

On the 11th, Tuesday, I took the sun in $88\frac{1}{4}°$, it had
$9\frac{1}{3}°$ declination; the latitude came to 9° 35′, and we were in
calm.

Wednesday, the 12th, I did not take the sun, but we
were becalmed in the neighbourhood of where we were the
the day before, or a little more.

On the 13th I took the sun in $89\frac{2}{3}°$; it had 9° 52′ declination; the latitude came to 10° 32′, and we were in the
neighbourhood of islands of which we do not know the
names, nor whether they are inhabited. They lie E.S.E.
and W.N.W. with the west cape of Timor, and from here
we took our course to the Cape of Good Hope, and went to
W.S.W.

[After this the course was W.S.W. for several days,
and there is nothing worthy of note till Tuesday, the 18th
of March, when the Victoria discovered Amsterdam Island.]

On the 18th of the said month (March), I took the sun in
$49\frac{1}{2}°$, it had 2° 55′ declination, the latitude came to be
37° 35′, and whilst taking the sun we saw a very high
island, and we went towards it to anchor, and we could not
fetch it; and we struck the sails and lay to until next day,
and the wind was W. ; and we made another tack to the
north under storm sails;[1] and this was on the 19th, and we
could not take the sun; we were east and west with the

---

[1] "Papahigos."

island, and it is in 38° [1] to the south, and it appears that
it is uninhabited, and it has no trees at all, and it has a
circumference of a matter of six leagues.

On the 20th of the said month, Thursday, I did not take
the sun, but we were east and west with the island, and we
went to N.W. and to N.N.W. and ¼ N.W., and for the whole
course I put down a matter of 15 leagues to the N.N.W.,
and in the latitude of 35½°.

On the 22nd of the said month I took the sun in 50¼°: it
had 4° 27′ declination; the latitude came to 36° 18′. The
day before we had struck the sails until the morning of the
said Saturday, and this day we set sail and went to the
N.W.

> .   .   .   .   .

On the 8th of the said month (May) I did not take the
sun; but, according to the run we had made, we thought
we were ahead of the Cape, and on this day we saw land,
and the coast runs N.E. and S.W. and a quarter east and
west; and so we saw that we were behind the Cape a
matter of 160 leagues, and opposite the river Del Infante,[2]
eight leagues distant from it in the offing; and this day we
were lying to with winds from the west and west-north-
west, and it was Thursday.

On the 9th I did not take the sun, but we made land
and anchored, and the coast was very wild, and we remained thus till next day; and the wind shifted to W.S.W.,
and upon that we set sail, and we went along the coast to
find some port for anchoring and taking refreshments for
the people who were most suffering, which we did not find.
And we stood out to sea, to be at our ease; and we saw
many smokes along the coast, and the coast was very bare,

---

[1] It is 37° 52′. This is the northernmost of the two islands, St.
Paul's and Amsterdam. The Dutch call the N. Island Amsterdam, and
the English call it St. Paul's in ordinary maps.

[2] The Great Fish River.

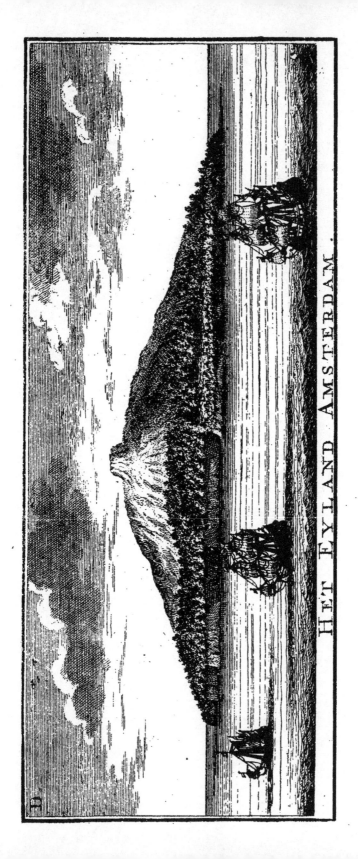

HET EYLAND AMSTERDAM.

Het Eyland St. Paulo.

without any trees, and this coast runs N.E. and S.W.: it is
in 33° latitude, and it was Saturday, 10th of May.

> •   • •   "   "   •

Friday, the 16th (May), I took the sun in 33¼°; it had
21° 6' declination; the latitude came to 35° 39', and we
were E.S.E. and W.N.W., with the Cape of Good Hope
twenty leagues off from it; and this day we sprung our
fore-mast and fore-yard, and we were all day hove to, and
the wind was W.

[The *Victoria* doubled the Cape of Good Hope between
the 18th and the 19th of May, and arrived] on the 9th of the
month of July, and anchored in the port of Rio Grande in
Santiago [of the Cape Verde Islands], and they received us
very well, and gave us what provisions we wanted; and
this day was Wednesday, and they reckoned this day as
Thursday, and so I believe that we had made a mistake of
a day; and we remained there till Sunday in the night, and
we set sail for fear of bad weather and the difficulty of the
port; and on the morrow we sent our boat on shore to get
more rice, which we wanted, and we were standing off and
on till it came.

On the 14th of July, Monday, we sent our boat on shore
for more rice, and it came at midday, and returned for more,
and we were waiting for it till night, and it did not come; and
we waited till next day, and it never came; then we went
near the port to see what the matter was, and a boat came
and told us to give ourselves up, and that they would send
us with a ship which was coming from the Indies, and that
they would put some of their people in our ship, and that
the gentlemen had so ordered. We required them to send
us our boat and men, and they said that they would bring
an answer from the gentlemen; and we said we would take
another tack, and would wait: and so we took another tack,
and we made all sail, and went away with twenty-two men,
sick and sound, and this was Tuesday, the 15th of the

month of July.   On the 14th I took the sun.   This town is
in 15° 10'.

September, 1522.

On the 4th of the said month, in the morning, we saw
land, and it was Cape St. Vincent, and it was to the north-
east of us, and so we changed our course to the S.E., to get
away from that Cape.

The manuscript has at the end :
V^{to} Simancas, 8 Setiembre, 1783, Muñoz.

D. Juan Bautista Muñoz, who died in 1822 or 1823, made a large
collection of transcripts from the Simancas and Seville archives, which
Navarréte made use of. In 1793 Muñoz published the first volume of
his *Historia del Nuevo Mundo*, which he never finished.

THE SHIP "TRINITY" AND HER CREW

After she parted company with the " Victoria".

From Navarrete.

AFTER the *Victoria* left Tidore, the crew of the *Trinity* commenced careening their ship, and took out of her and placed
in the store-house in Tidore their goods and the guns of
the *Conception*, which they had burned, and of the *Santiago*,
which was lost. Gonzalo Gomez de Espinosa determined to
leave in charge of these goods and factory the accountant,
Juan de Campos, as clerk; the officer, Luis del Molino; the
servants, Alonso de Cota, Genoese, and Diego Arias; and
Master Pedro, a bombardier.

Taking leave of the King of Tidore, the *Trinity* sailed
thence on the 6th of April 1522, with fifty men on the
muster-roll, and a cargo of nine hundred quintals of cloves.
The *Trinity* sailed for forty leagues to an island named
Zanufo, in 2 deg. 30 min. N. latitude, belonging to the King
of Tidore, thence to the open sea, where they calculated
they had two thousand leagues to run to Panama. In 20
deg. they fell in with an island, where they took in a native,
and continuing a northerly course to 42 deg., they met with
a storm which lasted five days, and they had to cut away the
castle at the prow; their poop was broken; their mainmast
was broken in two. The crews fell sick, and they returned
to seek the island from which they had taken the native;
but, not being able to fetch it, they arrived at another

twenty leagues distant from it.   This island was named
Mao, and is to the north of the island Botaha; they are
in 12 deg. and 13 deg.   This island was three hundred
leagues from the Moluccas, and they were a month and a
half in getting there; many of the crew died.   When they
arrived and anchored at the first land, which was Zanufo,
a vessel passed by which informed them that a fortnight
after the *Trinity* sailed, five or seven Portuguese sail had
arrived at Terrenate, whose captain was Antonio de Brito,
and that they were building a fortress there.   Barros states
that the first stone of this was placed by Antonio de Brito
June 24th, 1522.   The captain of the *Trinity* begged the
people of this vessel to take a man to Terrenate, who was
Bartolome Sanchez, the clerk of the ship, by whom he sent
a letter to the Portuguese captain, begging him, on the
part of His Majesty, to send him succour to prevent the
ship being lost, for his crew was sick and reduced in number.   Gonzalo Gomez, seeing that this was delayed, weighed,
and came to anchor in the port of Benaconora.   Simon
Abreu, and Duarte Roger, clerk of the King of Portugal's
factory, came there, with other people, in a caracora, and
after that came a fusta and caravel, with other armed Portuguese, who entered the *Trinity*, and gave to the captain a
letter from Antonio de Brito in answer to his, dated October
21st, 1522, which only said that people were going to
bring in his ship.   By an order which they brought from
Antonio Brito, they at once took from Gonzalo Gomez all
the letters, astrolabes, quadrants, and log-books which he
had made; they took the vessel and anchored her in the port
of Talangomi.   There were seventeen Castilians of sound and
sick in the vessel, and they took those that were well with
Gonzalo Gomez to the fortress, and next day took the sick
to the hospital.

Gonzalo Gomez complained of the violence done in taking
that which belonged to the emperor, and in his country.

They replied that he had done what the emperor, his lord, had commanded him; and they, what they ought to do by the instructions from the king, their lord. They asked him to give up the royal standard of Castile, and he answered that he could not do so, neither could he defend it, since he was in their power. Upon which they drew up some documents before a notary; and when they discharged the cargo of the ship, he asked the Portuguese to give him a certificate of what was in it, for him to render an account to His Majesty; and they replied that, if he asked for this often, they would give it him on a yard arm. In the fortress we found Juan de Campos, Diego Arias, and Alonzo, the Genoese, sick, who were three of those who had remained in Tidore with the goods of His Majesty. They said that the Portuguese had knocked down the factory-house and taken the cloves and receipts for cloves which were paid for, and all the rigging and fittings of the ships; Luis del Molino had fled, and Gonzalo Gomez called him to come to the fortress under safe conduct, but when in it they put him in irons; Master Pedro had died.

When the ship was in Tidore, the pilot, Juan Lopez Carvalho, died on the 14th February, 1522; and, between sailing thence and anchoring at Benaconora, there died in August, September, and October, thirty-one individuals, without counting three who ran away in the isle of Mao of the Ladrones.

The twenty-one Castilians of the ship and factory remained about four months as prisoners in Terrenate, until, at the end of February 1523, Captain Antonio de Brito gave them a passage to India, sending them to the island of Banda, which was a hundred leagues off, excepting the carpenter Antonio, and the caulker Antonio Basazaval, whom he said that he required. The clerk of the factory, Juan de Campos, and three other Castilians, went in a junk, of which nothing was known nor what became of those persons. The Castilians remained in Banda about four months; from thence they were conducted to Java, and coasting it they arrived at a city named Agrazue. Agrazue was a town of thirty thousand inhabitants, Mussulmans, of great trade, to which porcelain, silks, and other Chinese goods were brought from Borneo and other parts.

From Agrazue they went to Malacca, two hundred leagues distant, where Jorge de Albuquerque was captain.

They were about five months at Malacca. Four Castilians died there at the end of November 1524. The ship-boy, Anton Moreno, remained there, who was, they said, the slave of a sister of Jorge de Albuquerque, and the rest went on to India. They were twenty-five days in reaching Ceylon, which was three hundred leagues, and they went a hundred leagues more to Cochin. The clerk, Bartolomé Sanchez, and two others, went in a junk, of which nothing more was heard. In Cochin they found that the ships for Portugal had sailed a short time before their arrival, and they had to wait a year for the passage of the spice ships.

After they had been ten months in Cochin, without obtaining leave to embark, the seaman, Leon Pancaldo, and Bautista Poncero, master of the ship *Trinity*, fled secretly in the ship *Sta. Catalina*, which left them in Mozambique. There they were arrested and put on board the ship of Diego de Melo to be taken to the Governor of India, but contrary winds did not permit her departure; and, having been allowed to go ashore, Bautista Poncero died, and Leon Pancaldo hid himself in the ship of Francisco Pereira, which was going to Portugal. He remained hid till they got a hundred leagues from Mozambique. When they arrived at Lisbon they put him in prison, from which the king commanded him to be set free.

At this time, D. Vasco da Gama arrived in India as Viceroy, and the Castilians begged for leave to embark in the ships which were going to Portugal, but he would not give it. The Viceroy died in twenty days, and they elected in his stead D. Enrique de Meneses governor of Goa, who came to Cochin. Two Castilians died there, and those that remained had to wait for another year.

Gonzalo Gomez had done homage and could not get away until after constant recourse and petitions to the governor, D. Enrique de Meneses, who gave him leave, as also to the seaman, Gines de Mafra, and to Master Hans, a bombardier, when it was known there that the King of Portugal was married to Da. Catalina, sister of His Majesty the Emperor. These three individuals left Cochin in the Portuguese ships, and when they arrived at Lisbon they put them in the Limoneiro or public prison, where Master Hans died. Gonzalo Gomez and Gines de Mafra remained there about seven months, until they were set free by letters from His Majesty; but Gonzalo Gomez[1] was set free twenty-seven days before Gines, whom they supposed to be a pilot, having found some log-books in his box and two other (books), which Andres de San Martin, pilot of His Majesty, had made, which books and other writings they took, and would not return to him.

From their departure from Terrenate, in the Moluccas, to Lisbon, inclusively, there died eight individuals. What became of seven was unknown; two remained in the Moluccas; one in Malacca; and three reached Spain, besides the licentiate and priest, Morales.

Gaspar Correa says (tome iii, p. 109) :—

" In this year 1527, one Sebastian Gabato, a Basque, and a great pilot, sailed from Seville as captain-major of two ships and a caravel, who was ordered by the Viceroy of the Antilles to go and take in cargo at Maluco, and recover

---

[1] This Gomez was the alguazil who assisted Magellan so much in putting down the mutiny in the port of St. Julian.

R

the property of the Castilians, which he might find belonging to the ship of the fleet of Fernan de Magalhães which
put in in distress; and if he found any things in the possession of the Portuguese, he was to ask for them and require them from the captains on behalf of the emperor, with
all urbanity : and if they did not choose to give them up,
he was to ask for documents, with protests, which he was
to bring to the emperor for him to do in the matter what
might be for his service.   This fleet sailed from Seville,
and never more was any news heard of what became of it,
nor what end it had.   This only was known, that this fleet
had thus sailed this year, through other Castilians, who
later arrived at Maluco in another fleet, as I will relate
further on in its place."

[Correa relates, in his Tom. iii, cap. xiv, that Charles V sent a fleet
of five ships in 1527 to Maluco under Fray Garcia de Loaysa, and
that only one ship under Captain Martim Inhigo reached Maluco: he
then describes the disputes and skirmishes between the Castilians and
Portuguese.]

THE MUTINY IN PORT ST. JULIAN.

NAVARRETE gives, No. XX of his documents relating to Magellan, a copy of a document presented on Wednesday, the 22nd of May, 1521, by a servant of Diego Barbosa, on behalf of Alvaro de Mezquita, to the Alcalde of Seville, dated April 26th, 1520, which were the informations taken in Port St. Julian by Martin Mendes, clerk of the *Victoria*; Sancho de Heredia, king's notary; Gonzalo Gomes de Spinosa, Alguazil-mayor or chief constable of the fleet: he could not write, and Domingo de Barruty signed for him.

These informations were taken in consequence of a petition from Alvaro de Mezquita, captain of the *S. Antonio*, to Magellan, complaining of Gaspar de Quesada, captain of the *Conception*, and Juan de Cartagena, with about thirty armed men, having seized him the night of Palm Sunday, April 1st, 1520, and having locked him up in the cabin of Geronimo Guerra, the clerk of the *S. Antonio*. This petition was presented to Magellan when he was on shore, after hearing Mass on Sunday, the 15th of April, and he gave orders to the two clerks and Alguazil to make an inquiry on board the *S. Antonio*. His order was dated April 17th, and signed by himself and Leon de Speleta, clerk of the flag-ship. The informations taken on board the *S. Antonio* were dated Thursday, the twenty-sixth April, 1520

No. XXI of Navarrete is a letter from Juan Lopez de Recalde to the Bishop of Burgos, of May 12th, 1521, giving him an account of the arrival of the *S. Antonio* at Seville,

R 2

6th May, 1521, commanded by Geronimo Guerra, a relation
and servant of Christoval de Haro, and of the execution of
Gaspar de Quesada and others. This letter relates the story
of the mutineers and those who turned back from difficulty
and danger, and is naturally unfavourable to Magellan.

According to Navarrete, the desertion of Magellan's fleet
by the ship *S. Antonio*, was caused by Esteban Gomez, a
Portuguese pilot, who, from rivalry with Magellan, and
envy at seeing others promoted instead of himself, after the
executions, got up a conspiracy on board the *S. Antonio*,
and proposed to return to Spain. The mutineers put
Alvaro de Mezquita in irons; they then went to the coast
of Guinea, and thence to Spain. When the *S. Antonio*
arrived at Seville, Alvaro de Mezquita was handed over to
the authorities and kept in prison until the ship *Victoria*
arrived. Esteban Gomez, Juan de Chinchilla, Geronimo
Guerra, and Francisco Angulo, were also arrested; and
Magellan's wife and family were put under surveillance to
prevent their going away to Portugal. According to
Herrera, Juan de Cartagena and the priest, who were left
behind, did not come away with the *S. Antonio*, and orders
were given to send and look for them.

More ample details of the suppression of the mutiny are
given by Gaspar Correa in the following account of Magellan's voyage, in his *Lendas da India* (tome II, cap. xiv) :—

"Ferdinand Magellan went to Castile to the port of Seville,
where he married the daughter of a man of importance, with
the design of navigating on the sea, because he was very
learned in the art of pilots, which is that of the sphere. The
emperor kept the House of Commerce in Seville, with the
overseers of the treasury, with great powers, and much seafaring traffic, and fleets for abroad. Magellan, bold with
his knowledge, and with the readiness which he had to annoy
the King of Portugal, spoke to the overseers of this House

of Commerce, and told them that Malacca, and Maluco, the
islands in which cloves grew, belonged to the emperor on
account of the demarcation drawn between them both [the
Kings of Spain and Portugal]: for which reason the King
of Portugal wrongfully possessed these lands: and that he
would make this certain before all the doctors who might
contradict him, and would pledge his head for it. The
overseers replied to him, that they well knew that he
was speaking truth, and that the emperor also knew it,
but that the emperor had no navigation to that part, because he could not navigate through the sea within the
demarcation of the King of Portugal. Magellan said to
them: 'If you would give me ships and men, I would show
you navigation to those parts, without touching any sea or
land of the King of Portugal; and if not, they might cut off
his head.' The overseers, much pleased at this, wrote it to
the emperor, who answered them that he had pleasure in
the speech, and would have much more with the deed; and
that they were to do everything to carry out his service,
and the affairs of the King of Portugal, which were not to
be meddled with; rather than that everything should be
lost. With this answer from the emperor, they spoke with
Magellan, and became much more convinced by what he
said, that he would navigate and show a course outside of
the seas of the King of Portugal; and that if they gave him
the ships he asked for, and men and artillery, he would fulfil what he had said, and would discover new lands which
were in the demarcation of the emperor, from which he
would bring gold, cloves, cinnamon, and other riches. The
overseers hearing this, with a great desire to render so great
a service to the emperor as the discovery of this navigation,
and to make this matter more certain, brought together
pilots and men learned in the sphere, to dispute upon the
matter with Magellan, who gave such reasons to all, that
they agreed with what he said, and affirmed that he was a

very learned man. So the overseers at once made agreements with him, and arrangements, and powers, and regulations, which they sent to the emperor, who confirmed everything, reserving specially the navigation of the King of
Portugal ; thus he commanded and prohibited, and ordered
that everything which Magellan asked for should be given
him. On this account, Magellan went to Burgos, where the
emperor was, and kissed his hand, and the emperor gave
him a thousand cruzados alimony for the expenses of his
wife whilst he was on his voyage, set down in the rolls
of Seville, and he gave him power of life and death[1] over
all persons who went in the fleet, of which he should be
captain-major, with regard to which he assigned him large
powers. So, on his return to Seville, they equipped for
him five small ships, such as he asked for, equipped and
armed as he chose, with four hundred men-at-arms, and
they were laden with the merchandise which he asked for.
The overseers told him to give the captaincies, with regard
to which he excused himself, saying that he was new in the
country and did not know the men; and that they should
seek out men who would be good and faithful in the emperor's service, and who would rejoice to endure hardships
in his service, and the bad life which they would have to go
through in the voyage. The overseers were obliged to him
for this, and held it to be good advice, and decided to inform
the captains they might make, and the crews they might
take, of the powers which he had received from the emperor.
This they did, and they sought in Seville for trustworthy
men for captains, who were Juan de Cartagena, Luis de
Mendoça, Juan Serrano, Pero de Quesada. This fleet
having been fitted out, and the crews paid for six months,
he sailed from San Lucar de Barrameda in August of the
year 1519. So he navigated to the Canary Islands, and
took in water; whilst he was there a vessel arrived with

_____
[1] Literally, of cord and knife.

letters from his father-in-law,[1] in which he warned him to keep a good watch for his personal safety, because he had learned that the captains whom he took with him had said to their friends and relations, that if he annoyed them they would kill him, and would rise up against him. To this he replied, that he would do them no injuries so that they should have reason to act thus; and on that account he had not appointed them, but the overseers, who knew them, had given them; and whether they were good or bad, he would labour to do the service of the emperor, and for that they had offered their lives. The father-in-law showed this answer to the overseers, who greatly praised the good heart of Magellan.

"He sailed from the Canaries of Tanarife, and made the Cape Verde, whence he crossed over to the coast of Brazil, and there entered a river which is named Janeiro. There went, as chief pilot, a Portuguese named Joan Lopes Carvalhinho, who had already been in this river, and took with him a son whom he had gotten there of a woman of the country. From this place they went on sailing until they reached the Cape of Santa Maria, which Joan of Lisbon had discovered in the year 1514; thence they went to the river San Julian. While they were there taking in water and wood, Juan de Cartagena, who was sub-captain-major, agreed with the other captains to rise up, saying that Magellan had got them betrayed and entrapped. As they understood that Gaspar de Quesada was a friend of Magellan's, Juan de Cartagena got into his boat at night, with twenty men, and went to the ship of Gaspar Quesada, and went in to speak to him, and took him prisoner,[2] and made

---

[1] Diogo Barbosa.

[2] Correa seems to have made a mistake here. Quesada helped to make Alvaro de Mezquita, Magellan's relation, and captain of the *S. Antonio*, a prisoner; but what Correa relates may have been part of the plot and a stratagem of Juan de Carthagena.

a relation of his captain of the ship, in order that all three might go at once to board Magellan and kill him, and after that they would reduce the other ship of Joan Serrano, and would take the money and goods, which they would hide, and would return to the emperor, and would tell him that Magellan had got them entrapped and deceived, having broken faith with his instructions, since he was navigating in seas and countries of the King of Portugal: for which deed they would get first a safe conduct from the emperor. So they arranged matters for their treason, which turned out ill for them.

"Magellan had some suspicion of this matter, and before this should happen, he sent his skiff to the ships to tell the captains that the masters were to arrange their ships for beaching them to careen them; and with this pretext he warned a servant of his to notice what the captains answered. When this skiff came to the revolted ships they did not let it come alongside, saying that they would not execute any orders except those of Juan de Cartagena, who was their captain-major. The skiff having returned with this answer, Magellan spoke to Ambrosio Fernandes,[1] his chief constable, a valiant man, and gave him orders what he was to do, and to go secretly armed; and he sent a letter to Luis de Mendoça by him, with six men in the skiff, whom the chief constable selected. And the current set towards the ships, and Magellan ordered his master to bend a long hawser,[2] with which he might drop down to the ships if it suited him. All being thus arranged, the skiff went, and coming alongside of Luiz de Mendoça, they would not let him come on board. So the chief constable said to the captain that it was weakness not to bid him enter, as he was one man alone who was bringing a letter. Upon which the captain bade him enter. He came on board, and giving him the

---

[1] His name was Gonzalo Gomes de Spinosa; he returned to Spain.
[2] " Que fizesse grande toa."

letter, took him in his arms, shouting : 'On behalf of the
emperor, you are arrested !'"   At this the men of the skiff
came on board with their swords drawn ; then the chief
constable cut the throat of Luis de Mendoça with a dagger, for he held him thrown down under him, for so Magellan had given him orders.   Upon this a tumult arose, and
Magellan hearing it, ordered the hawser to be paid out, and
with his ship dropped down upon the other ships, with his
men under arms, and the artillery in readiness. On reaching
the ship of Mendoça, he ordered six men to be hung at the
yard-arms, who had risen up against the chief constable, and
these were seized upon by the sailors of the ship, of which
he at once made captain, Duarte Barbosa, a Portuguese, and
a friend of his : and he ordered the corpse of Mendoça to
be hung up by the feet, that they might see him from the
other ships.   He then ordered Barbosa to prepare the men
for going and boarding one of the other ships; and to avoid
doing the harm which it was in its power to have done, and
since he was a Portuguese, and the crews belonged to the
emperor, he used à stratagem, and spoke secretly to a sailor,
whom he trusted, who fled to the ship of Cartagena, where,
at night when the current set for Magellan's ship, which
was astern, the sailor seeing his opportunity, cut the cable
or loosed the ship of Cartagena, so that it drifted upon that
of Magellan, who came up, shouting : 'Treason ! treason !'
Upon which he entered the ship of Cartagena, and took
him and his men prisoners, and made captain of the ship
one Alvaro de Mesquita, whom Cartagena had arrested and
put in irons, because he found fault with him for the mutiny
which he was making.   Seeing this, the other ship at once
surrendered. He ordered Cartagena to be quartered, having
him publicly cried as a traitor ; and the body of Luis de
Mendoça also was quartered ; and he ordered the quarters
and the executed men to be set on shore, spitted on poles.
So the Castilians had great fear of him, for he kept the

mutineers prisoners in irons, and set to the pumps; during three months that he remained in this river, in which he careened and refitted his ships very well.

" When he was about to set sail, he ordered the prisoners to be set at liberty, and pardoned them, and he sent them to go along the shore, following the bank of the river until they found the headland from which they could see the sea on the other side; and whoever returned to him with this news he would give him a hundred ducats as a reward for good news. These men went for more than forty leagues, and returned without news; and they brought back two men, fifteen spans high, from a village which they found. He then sent Serrano, because his vessel was the smallest, to go along the river to discover its extremity; and he went with a strong current, which carried him without wind. And, going along thus, his ship grounded on some rocks, on which it was lost, and the boat returned laden with the crew. Magellan sent the boats thither, and they saved everything, so that only the hull was lost. Then he ordered two priests, who had taken part in the mutiny, to be set on shore, and a brother of Cartagena, whom he pardoned at the petition of Mesquita, and he left them thus banished.

" Then he sailed from the river and ran along the coast until he reached a river, to which they gave the name of Victoria, and which had high land on either side. From this river Mesquita's ship ran away, and it was not known whether they had killed him, or if he had gone of his own accord; but an astrologer and diviner told him that the captain was a prisoner, and that they were returning to Castile, but that the emperor would do them an injury.

" Then Magellan, with the three ships which he had, entered the river, through which he ran for more than a hundred leagues, and came out on the other side into the open sea, where he had a stern wind from the east, with which they ran for more than five months without lowering their sails, and they fetched some uninhabited islands, in one of which they found some savages, who lived in huts underground. They went to another island where they gave them gold for its weight of iron, by which means they collected much gold: the people also were of a good disposition, and had a king. They were well governed people, who were at war with other neighbours who were more powerful than themselves; for which reason the king became Christian, with all his people, in order that Magellan might assist him against his enemies. This Magellan offered to do, and with his armed men, and the people of the country, he went against the enemy, of whom he killed many, and burned a village. The enemy got assistance from others, and many came to fight with Magellan, who defeated them, and the struggle was a severe one. They acted with cunning, for they had placed ambuscades of men hidden in the bush, who, seeing the Castilians wearied, came out against them and killed many, and another ambuscade came out of the bush to seize the boats, which were on the beach without men: then the king came out, and fought with them, and defended the boats, and brought off the men.

"The king who had fled, seeing himself defeated, plotted treachery with the Christian king, and made an agreement with him to give him his daughter in marriage, and plighted his troth to him, that when he died, for he was already old, all would remain to him, and they would always live as friends; because the Castilians would depart, and if he did not act thus he would always make war on him: and this was with the condition that he was to find him means for killing the Castilians. And the Christian king, like a brutal man, consented to the treachery, and prepared a great feast and banquet for carrying it out, to which he invited Magellan, who went to the banquet with thirty men, of the most honourable and well dressed: while they were enjoying themselves at the banquet, the armed enemies entered, and killed Magellan, and all the Castilians, and none of them escaped, and they stripped Serrano, and dragging him along, brought him to the beach, where they executed him, and killed him thrown down on the ground.[1]

"Those who were in the ships, seeing the misfortune on shore, which the sailors who had gone in the boats related to them, raised up from among them as captain, Carvalhinho, the pilot of the flag-ship, whom all obeyed. He ordered one of the ships, which was very leaky, to be stripped, and set fire to it in the midst of the sea, so that the people on shore should not profit by the iron, and he made captain of the ship of Serrano one Gonzalo Gomez d'Espinosa, who was a relation of the astrologer,[2] who also died with Magellan, and did not divine the evil which befel him.

"The two ships departed thence, running between many islands, and they went to one which had much very fine cinnamon. From this place they went running through many islands to the island of Borneo, where they found in the port many merchant junks from all the parts of Malacca, which made frequent visits to Borneo. Here Carvalhinho sent a present to the king of scarlet cloth, and coloured silks, and other things, with which the king was much pleased, and he did him great honour, and gave him leave and safe conduct to remain on shore for twenty days, for such was their custom to give to new people, the first time that they came to their port, in which they could buy and sell freely as much as they pleased. But the king, knowing how much goods the ships contained, got up a plot to kill them, and take the ships. This treachery was concerted by the king with the Javanese who were in the port in large junks; and for this object the king showed great honour to those who went on shore, and sent refreshments to the ships, and leave

---

[1] The reader will observe that this account of Magellan's death is incorrect.

[2] Andres de San Martin.

to remain in the port as long as they pleased. Carvalhinho became suspicious at this, and ordered good watch to be kept day and night, and did not allow more than one or two men to go ashore. The king perceiving this sent to beg Carvalhinho to send him his son who had brought the present, because his little children who had seen him, were crying to see him. He sent him, very well dressed, with four men, who, on arriving where the king was, were ordered by him to be arrested. When Carvalhinho knew this he raised his moorings, and with armed men went to board a junk which was filled with many people and ready to sail. They entered this junk and plundered much gold and rich stuffs, and captured a son of the King of Luzon, who was captain of the junk and of three others which were in the port, and who had come in them to marry a daughter of this King of Borneo. They found in this junk valuable things of gold and jewellery which he had brought for his wedding; and they found there three girls of extreme beauty, whom Carvalhinho took care of, saying that he would take them to the emperor: at which all rejoiced. But he did not act thus, but slept with them, so that the Castilians were near killing him; but he divided with the Castilians so liberally that they became friends; for he agreed with the bridegroom, that he and his people should escape by night, and for that should give him much wealth of precious stones, and by night they got away by swimming; and Carvalhinho pretended to have been asleep, and woke up complaining of the watch. But the Castilians understood the deceit, and took Carvalhinho and put him in irons, and took from him all he had, and raised up as captain one Juan Bautista, master of the ship, because he understood pilot's work.[1]

"Thence they sailed and went to Maluco, Ternate, and

---

[1] Probably the Genoese pilot, whose narrative commences this volume.

Tidore, where they took to the kings the presents which
Magellan had set apart for them. They paid them great
honour, and received them hospitably, for they also gave to
their ministers ; and to the kings they gave an embassage
on the part of the emperor, relating to them his magnifi-
cence, so that both soon obeyed him, and did homage as
vassals for ever; and they established trade and prices for
buying and selling, and established factories on shore, and
began to collect cloves, and very much was brought to
them, because the Castilians gave what they asked, for they
had a superfluity of merchandise ; thu they became lords
of the land.   As the ships were much injured, they patched
them up a little, the best they could, and hastened to fill
both ships with cargo, which they did in one month.
When they were about to sail there came to the Castilians a
Portuguese, named Juan de la Rosa, who had come to
Ternate, saying he was a pilot, and would take them to
Castile, upon which they agreed with him to give him fifty
quintals of cloves in each ship, because he said he would
take them to the island of Banda, which had more riches
than Maluco.   So the Castilians rejoiced greatly at taking
this man back to the emperor, for the greater certainty as
to their discovery.   This Juan de la Rosa warned the
Castilians that they would come from India and seek for
them, and kill them all, for this was spoken of in India.
To this the Castilians gave much credit, and on that account did him great honour.   They settled with the King
of Tidore to leave with him a factor with the merchandise,
which they had, because many ships would soon come, sent
by the emperor; for which reason they should have much
cloves collected together.   They then set sail, making de
la Rosa captain of the ship of Carvalhinho.

" When they were at sea they freed him from his irons,
from the need they felt for his navigation, and they went to
the island of Banda, where they restored to Carvalhinho

his captaincy, and they went to Banda, where they took samples of nutmeg and mace, as they had nowhere to take in cargo of it. All having been consulted, they set sail to make for the Cape of Good Hope, and navigate thence to Castile, for they did not dare take any other course. Setting sail with this design, they met with hard weather, with which the ship of Carvalhinho put into port, and that of la Rosa continued her course. Carvalhinho put into Maluco, where he discharged half the ship's cargo, and heeled her over, and repaired her as well as possible; this he did in twenty days, and again set to taking in cargo and departing; but he fell ill with the labour, and died on setting sail. They made Gonzalo Gomez d'Espinosa captain of the ship again, and he, by the instructions of Carvalhinho, took a course to search for the river (strait) through which they had come; but when at sea, the ship again took in so much water, that they ran before the wind to beach her on the first land they made, which was in Batochina, where they beached the ship, and saved from her no great quantity of goods. Whilst they were at this juncture D. Gracia Anriques arrived at Maluco, with a ship to take in cloves, which came from Malaca, and learning how these Castilians were there he sent to call them under his safe conduct, that they should all come, because if they did not he would hold them as enemies, and would go at once and fetch them. The Castilians therefore, constrained by fortune, went to where D. Gracia was, like as men who were lost, so that D. Gracia had compassion upon them, and gave them a good reception, and supplied them with necessaries, and having laden his ship, he embarked them all with him, and they were more than thirty, and he took them to Malaca, where Jorge d'Albuquerque was captain, who ordered the factor to give them provisions for their maintenance, and in the monsoon to send them to India, where D. Duarte [de Meneses] was governor. He com-

manded those who chose to be written down in the rolls for
pay, and he forbade the ships of the kingdom to take them,
that they might not return to Castile ; and in fact all died,
only Gonzalo Gomes d'Espinosa passed to Portugal in the
year 1525, and he was made a prisoner in Lisbon, and set
at liberty by a letter which the empress sent to the king.

" The other ship followed its course, so that la Rosa made
the Cape of Good Hope, and while she was going near the
land Pero Coresma, who was going to India in a small ship,
met her, and spoke her ; and he was told she belonged to
the emperor, and came from Maluco, and it did not come
into his understanding to send her to the bottom, that she
might not return to Castile, and the ship entered the
watering place of Saldanha, and thence fetched Cape Verde,
where they went ashore to get wood and water ; there
some Portuguese, learning that the ship came from Maluco,
took the boat when it came ashore, with twenty Castilians ;
and as there was no ship in the port they got into a boat to
go and capture the ship ; but the ship seeing the boat come
with armed men, for the arms glittered, weighed and set
sail for Cape St. Vincent, and thence entered San Lucar
with thirteen men, for now there were no more, and it
arrived in the year 1521.   From Cape Verde they wrote to
the king about the Castilians, who remained there ; the
king ordered that they should let them go till they died,
but never to allow them to embark for any port ; and so it
was done."

COST OF MAGELLAN'S FLEET.

From Navarrete, Document No. XVII.

THE *Conception* was of ninety tons.
  „ *Victoria*   „ eighty-five tons.
  „ *S. Antonio* „ a hundred and twenty tons.
  „ *Trinity*   „ a hundred and ten tons.
  „ *Santiago* „ seventy-five tons.

SUMMARY :
Maravedis.

Five ships, with rigging, artillery, and arms, cost 3,912,241
Five ships, of 445 tons, five more or less, which makes each ton come to a cost of 8,791½ *maravedis.*

Various necessaries	415,060
Provisions, biscuit, wine, oil, fish, meat, cheese, vegetables, and barrels	1,585,551
Four months pay for 237 persons	1,154,504
Merchandise	1,679,769
Total	8,751,125

THE END.

✠

Senhor.

Acerqua do negoceo de fernam de magalhaes eu tenho feito e trabalhado quanto deus sabe, como lhe largamente tenho esprito, e agora estando xebres doente falei niso muito ryjo a el Rei apresentando lhe todolos enconuinientes que neste caso auia, apresentando lhe alem das outras cousas, quam fea cousa era e quam desacostumada receber hum Rei os uasalos doutro Rei seu amigo contra sua vontade que era cousa que antre caualeiros se nom acustumaua e se auia por mui grande erro e cousa mui feia e que eu nom acabaua em ualhadoly de lhe oferecer uosa pesoa e reinos e senhorios quando ele ja recebya estes contra uoso prazer que lhe pedia que oulhase que nom era tempo pera descontentar uosalteza e mais em cousa que lhe tam pouco inportaua e tam incerta e que muitos uasalos e omens tinha pera fazer seuos descobrimentos quando fore tempo e nam c os que de uosalteza uinham descontentes e de que uosalteza nom podia de deixar de ter sospeita que auiam de trabalhar mais por uos desseruir que por ninhũa outra cousa e que su alteza tinha ainda agora tanto que fazer em descobrir seuos reinos e senhorios e em os asentar que lhe nom deuiam de lembrar taes nouidades de que se podiam seguir escandolos e outras cousas que se bem podiam escusar apresentando lhe tambem quam mal isto parecia em anno e tempo de tal casamento e acrecentamento de divido e amor. E que me parecia que uosalteza syntiria muito saber que estes omens lhe pedem licença e nom lha dar pera

b

se tornarem que eram ja douos males recebedos contra sua
uontade e telos contra uontade deles que eu lhe pedia polo
que compria a seu seruiço e de uosalteza que de duas fizese
hūa ou lhe dese licença ou sobre-esteuese neste negocio
este anno em que se nom perderia muito e se poderia
tomar tal meio como ele fore seruido e uosalteza nom
recebese desprazer do modo com que se isto faz.

Ele senhor fycou tam espantado do que lhe dyse que eu
me espantei e me respondeo as milhores palauras do mundo
e que ele por ninhūa cousa nom queria que se fizese cousa
de que uosalteza recebese desprazer e muitas outras boas
palauras e que eu falase com ho cardeal e que lhe fizese
relaçam de tudo.

Eu senhor o tynha ja bem praticado com ho cardeal que
he a milhor cousa que qua ha e lhe nom parece bem este
negoceo e me prometeo de trabalhar quanto podese por se
escusar Falou com el Rei e chamaram per isto ho bispo de
burgos que he o que sostem este negocio. E asy huns
douos do conselho tornaram a fazer crer a el Rei que ele nom
eraua nisto a uosalteza porque nom mandaua descobrir
senam dentro no seu lemite e mui longe das cousas de
uosalteza e que uosalteza nom auia dauer por mal de se
seruir de douos uasalos seuos homens de pouca sustancia
seruindo se uosalteza de muitos dos naturaes de castela
alegando outras muitas razões. In fim me dise o cardeal
que o bispo e aqueles insistiam tanto nisto que por ora el
Rei nom podya tomar outra detriminaçam.

Tanto que xebres foi sam lhe tornei a presentar este
negoceo como digo e muito mais ele da a culpa a estes
castelhanos que pōi el Rei nisto e com tudo que ele falara a
el Rey e nos dias pasados o requeri muito sobre isto e
nunca tomou detriminaçam e asi creio que fara agora a mim
senhor parece me que uosalteza pode recolher fernam de
magalhāes que sera grande bofetada pera estes que polo
bacharel nom dou eu muito que anda casi fora de seu syso.

E fiz diligencia com dom jorge acerqua da yda laa do seu alcayde e ele diz que hira em toda maneira asy senhor que isto esta desta maneira e com tudo eu nunca deixarei de trabalhar nisto o que poder.

E nom cuide vosalteza que dise muito a el Rei no que lhe dise porque alem de ser tudo verdade o que dise esta gente como dygo nom sente nada nem el Rei tem liberdade pera dy sy fazer ate ora nada e por iso se deue de syntyr menos suas cousas. noso senhor a uida e estado de vosalteza acrecente a seu santo seruiço. de saragoça terça feira a noyte xxviii dias de setembro [1518].

Beijo as mãos de uosa alteza,

ALUARO DA COSTA.

(Torre do Tombo, Gav. 18, Maç. 8, No. 38.)

No. II.

Señor,

em xv deste Julho p chavascas moço dest'beyra R. duas cartas de vosa alteza hũa de xviij e outra de xxix do mes pasado que entendy e sem a seg^da Resumyr Respondo a vosa alteza.

Sam agora vindos em companhia a esta cidade xpovã de harõo e J° de cartajena feitor moor darmada e capitam de hũ navio e o tesourey° e esc'vã desta armada e nos Regim^tos que trazem ha cap^os contrarios ao rregm^to de frnã de magalhães E vistos p̃llo contador e feitores da casa da contr-taçam como posam mall engulyr as cousas de magalhãees foram logo da opiniam dos que nova^mte vieram.

E juntos mandarū chamar frnā de magalhaēes e
q̃seram dele sabr̃ a ordem desta armada e a causa
por que na q^rta nāao ño ya capitā som^{te}
carvalho que era piloto e nō capitam, dise
que elle a queria asy levar p̧a levar o foroll
e as vezes se pasar aela.

E lhe diseram que levava m^{tos} portugeses e que
nō era bem que levase tantos Respondeo que
ele faria na armada o q̃ q̧sese sem lhe dar co^{ta}
e que elles o no podiam faz^r sem a darē a elle pa-
saranse tantas e tam mas Rezoēes q̃ os feitores
mandarā pagar soldo a jente do maar e darmas
e nō a nēhūes dos portugeses q̃ frña de magalhaēes e Ruy faleiro tem p̧a levar e
a ysto se fez correeo a corte de castela.

E por eu v̄r a materia aberta e t̄po bē conve-
niente p̧a diz^r o que me vosa alteza mādo
me fuy a pousada de magalhaēes onde o achey
conçertando cortiços e arcas com vitoalha de cons^r-
vas e out^{as} cousas ap^rtey o fingindo que
p̃llo achar naquele acto que me pareçia
conclusā da obra de seu māao p̧posyto e por
que esta seria a derradr^a fala q̃ lhe faria lhe
queria rreduzir a memoriam quantas vezes
como bom portuges e seu amygo lhe avia
falado cont^{ra}riando lhe o tam grande erro
como fazia.

E despois de lhe pedir p̧dam se algūu escandalo
de my Reçebese na p̃tica, lhe trouxe a memoria
quantas vezes lhe avia falado e quā bem me
senp̃ Respondia e que segundo sua Reposta
senp̃ eu esperey q' o fim nō fose con tā
grande dess^rviço de vosa alteza e o que lhe
senp̃ disera era que visse que este caminho tinha tantos perigos como a Roda de Santa C^{na}

e que o devya deixar e tomar o coy'brãao[1] e tor-
nar se a sua natureza e a g̅ça de vosa alteza
donde senp̃ Reçeberia m^ce. nesta fala entrou
meter lhe todolos temores q̃ me pareçerã e erros
que fazia dise me q̃ elle n̅o poderia ja all
faz^r por sua honrra senã seguir seu caminho, eu
lhe disse que ganhar onrra indyvidam^te e adq̃ri-
da com tanta infamia n̅o era sab^r ne̅ honrra
mas antes p^ri̅v̅ãça de sab^r e d onrra por que fose
çerto q̃ a jente castelhana p^ri̅nçipall desta çidade
falando nele o aviam por h̅ome vyll e dè mãao
sangue poys em dess^rviço de seu v̅dad^ro Rey
e señor aceptava tall enpsa quanto mais semdo
p̃ ele levantada e ordenada e Requerida, que
fose ele certo que era avida por treedor
por hyr cont^ra o estado de vosa alteza, aquy
me Respondeo que ele via o erro que fazia
porem que ele esperava g̅dar muyto o s^rvi-
ço de vosa alteza e faz^r lhe muito s^rviço em sua
yda. Eu lhe dise que que̅ lhe louvase tall
diz^r o n̅o entenderia, por que caso q̃ ele n̅o
tocase a conq̃sta de vosa alteza como qr̅ q̃
achasse o q̃ dizia luogo era em grande dano
das rrendas de vosa alteza, e que este Reçebia todo o rregno e jenero de p^as [2] e que mais virtuoso
pensam^to era o que ele tinha quando me
disse que se vosa alteza mandase q̃ se
tornasse a portugall q̃ o faria sem out^ra
çerteza de merçee e que quando lha n̅o fizese
que hy estava essa serradoosa e sete v^as [3]
de pardo e h̅uas contas de bugalhos que

[1] Road to Coimbra—straight road.
[2] Pessoas.
[3] Varas.

entū me pareçia q̃ seu coraçā estava na·
vʳdade do que compria a sua honnra e conçy-
ençia, o q̃ se falou foy tanto q̃ se nō pode esc̄ver.

a q̃ⁱ sᵒʳ me começou a dar synall dizendo que lhe
dissese mais que ysto nō vinha de my e que
se v. alteza mo mandava q̃ lho disṡese e a mᶜᵉ·
q̃ lhe faria, eu lhe disse q̃ eu nō era de tantas
toneladas p̣ q̃ v. alteza me metese em tall
acto mas eu como outᵃˢ mᵗᵃˢ vezes lho dezia
aquy me q̃ⁱs honrrar dizendo q̃ se o q̃ eu come-
çey com ele levara avante sem antʳᵉvir outᵃˢ
p̣ᵃˢ q' vosa alteza fora s̄vido mas q' nᵒˡ Ribeiro
lhe disera hūa cousa e q' ño fora nada e Joam
mendez outʳᵃ q' nō atara e diseme a merçee q'
lhe prometian da p̣te de vosa alteza, aqⁱ ouve
grande amiserarse e diz' que bem sentia tudo mas
que nō sabia cousa p̣a que cō rrezam deixase
hūu Rey que tanta mᶜᵉ lhe avia feito. e eu
lhe disse q' por faz' o que devia e nō p̣der
sua honrra e a mᶜᵉ q' vosa alteza lhe faria
que seria mais çerta e cō mais verdadeira
onrra. E que pesasse ele se a vinda de pur-
tugall q' fora por çem rrēs mais ou menos
de morida q' v. alteza lhe deixara de dar por
nō quebrar sua ordenança, com virem
dous rregmᵗᵒˢ contrarios ao seu, e ao q' ele
capitolou cō el Rey dō carlos, e veria se
este despʳᵉzo p̣essa mais p̣a se hyr e fazʳ
o que deve se vyr se por o q' se veeo.

fez grande admiraçā de eu tall sabr̃ e aquy
me disse a vᵉʳdade e como o correo era p̣ʳtido
q' eu ja tudo sabia. E me disse que
çerto nō aberia cousa por q' elle desse cō

¹ Nuno.

a carga em tr̃ra senā tirando lhe algūa
coussa do capitolado; porem q' p^rm° abia
de veer o que lhe vosa alteza faria. eu lhe
disse q' mais q'ria veer q' os rregm^{tos} e Ruy
faleiro q' dezia abertam^{te} q' nō avia de seguir
seu foroll e que avia de navegar ao sull
ou nō hira na armada, e que ele cuidara
q' hia por capitā moor e que eu sabia que
avia out^{os} mandados em cont^{ra}iro os quaees
elle nō saberia senā a t̃po que nō pudese
Remedea^r sua onrra; e que nō curasse do mell
que lhe punha p̃llos beiços o bp̃o de burgos
e que agora era t̃po por ysso q' visse se
o queria faz^r e que me desse carta p̨a vossa
alteza e que eu por amoor dele yria a vossa
alteza a faz^r seu p̨^rtido, por que eu n'o tinha
nehūu Recado de vosa alteza p̨a em tall entē-
der som^{te} falava o q' me pareçia como out^{as} vezes
lhe avia falado. dyseme que nō me dezia na-
da ate veer o rrecado q' o correo trazia e nisto
concludymos eu vigiarey com toda minha
posybilidade o s^rviço de v altēza.

neste paso me parece bem que saiba vosa alteza
que he çerto que a navegaçā q' estes esperā
faz^r el Rey dom carlos a sabe e fernā de
magalhaēes asy mo tem dito e pode aveer
quem tome a emp^{re}sa que faça mais dano.
faley a rruy faley^{ro} p̨ duas vezes nunca me all
Respondio senā que como faria tall cont^{ra}
el Rey seu señor q' lhe tanta m^{ce} fazia a todo
o que lhe dezia nō me rrespondia all, pareçe
me que esta como homē torvado do Juizo
e que este seu famyliar lhe despontou
algūu sabr̃ se o nele avia pareçeme
q' movido fernā de magalhaēes q' Ruy faley^{ro}
seguira o q' magalhaees fiz^r.

s^{or} os navios da capitania de magalhaẽes sam cinq^o
·s. hūu de cx toneladas os dous de lxxx cada
hūu e os dous de lx cada hū pouco mais ho
menos, sam muy velhos e Remēdados por
que os vy em monte corregeer, ha onze
messes que se correjeram e estā na agoa
agora calafetam asy nagoa eu entrey
neles algūas vezes e çertefico a vosa alteza
que pa canari^a navegaria de maa vontade neles, por q' seus liames sam de sebe.

hartelharia que todos çinq'^o levā sam lxxx tiros
muy pequenos som^{te} no maior em q' ha de hyr
fernam de magalhaẽs estam quat^o v^{er}ços de ferro
nō bōos p toda a jente que levā em todos
çinq'^o sam ii^cxxx homẽs todo los mais tem
ja Reçebido o soldo som^{te} os portugeses que
nō querē Reçebr̃ a mill R̄s, ag^rdan que venha
o correo por que lhes disse magalhaẽes que
ele lhes farya acrecētar o soldo e levā mā-
tym^{tos} pa dous anos.

capitam da p^rm^a nāao fernā de magalhaẽes e
de segunda Ruy faley^o da 3ra J^o de cartagena
q' he feitor moor darmada da 4^a quesada
c^{ri}ado do arçobpo de sevilha a 5^a vay sem capitam sabido vay nella por piloto carvalho
portugues, nesta se diz que ha de meteer
por capitā desque forē de foz ē fora ha
alv^o da mizq'ta d est^{re}moz que caa estaa
os portugeses que ca vejo pa hirem
§ o carvalho piloto
§ estevā gomez piloto
§ o sserrāao piloto
§ v^{co} p^{re}to galego piloto ha dias q' caa vive
§ alv^o da myzq'ta d es̄moz
§ martȳ da myzq'ta d estremoz

§ fr^{co} d a^o seca f^o do c^{dor} do rrosmaninhall

§ xpovā ferr^a f^o do c^{dor} de castelejo

§ martim gill f^o do Juiz dos orfãaos de lixboa

§ po d abreu c^{ri}ado do bp̃o de çafy

§ duarte barbosa sobr^{i}nho de di^o barbosa c^{i}ado do bp̃o de
çiguença

§ ant^o frrz q' vivia na mouraria de lixboā

§ luis a^o de beja q' foy c^{r}ado da s^{ra} Ifante q' đs tem

§ J^o da silva f^o de n^o da silva da ilha da madeira
este me disse senp̃ q' n'o avia de hyr salvo se
vosa alteza o ouvese por seu s^{r}viço e anda como
diçipulo encuberto.

§ o faleiro tem caa seu pay e may e irmãaos hū
deles leva consigo.

out^{ra} jente miuda de moços destes tambē dizē
q' am de hyr de que farey memoria a vosa
alteza se mandar quando forē.

a q^{i}nta p̃te desta armaçā he de xpovā de haroo
q̃ nela meteo m̄j^1 ducados Diz caa q̃ vosa
alteza lhe mādo la tomar $\overline{xx}^2$ $+$^{dos} de fazē-
da elle daa caa os avisos d armada de
vosa alteza asy da feita como da que
se faz soube q̃ p hūu c^{ii}ado seu q̃ la
tem. avendo se as cartas deste podria vosa
alteza sabr̃ p que via sabia estes sec^{re}tos.

as mercaderias que levā sam cobre azouge
panos baxos de cores sedas baxas de cores
e marlotas feitas destas sedas.

certificasse que p̃tira esta armada p̃a baxo
em fim deste Julho mas a m̄y nō mo pareçe
asy nē ate meado agosto, posto que o correo
venha mais çedo.

a rrota que se diz que han de levar he dir^{to}
ao cabo fryo ficando lhe o brasy a māo dir^{ta}

<hr>

^{1} 4,000. ^{2} 20,000.

ate pasar a linha da ptiçã e daly navegar
ao eloeste e loes noroeste dir'ᵒˢ a maluco
a quall tr̃ra de maluco eu vy asentada na
poma[1] e carta que ca fez o fᵒ de Reynell
a quall nō era acabada quando caa seu pay
veo por ele, e seu pay acabou tudo e
pos estas tr̃ras de maluco e ꝑ este pa-
deram se fazem todallas cartas as
quaēes faz diᵒ Ribeiro e faz as agulhas
quadrantes e esperas porem nō vay nar-
mada nem q̃r mais q̃ ganhar de comeer
ꝑ seu engenho.

    desd este cabo frio ate as Ilhas de maluco ꝑ
esta navegaçam nō ha nēhūas tr̃ras asentadas
nas cartas que levā pʳᵃza a d's todo poderoso
que tall viajem façā como os corterrāes, e vosa
alteza fique descansado.   e seja senpʳᵉ asy ē-
vejado como he de todolos pʳⁱnçipes.

    Señnor outʳᵃ armada se faaz de tres navios
podres peq̃nos em que vay por capitam
andres ninho este leva outᵒˢ dous navios
pequenos lavrados em peeças dētro nestes
velhos este vay a tr̃ra fyrme q̃ descobʳⁱo pᵉ
ayres, ao porto de larym e daly ha de
hyr por tr̃ra xx legoas ao maar do sull
donde se ha de levar ꝑ tr̃ra os navios
lavrados com a enxarçeea dos velhos e
armalos neste maar do sull e descobʳⁱr
com estes navios mill legoas e mais nā
contʳᵃ o eloeste, as costas da tr̃ra q̃
se chama gataio e nestas ha de hyr
por capitam moor gill gl̃z contador
da Ilha espanhola e vam ꝑ dous años.

    partindo estas armadas se faz loguo

---

[1] Globe.

outra de quat° navios pa hyr segundo
se díz na esteira de magalhaēes porē
como ainda ysto nō este posto em gōço
de se faz^r nō se sabe cousa¹ cousa¹ çerta
e esto ordena xpovā de harōo o que se
mais pasar eu o farey sabr̃ a vosa
alteza.

    as novas da armada que el Rey dom carlos mā-
da faz^r pa se defender ou ofender a frança
ou hyr ao empereeo como se diz escuso esc^{re}ver
a vosa alteza por que de n° Ribeiro que he
em cartagena as tera vosa alteza mais certas
mas ha nova çerta nesta cidade p cartas que
el Rey de frança divulga que el Rey dō carlos
nō ha de seer emperador e que ele o ha de
sser o papa ajuda el Rey de frança p via
onesta conçede lhe quat° capelos pa que
os desse a quē ele q̃ᶦsesse diz se que el Rey
de frança os tem pa daar a quē os ele-
gedores do empereo q̨ᶦserem donde se çerte-
fica que ou el Rey de frança sera emperador
ou quē ele q̃ᶦs°r, o que mais pàsar nestas
armadas eu terey especiall cuidado de o faz^r sabr̃
a vosa alteza ainda q̃ eu estava ja frio nisto por
que me pareçeo q̃ yosa alteza o q̃ria p outrē sabr̃
por que vy caa n° Ribeiro e out^{as} p^{as} q̃ comigo
falavā p modo disymulado querendo sabr̃
de m̄y.   beeso as m̄aaos de vosa alteza, de sevilha
a xviij de Julho de 1519.

                                 SEBASTIĀ ALURZ.

¹ Sic.

✠

el Rey

Fernando de magallañs e Ruy falero cavalleros de la ordem de Santiago ñros capitañs generales della armada q' mandamos hasẽr para yr A descobrir e a los otros capitañs particulares de la ďha armada e pilotos e maestr̃s e contra-
maestres e marineros de las naos de la ďha armada por quanto yo tengo porcierto segund la mucha informaciõ que he a-
vido de personas que por esperiencia lo An visto q' en las islas de maluco ay la especieria e principalment' ys a buscar con esa ďha armada e my voluntad es que derechament' sigais el viage a las ďhas islas por la forma e man'a
que lo he dicho e mandado A vos el ďcho fernando de magallañs porende yo vos mando A todos e a cada uno de vos
q' en la navegacion del ďho viage sigais el parecer determinaciõ del ďho fernando de magallañs para que an͡ts e
primero que a otra parte alguna vais A las ďhas islas de maluco sin que en ello Aya ninguna falta porq' asy cun-
ple A ñro servicio e despues de fecho esto se podra buscar lo demas que convenga conforme A lo q' llevais mã-
dado e los unos ny los otros non fagaďs nyn fagan ende Al por alguna man'a so pena de ₱dimy^to de biens e las
₱sonas a la n̄ra merced fecha en barcelona a diez e nueve dias del mes de abril año de myll e quiniẽtos
e diez e nueve años

yo el rey

por mandado del rey fr̃r̃eo de los covos

p̃a q' los del armada sigan el parecer y determynaciõ de magallañs p̃a q' an͡ts y p^mo q' a otra
₱t vayã a la especerya.

No. IV.

Moradias da casa real—Maç. 1—L⁰. 7, f⁰. 47, v⁰.

------

fernan de magalhaēs f⁰ de p⁰ de
magalhaēs avera onze dias de Janʳᵒ
deste ano e deze seys dias de mayo e
todo Junho a dous mill e trezentos
e doze r̃s pʳ mes cō cᵈᵃ arqʳᵉ pʳ dia   v̄ lxvi r̄s
R⁰ o sobrino ē xiiij denʳᵒ de v⁰ xx v
pa ē ꝑte de tres meses q̃ lhe
ainda deve do ano de vynte e tres
dos q̃tro meses ij lhe māda-
va dar de q̃ tē avydo hū. mes
segᵈᵒ se tudo q̃tē ē hu escryto
seu q̃ lhe deles e de mays t̄po
deu de q̃ ja he pago somᵗᵉ dos tres
meses q̃ lhe ainda devia R⁰ os cynq̃⁰
mill e sesenta e seys Rˢ ēcyma'
q̃teudos.

BASTM
DA COSTA.   x̄iii ij⁰ lxxxiij
                                   FERNĀ ROIZ.

No. V.

M D. xxiv de mense Augusti.

Serenissimo Principe, et excellentissimi Signori,

Supplico jo Antonio Pigafetta Vicentino Cavallier hiero-solimitano che desiderando veder del mondo nelli anni passati, ho navicato cum le caravelli de la Maiesta Cesarea, che sono àndate a trovar le Isole, dove nascono le specie nelle nove Indie, nel qual viazo ho circumdato tutto il mondo à torno et per esser cosa, che mai homo lha fatta, ho composto un libreto de tutto el ditto viazo, qual desidero far stampir. Et per ho suplico de gratia che per anni xx alcun non possi stampirlo, salvo chi voro io, sotto pena à chi el stampasse, o stampato altrove el portasse qui, oltra e^l perder li libri de esser condenato lire tre per libro, et la executione possi esser fatta per qualunque magistrato de questa cita à chi sara fatta la conscientia et sia divisa la pena, un terzo al arsenal de la sublimita vostra, un terzo al acusador, et un terzo à quelli che farano la executione, alla gratia sua humiliter mi ricomando.

Die v^{to} Augusti.

Aloys de priolis
m^s dan d eq's
jo Emiliano
Lazar. mocenigo

Consil. ✝

	de parte	152
	de Non	6
	non sync	2

(Senato Terra, reg. 23, p. 124.)

INDEX.

GENERAL INDEX.

d

WRITERS QUOTED.

NAMES OF PERSONS.

ERRATA.

Page 11, Note, *for* "Massana", *read* "Massaua".

„ 57, Note, „ "Seameux", „ "Scameux"

„ 234, Note, *after* "Great Fish River", *insert* "or the Keiskamma River".

T. RICHARDS, PRINTER, 37, GREAT QUEEN STREET.